Beyond Eastern N(

Beyond Eastern Noir

Reimagining Russia and Eastern Europe in Nordic Cinemas

Anna Estera Mrozewicz

EDINBURGH
University Press

For Steen and August

Edinburgh University Press is one of the leading university presses in the UK. We publish academic books and journals in our selected subject areas across the humanities and social sciences, combining cutting-edge scholarship with high editorial and production values to produce academic works of lasting importance. For more information visit our website: edinburghuniversitypress.com

Edinburgh University Press Ltd
The Tun – Holyrood Road
12 (2f) Jackson's Entry
Edinburgh EH8 8PJ

First published in hardback by Edinburgh University Press 2018

Typeset in Monotype Ehrhardt by
Servis Filmsetting Ltd, Stockport, Cheshire,
and printed and bound by CPI Group (UK) Ltd, Croydon, CR0 4YY

A CIP record for this book is available from the British Library

ISBN 978 1 4744 1810 2 (hardback)
ISBN 978 1 4744 5226 7 (paperback)
ISBN 978 1 4744 1811 9 (webready PDF)
ISBN 978 1 4744 1812 6 (epub)

This publication has been subsidised by the National Science Centre in Poland, grant no. DEC-2011/03/D/HS2/00785.

Contents

Figures

Acknowledgements

My excursion into Nordic Eastern noir and beyond began in 2009, when I applied to The Danish Council for Independent Research (FKK) and received funding for my research project *Eastern Bloc Noir. Imaginations of 'Eastern Europe' in Danish Literature, Film and Visual Arts 1980–2009*. Since then, the project has evolved and stretched over a longer period than I originally expected, partly because the research led me ways I had not imagined and partly because of other professional commitments along the way. Over these years, I have had the enormous pleasure of meeting and collaborating with people working in various places, languages, cultures and academic disciplines – colleagues and friends who offered me their interest, time, support and encouragement. I am deeply thankful to Irina Souch for her invigorating suggestions, intellectual support and friendship; Ewa Mazierska for helpful and stimulating exchange of thoughts; Hans Hertel for his *Østblok noir*, valuable criticism and for being a dear friend and someone I can always rely on; Finn Hauberg Mortensen (†), former Head of the Department of Nordic Studies and Linguistics (now NorS) at the University of Copenhagen, for providing me with access to facilities, a work environment and, crucially, for pointing me in the right direction in the earliest stages of my project; Thomas Anessi for his editing and insightful comments, which helped my writing process invaluably – and for always being on time; Anders Marklund and Kimmo Laine for their constant helpfulness, which eased my explorations of Swedish and Finnish cinemas; all my colleagues at the Department of Film, Media and Audiovisual Arts at Adam Mickiewicz University in Poznań, especially Marek Hendrykowski, Head of the Department when I was first appointed assistant professor, Mikołaj Jazdon and Krzysztof Kozłowski, all three of whom offered me advice, criticism and encouragement, as well as Wojciech Otto, Head of the Department, for providing me with the time to work on this book, and Tomasz Mizerkiewicz, Dean of the Faculty, for financing the purchase of illustrations. I am also grateful to the institutions that opened their doors to me, where I enjoyed stimulating and intense research trips, and where I met wonderful people, many of whom became my dear friends: the Department of Nordic Studies and Linguistics at the

University of Copenhagen; the Amsterdam School for Cultural Analysis (ASCA) at the University of Amsterdam; and the Centre for Baltic and East European Studies (CBEES) at Södertörn University in Stockholm. I owe thanks to Tommi Partanen from the National Audiovisual Institute (KAVI) in Helsinki and to Tore Dybing Myklebust from the National Library of Norway (NB) for their invaluable help in providing me with a number of images reproduced in this book; as well as to the librarians at the Reading Room West of the Royal Library in Copenhagen, especially Ole Henrik Sørensen, for their competence and kindness. I am indebted to the research service at The Swedish Media Database (SMDB) for supplying me with access to a considerable number of films. I am also grateful to the National Science Centre (NCN) in Poland for funding my research. Parts of Chapter 3 and Chapter 4 build on material previously published in the *Journal of Scandinavian Cinema* (Mrozewicz 2013a; 2016), and parts of Chapter 5 build on material previously published in *Panoptikum* (Mrozewicz 2017). I am very grateful to the editors of these journals for granting me permission to further develop my thoughts and arguments on the basis of these articles. Also thanks to my publisher for making this book possible and to the anonymous reviewers of the book for their insightful critique. Although there are too many to mention here by name, I would also like to thank all the filmmakers, colleagues and others that have granted me access to their works and been so very helpful. Many thanks also to my family for being there for me all along.

Lastly, I wish to thank Steen Ulrich, the person who has been with me at every stage of this journey. I am deeply grateful for your patience and loving support, transformative criticism, broadening of my worldview and being with me through it all. Without you, this journey, during which Poland and Denmark became one for me, would not have happened. I dedicate this book to you and to August, who lent me strength in the final phase, promising a good new beginning.

Having had such wonderful support and encouragement along the way, it is important to state that the responsibility for any flaws in this book is mine alone.

INTRODUCTION

The Iron Curtain Effect:
Nordic Eastern Noir

In the feature-length docudrama *1989* (Denmark 2014), by Danish director
Anders Østergaard and Hungarian filmmaker Erszébet Rácz, the camera
traces an East German couple's fateful border crossing from Hungary to
Austria. The scene takes place in August 1989. Kurt-Werner Schulz, his
partner and their child are attempting to escape from the Eastern Bloc.
The scene is set at night, as the family walks in darkness through tall
cornfields, led by a local Hungarian man. The severely limited visibility,
wobbly hand-held camera focused solely on the nearest elements (corn
leaves and the ground), and the sounds of breathing and footsteps, as well
as the fact that the refugees do not understand their Hungarian guide, all
create an atmosphere of disorientation and fear. Suddenly, warnings are
shouted in the distance. Kurt-Werner is shot dead. A blurred frame shows
him lying on the ground, after which it fades to black. A few weeks afterward, the Hungarian–Austrian border is opened, and a couple of months
later, the Berlin Wall 'falls'. Schulz thereby becomes 'the last victim of the
Iron Curtain'.

 1989 is about the remarkable end to the Cold War. It is told from a
contemporary perspective, marked by far-reaching reconstructions and
the directors' highly creative take on archival materials. The escape scene
is reconstructed using cinematic means normally applied in fiction films.
It adheres to well-known depictions of crossings of *the* border that defined
European reality for almost fifty years and embodied the 'geography of
fear' associated with the Cold War (see Loshitzky 1997: 277).[1] The border
crossing serves as a point of no return for the refugees and is the climax in
the narrative structure of the film. It is connected with danger, pain and
death. Moreover, the border denotes the edge of one world and the beginning of another, thus creating a clearly defined separation of the two sides.
The use of the gun by the guards signifies the militarisation of the border
and the prison-like confinement of those on the Eastern side. Ultimately,
the border is invisible and yet acutely present.

The border is not simply a physical barrier. Rather, it is both real and imagined; the imagined is conveyed through cinematic means that enhance the act of border crossing both dramatically and emotionally (cf. Mrozewicz 2013b). Moreover, the scene combines what are sometimes defined as 'hard' and 'soft' borders (see Eder 2006). The hard border – institutionalised and secured by legal texts – is embodied by the guards. The soft border is encoded in the landscape that continues from Hungary to Austria regardless of the (hard) border. The soft border is also incarnated by the refugees, who refuse to accept its hardness. The scene belongs to the narratively constructed, imagined realm – to the aggregation of images of borders within Europe, accumulated throughout history. Klaus Eder describes it as a 'narrative construction of the boundaries of Europe', defining 'stories that people tell each other, thus creating a space of narrative fidelity. Telling stories implies a social relationship and implies a space within which such stories circulate. This symbolic space is bordered by "shared stories"' (2006: 256). Films are such shared stories, narrated within a community and delineating its borders.

This book examines cinematically rendered 'narrative constructions' of (not just physical) borders, especially the changing dynamics and nature of European borders after 1989, but also of the old East/West divide. The focus is on the 'shared stories' that have comprised the Nordic cultural imagination since 1989. My thesis is that the border that both divided and connected the Nordic countries with the Eastern Bloc has significantly influenced the Nordic cultural and thus audiovisual imagination regarding Russia and Eastern Europe. This border combined material and imaginary realms, generating a hegemonic master narrative defined here as 'Eastern noir', which exploded in Nordic cinemas after 1989. This narrative has its roots not only in the Cold War, but also in the pre-War imaginations and long-established discourses on Russia and Eastern Europe, as well as being firmly embedded in post-1989 socio-political contexts. Eastern noir encapsulates the pervading negative stereotypes about Russia and Eastern Europe and the hierarchical, vertical and binary 'us'/'them' logic. I argue that Russia and Eastern Europe serve as an important, though not always recognised, screen onto which the Nordic countries project themselves. These Nordic cinematic imaginations of Russia and Eastern Europe fall into two main categories: a *border discourse* that consolidates Eastern noir narratives and *boundary discourses*, which, oriented towards a horisontal and non-hierarchical imaginary of the Nordic/Eastern connections, pluralise and destabilise hierarchical divisions. The first can be perceived as rooted in the Cold War universe, with its pronounced national divisions, whereas the other(s) anticipate and reflect upon an increasingly globalised world with a less consensual understanding of borders. These two types of discourses, which constitute two poles of a continuum rather than occurring separately, are explored in each of the six chapters comprising this book in relation to an issue representing the most frequently recurring tropes or ways of approaching the eastern neighbours in Nordic films: as a crime scene; through the figures of the spy, the soldier and the Polish plumber; and by means of reference to the Baltic Sea, guilt and shame.

My method is based on a close analysis of cinematic and televisual works in view of patterns and treatments of these themes both across time and employing a synchronic perspective. The focus is thus on the immanent features of a film or television series – including the treatment of the theme, narrative patterns, types of characters and the working of aesthetics (*mise-en-scène*, cinematography, editing, genre) – rather than on production, audience reception and distribution. As a consequence, this book does not have film-historical aspirations, although I pay careful attention to historical, geopolitical and socio-cultural circumstances. I also offer a brief historical overview of representations of Russia and Eastern Europe in the following sections of this Introduction. Yet, rather than discussing the external conditions of a film, the primary focus of my analysis is on the realisation of a theme or a convention within the cinematic representation itself. My aim is to show not only how wide-ranging, but also (and especially) how complex these narratives are. Therefore, close attention is paid to a limited number of films in each chapter, rather than giving brief coverage to a large number of works. Throughout the analyses, I engage with relevant concepts which serve as tools for specifying border/boundary discourses in relation to the themes analysed in the chapters, asking questions about the functions of Russia(ns) and Eastern Europe(ans) in Nordic cinematic representations and the critical operations they are involved in. What do these narratives do to the idea of *Norden?* How are stereotypical discourses unsettled and in what ways are they reinforced? What is *Nordic* about the representations of Russia and Eastern Europe in Nordic cinemas? What are the internal differences in the approaches to the eastern neighbours within the Nordic countries? First, however, I will explain the notions structuring the conceptualisation of this book, the key concept among which is that of the border.

Norden's Iron Border

While the notion of shared stories evoked earlier could imply stories that define a community's centre, I focus not only on central, but also marginal, stories – those not shared by all, removed from the hub of mainstream narratives. One such hub may be denoted as Berlin-centric optics, neatly epitomised by Østergaard and Rácz's docudrama. Famously, the border that came to define the bipolar Cold War order was designated by Winston Churchill as the Iron Curtain (Churchill 1946). From 1961, after the erection of the Berlin Wall by the East German government, the 'Wall' concretised this metaphor and practically became synonymous with the Iron Curtain. But although Berlin and the divided Germany made up the front line during the Cold War, becoming symbols of the twentieth century with its 'geographical dichotomy of freedom/repression' (Loshitzky 1997: 276), and despite Churchill's description of the Polish town of Stettin as the Baltic terminus of the Iron Curtain, it is important to remember that the Iron Curtain cut vertically across Europe from its utmost northern outposts on the Arctic coastline of Norway/Russia to Romania and Bulgaria in the south. Between 1944 and 1991, two Nordic countries, Norway and Finland, shared a direct land border with the Soviet Union; Norway, moreover, was the only member of the North Atlantic defence alliance NATO in Europe to share a border with the USSR. This border, around 196 km long, made Norway, and especially Finnmark – Norway's extreme northeast county bordering with the Murmansk Oblast – a geopolitically strategic location during the Cold War. Finland's border with Russia comprised around 1,340 km of the Iron Curtain. Across the Gulf of Finland, Finland lay close to the Baltic countries (then part of the USSR), whereas its capital Helsinki was only a short distance from Leningrad (today St Petersburg). Although Sweden and Denmark did not share a land border with the Eastern Bloc, the Baltic Sea provided a common connection. Sweden controlled large parts of the Baltic due to its long eastern coastline; Denmark, like Norway a NATO member since 1949, was a neighbour to both East Germany and Poland.

In other words, four Nordic countries – Norway, Finland, Sweden and Denmark – were adjacent to the Eastern Bloc, in part, joined by the Baltic; their eastern and southern borders were part of the Iron Curtain. These countries were thus neighbours to the Soviet Union and the Eastern Bloc. This neighbourliness forced the Nordic countries to develop a security model denoted by political scientists as the 'Nordic balance', based on a greater degree of disengagement and a lower level of tension than in the rest of Western Europe (see Wæver 1992; Brundtland 1966). At the same time, each of the four countries developed its own security policy. This position and these policies influenced social and cultural life in the Nordic region, not least its cultural imagination of the Cold War (see Bastiansen and Werenskjold 2015: 9–10).

The geopolitical border dividing and connecting *Norden* with the (former) Eastern Bloc is crucial for understanding the conceptualisation of the current book and its focus on the Nordic cultural imaginations of neighbouring Russia and Eastern Europe in the age of permeable borders (post-1989) as represented in films from these four Nordic countries. Here, I understand the neighbouring areas to include Russia, the three Baltic states (Estonia, Latvia and Lithuania), Poland and the area of the former German Democratic Republic (GDR). This book demonstrates that the borders the Nordic countries once shared with the Communist Bloc and now share with Russia and its Eastern European neighbours (some across the Baltic) have been significant for constructing and renegotiating the Nordic 'self' over the last three decades.

Beyond Eastern Noir represents a first attempt to shed light on the Nordic region's cinematic constructions of Russia and Eastern Europe. The book does not present an in-depth analysis of each of the Nordic countries individually, but it does look at variations between them and discusses possible explanations for these similarities and differences. The term *Nordic* denotes here Finland and the three Scandinavian countries: Denmark, Sweden and Norway.[2] Although in the English-speaking world, the term *Scandinavia* is used interchangeably with *Norden* (literally, 'the North', denoting Denmark, Norway, Sweden, Finland, Iceland and the autonomous island territories of Greenland, the Faroe Islands and Åland), in the present context it is important to distinguish between the Finnish and Scandinavian (Danish, Norwegian, Swedish) imaginations of Russia and Eastern Europe, not only due to cultural and linguistic differences, but also due to Finland's precarious geopolitical position in relation to Russia and the Soviet Union.[3] It should also be remembered that the foreign perception of *Norden* as a relatively unified region, distinguished by a very specific organisation of society, 'was gradually incorporated in self-understanding in Scandinavia/*Norden*' (Sørensen and Stråth 1997: 21). *Norden* should thus be seen as a cultural construction. Accordingly, the 'Nordic self' is by no means treated here as a homogenous entity, although *Norden* is understood as a region rather than an amalgam of the constituent countries.

If the term *Norden* is not unproblematic, the notion of Eastern Europe remains definitely thorny. In the Western world, it is typically applied as an umbrella term covering all member countries of the previous geopolitical formations of the Warsaw Pact and the Federal People's Republic of Yugoslavia (see Mazierska et al. 2014: 1). Yet it cannot be ignored that the vast area encompassed by this term is highly differentiated; indeed, rather than a single Eastern Europe, it includes many 'Eastern Europes'. In a much narrower sense, the term Eastern Europe describes the territory located between the Iron Curtain and the Soviet Union (Piotrowski 2009: 7). Both understandings, the broad and the narrow, include countries such as Poland, the Czech Republic and Hungary, who tend to perceive themselves as 'Central' or 'East-Central' Europe, thereby conveying their desire to distance themselves from Russia and the Soviet Union. However, as both Ewa Mazierska and Paul Coates observe, these terms 'did not enter cultural discourses after the fall of communism' (Mazierska 2010: 6; see Coates 2000). At the same time, the three Baltic countries tend to perceive themselves as a part of 'Central-Northern Europe', looking towards the North in an attempt to construct a new regional identity that transcends the East/West binary (see Šukaitytė 2015). We should also remember that the idea of Eastern Europe is much older than the twentieth-century geopolitical perturbations. Larry Wolff proves in his seminal book *Inventing Eastern Europe* that 'Eastern Europe' was already mapped and constructed by Western travellers and intellectuals during the Enlightenment (Wolff 1994). Like today, there was no agreement then as to Eastern Europe's precise borders; however, Russia was included within these borders.

The notion of Eastern Europe employed in this book, which focuses on the Nordic countries' neighbours across the former Iron Curtain, is limited to the Baltic Sea region. Thus, what is of interest here is the Eastern European side of the Baltic Sea and the countries constituting it. At the same time, I differentiate between Russia and Eastern Europe, first, because Russia dominates quantitatively in Nordic cultural and cinematic imaginations, and second, because the connotations Russia evokes differ greatly from those related to the other Eastern European neighbours – an issue addressed more thoroughly in Chapter 1. It should be added that the everyday use of the term 'Eastern Europe' in the Nordic countries does not encompass Russia.

Focusing on Russia and the Baltic Sea region, I argue that common borders have instigated tensions – both historically and imaginatively – which underlie many Nordic narratives about these areas. The focus on the period after 1989 (and the dissolution of the Soviet Union in 1991) is motivated by the fact that these borders have become increasingly porous as political lines of division. I explore whether and how this porousness has influenced the Nordic imagination of these eastern neighbours and how it is charted in Nordic cinemas. Moreover, I tentatively view the last nearly thirty years as a partly closed historical chapter that started with the end of the Cold War and concluded due to the recent return of a (new) Cold War rhetoric in relations between Russia and the West, including the Nordic countries.[4] Russia's aspirations to revive its superpower position and other world developments (waves of migration, the wars in Ukraine and Syria, terror attacks in Europe and the US) have sparked a revival of eschatological and polarising discourses. In view of the above, the period may be seen as a distinct historical entity, the 'iron' border returning to public discourse.

However, before we move to discuss this period, let us first briefly look at the 'pre-history' of the Eastern neighbours on the Nordic screen in order to get an overview of the most important elements in its chronology.

Eastern Neighbours in Nordic Cinemas Before 1989

The metaphor of the Iron Curtain, describing the divided, bipolar world of the Cold War, spanned two conceptual realms: the material and the imaginary. From the Nordic perspective, what lay behind the 'curtain' was associated, above all, with the feared Soviet Bloc. It was an area scarcely visited, in spite of its physical proximity. This made it ripe for projections of various imaginations, represented in both literature and film. In Nordic cinemas, these imaginations came to figure noticeably only after the 'raising' of the curtain. A significant reason for this 'delay'[5] was a broadly understood culture of self-censorship in public communication in the Nordic countries during the Cold War, aimed at avoiding controversial topics related to the Soviet Union (Lounasmeri 2015: 85). Film, in particular, due to high production costs and technological complexity, was influenced by this self-censorship. Another reason was the fact that travel possibilities in the Eastern Bloc were limited.

It should be emphasised, however, that rich cinematic representations of *Norden*'s eastern neighbours precede the Cold War, reaching back to the silent era. Russia stimulated the Nordic imagination to the highest degree, inciting predominantly negative connotations. The perception of Russia as a threat has a long tradition in the Nordic countries, reaching back to the sixteenth century (Russo-Swedish War 1554–7) and consolidated during the Great Northern War (1700–21) the Finnish War (1808–9) and not the least the October Revolution (1917), due to the ruthless and bloody terror it brought. The fear of Russia (*rysskräck* in Swedish) can also be coupled with convictions about Russia's deep foreignness, especially when it comes to dictatorship and the terror it exerted on its own citizens (Alm 2008: 135–44), but also in terms of broader cultural differences. As ethnologist Owe Ronström explains, Russians 'are Orthodox, write in Cyrillic and speak a Slavic language. [. . .] Are they Europeans at all? [. . .] Besides, they are so many and we are so few. This is the source and fuel of *rysskräck*' (Ronström 2009: 124).[6]

During and shortly after the revolution, a number of anti-revolutionary

films were made by Norwegian, Swedish and Danish directors, such
as *The Daughter of the Revolution* (*Revolutionens datter*, Ottar Gladtvet,
Norway 1918), *Heroes of Our Time* (*Vor tids helte*, Peter Lykke-Seest,
Norway 1918), *Jeftha's Daughter* (*Jefthas dotter*, Robert Dinesen, Sweden
1919) and *Christian Wahnschaffe* (Urban Gad, Germany 1921) (see Tybjerg
1999: 27–9). In the Danish director Carl Theodor Dreyer's *Leaves from
Satan's Book* (*Blade af Satans Bog*, Denmark 1921), the final part of the
four-part film is set in 1918, during the Civil War in Finland (1917–18),
in which the pro-Soviet Red forces fought against, and in the end lost
to, the non-socialist White Guard. The film's main character, Satan, is
here embodied by a devilish Bolshevik, who spreads hatred and destruction. Although the Red Guards consisted primarily of Finnish workers
(supported only by a few Soviet military units), many placed the blame
entirely on the Russians. In Dreyer's film, the communist threat embodied
by Satan endangers not only the Finnish nation, but also Christianity,
adhering to the recurring trope of 'oriental despotism', which imagines
Russia in opposition to Western civilisation (see Naarden and Leerssen
2007: 227). It is worth adding that Christianity resonates in the rhetoric of
Churchill's 'Iron Curtain' speech, in which 'the communist parties or fifth
columns constitute a growing challenge and peril to Christian civilization' (Churchill 1946; see Tybjerg 1999). The trope of Russians as despots
and barbarians threatening 'our' civilisation is central to what I denote as
Nordic Eastern noir, discussed later in this Introduction and in Chapter 1.

    The Swedish fear of Russia found monumental expression in a his-
torical drama directed by John W. Brunius, *Karl XII*, released in 1925,
at a time of heated debates over defence and reductions in the military in
crisis-ridden Sweden. Reviving national myths of the bygone greatness
of the Swedish kingdom, the film took a clear stance against demilitarisa-
tion (Furhammar 2003: 114). *Karl XII* renders the last glorious years of
Swedish dominion in the Baltic Sea region under the rule of Charles XII,
terminated by the fateful Battle of Poltava (1709), when the Swedes were
defeated by the Russians. Unlike many post-WWII films, here the Russian
enemy is not merely a nameless and faceless threat, embodied by distant
Russian soldiers. The plot closely follows Tsar Peter the Great, depicting him not simply as a despot with strong ambitions of expanding and
strengthening his empire and thereby making Russia more 'European'
than 'Asiatic', but also as a human being with doubts, desires and moments
of weakness. Such a double-edged rendering of Russians as brutal hordes
on the one hand and as open-minded and 'European' (although autocratic)
on the other captures an old trope in the Western imaginery of Russia as
representing either 'oriental despotism' or 'enlightened despotism' (Malia

1999; Naarden and Leerssen 2007: 227–9). This trope, as we shall see, reverberates in recent Nordic films on contemporary Russia (see especially Chapter 1). Interestingly, a Pole, the historical figure of General Stanisław Poniatowski, who was a supporter of Charles XII, is featured in Brunius' drama as the king's helper.

Regarding the 'Polish cause', another Swedish film from this period must be mentioned. *When Millions Roll . . . (När millionerna rulla . . .*, Lasse Ring 1924), set during WWI and the Bolshevik revolution, expresses clear sympathy for the Polish independence movement. Its agents are helped along by Swedish solidarity, and especially by a wealthy baron, who ends up marrying the Polish protagonist Irma – a character who is actively engaged in the Polish national cause. The film points to the similarity between Poland and Finland, both nations severely oppressed by Russia. Through its association with Finland, with which Sweden has historically close relations, Poland seems nearer and more familiar. The perceived familiarity of the Eastern European countries situated on the other side of the Baltic, in contrast to the hostile and more distant Russia, remains present in Nordic cinemas today (as discussed especially in Chapter 3), although Eastern Europeans tend to be lumped together with Russians (see Chapter 4).

The Finnish struggle against the 'Bolshevik hordes' is also a theme in Swedish director Gustaf Molander's drama *One Night (En natt,* Sweden 1931), which tells the story of two brothers, one of whom enrols in the White Guard, the other supporting the Red forces. Similarly, George Schnéevoigt's *Outlaw (Fredlös,* Sweden 1935) engages with the consequences of the Finnish War, from 1808 to 1809 (when Sweden lost Finland to the Russian Empire), in the territories annexed by Russia. Oppressed by a tyrannical Russian governor, the local people incite a revolt.

When Finnish film came into existence, Finland was still the Grand Duchy of Russia (1809–1917). Finnish film history and the ideology behind filmmaking in Finland are inseparable from the patriotic and nationalist aspirations of the Finnish people (see Soila et al. 1998: 31ff.). In the first decades of independence after the Civil War, the main challenge was to unite the divided nation under the rule of the victorious (conservative and anti-Soviet) political forces. As Tytti Soila notes, the Finnish film industry was owned by the patriotic middle class, and, as a consequence, 'this popular mass medium became a mediator of its values and goals, promoting the healing and homogenizing of the country' (Ibid. 45). During the silent film era, national anti-Russian sentiment was frequently expressed – for example, in the rural melodrama *The Bothnians (Pohjalaisia,* Jalmari Lahdensuo 1925), conflicts arise between Finnish peasants from Ostrobothnia and the Russian rulers; in *Fugitives from Murmansk* (*Muurmanin pakolaiset*, Erkki Karu 1927), a German protagonist fights against the Russians and returns to the newly independent Finland; *The Highest Victory* (*Korkein voitto*, Carl von Haartman 1929) expresses a deep mistrust towards, and fear of infiltration by, the Soviets. However, if compared to the following decade, these films only subtly expressed political attitudes. The 1930s in Finland were marked by rightist radicalism, persecution of communists and strong anti-Soviet views sanctioned by the authorities (see Meinander 2011: 63; Rosenberg 1995: 58). Towards the end of the decade, Finland's relations with its eastern neighbour became increasingly strained as the Soviet Union applied political pressure on Finland (see Soila et al. 1998: 48, 54). On-screen Russophobia escalated, and a number of manifestly anti-Soviet pro-nationalist propaganda films were produced, offering a retrospective view of Finland's relations with its eastern neighbour, such as *The Activists* (*Aktivistit*, Risto Orko 1939), *The February Manifesto* (*Helmikuun manifesti*, Yrjö Norta, T. J. Särkkä 1939) and *The Stolen Death* (*Varastettu kuolema*, Nyrki Tapiovaara 1938), all of which were set in historical periods of increased Russification in Finland (1899–1905 and 1908–17).

These films, along with other films set in the past, such as *The Great Wrath* (*Isoviha*, Kalle Kaarna 1939) and *Soldier's Bride* (*Jääkärin morsian*, Risto Orko 1938), depict Russians as thoroughly negative characters: dumb, drunk, filthy, primitive, violent and abusive towards women, who are raped in churches, evoking the trope of Russians posing a threat to Christianity and thereby to all of Western civilisation. In this period, anti-Russian views were commonly combined with anti-Semitism, as in *The Highest Victory* or *Soldier's Bride*, where Jewish spies serve the Soviets against the Finns. Moreover, the propagandist message of *Soldier's Bride* (similarly to its earlier version from 1931, directed by Kalle Kaarna) urges Finland to strengthen its ties with Germany, which points to the crucial political tensions in Finland during the 1930s (see Kääpä 2012: 89–90). It is worth noting that these fiercely anti-Russian films were imported to Sweden during WWII, when neutral Sweden leaned towards Germany (Soila et al. 1998: 179).

These anti-Russian films were banned shortly after WWII and re-released only in the mid-1980s, with the thawing of the Cold War. But although openly derogatory depictions of Russians nearly disappeared from Finnish post-war cinema due to Finland's 'friendship' with the USSR, a number of war films were made depicting Russians as the great enemy: most importantly, *The Unknown Soldier* (*Tuntematon Sotilas*), directed by Edvin Laine in 1955, based on the novel by Väinö Linna

(1954), as well as Rauni Mollberg's adaptation of the novel from 1985, and *Winter War* (*Talvisota*, Pekke Parikka 1989). Russian soldiers remain distant and anonymous in all these films.

During the Cold War, anti-Soviet views and Russophobia remained suppressed, especially in Finland. Nordic films, documentaries and television productions about Russia or the Soviet Union were either limited by self-censorship or tainted by left-wing attitudes, which flourished in the Scandinavian countries and Finland in the late 1960s and 1970s.[7] Examples of self-censorship can be observed in Swedish so-called 'civil defence films' (*civilförsvarsfilm*), made between the 1940s and 1970s with the aim of instructing citizens on how to behave in case of a nuclear attack. Strikingly, these films did not include a clear image of the enemy, who often was simply absent (Cronqvist 2008: 178).[8] The neutral Sweden adopted a cautious policy of non-alignment, but was nevertheless compliant towards the USSR, as well as regarding the annexation of the Baltic countries. This compliance was proved by the controversial and hotly debated extradition of Baltic war refugees from Sweden to the USSR in 1946. In 1970, left-leaning director Johan Bergenstråhle made a film about these events, *A Baltic Tragedy* (*Baltutlämningen*), based on the acclaimed documentary novel by Per Olov Enquist (Enquist [1968] 1973). Politically, the film is ambiguous and does not condemn the extradition (see Wright 1998: 204–5). Another example of these leftist tendencies in Swedish cinema are the films by director duo Olle Häger and Hans Villius, authors of historical documentaries often concerning highly charged political issues, such as *Stalin. Portrait of a Dictator* (*Stalin. Porträtt av en diktator*, 1970). Even though the film is critical of Stalin, the filmmakers were accused – by a conservative journalist – of remaining silent about some uncomfortable facts concerning the Soviet Union (Ludvigsson 2003: 227). But even in a strongly left-oriented film like the famous Swedish quasi-documentary *I Am Curious – Yellow* (*Jag är nyfiken – gul*, 1967) by Vilgot Sjöman, the Swedish *rysskräck*, or *kommuniströdsla* (the fear of communism) (see Cronqvist 2004: 72), is mentioned directly. The main protagonist, Lena, who espouses radical leftist views, says openly that she 'feared the Soviet Union and China'. Likewise in Finland, the leftist climate influenced cinema, which consequently became interested in the working class and revisions of recent history (for example, the Civil War, long called the War of Independence, was redefined as the Class War). An example of a film adhering to the official political (pro-Soviet) line is Pirjo Honkasalo and Pekka Lehto's *Two Forces* (*Kainuu 39*, 1979), which combines fiction and documentary to depict historical events in a Finnish village on the border with Russia that cooperated with the Soviets in 1939. A Swedish film depicting post-war migration of guest workers to Sweden in the 1950s, *Seppan* (Agneta Fagerström-Olsson 1986) (see Wright 1998: 282), features a Polish girl and a Russian boy. These two children have been brought together by their parents' affair, which reflects the tendency in Nordic cinemas to connect the Eastern European neighbours with Russia.

For Norway, which was occupied by the Germans from 1940 to 1945, the war is a significant part of their discourse on national identity. The genre of occupation (docu)drama emerged in the 1940s and continues today (Iversen 1998: 123; 2012). In these war dramas, Russians are scarcely represented. The enemy was predominantly Nazi, typically 'faceless, never individualized or assigned a significant role in the film' (Iversen 2012: 242). *Under a Stone Sky* (*Under en steinhimmel*, Norway, USSR 1974), directed by Knut Andersen, Igor Maslennikov and Stanislav Rostotsky, merits mention here, as it tells a story of Norwegian civilians hiding in mining tunnels during the German razing of Finnmark in autumn 1944, who are rescued by Soviet troops. It is noticeable that in relation to the history of Finnmark, and notably in post-Cold War films, Russians are depicted ambiguously – not only as a threat, but also as neighbours, supporters and allies, mainly against the Nazis (see Chapter 2). In Denmark, Russian soldiers were associated with the occupation of the island of Bornholm between May 1945 and April 1946 and with the bombing of its two major cities, Nexø and Rønne. Strikingly, in the Danish documentary *Russians on Bornholm* (*Russerne på Bornholm*, Ole Askman 1987) Russian soldiers are represented in a positive light, and the bombing is justified as necessary because of the German occupation. The fear that Russians would stay permanently on Bornholm, widespread among Danish society and politicians (Lauridsen et al. 2011: 140), is disavowed in the film as unfounded.[9]

East Germany also attracted attention, especially in Denmark. In the beginning of the 1970s, several films where made on the GDR, typically focusing on the socialist way of life rather than expressing critique of the Stasi-state, such as the leftist activist Tørk Haxthausen's social documentaries *A Berliner Family* (*En berliner familie*, Denmark 1971), about the everyday life of an East German engineer, and *GDR – Middle Class and Socialism* (*DDR – middelstand og socialisme*, Denmark 1971), about a factory owner and member of the GDR parliament, 'a capitalist in the socialist state'. A similar ideological spirit is expressed in Haxthausen's documentaries about Soviet Russia: *Workers in Moscow* (*Arbejdere i Moskva*, Denmark 1968) and *USSR on the Way to Communism* (*USSR på vej til kommunisme*, Denmark 1968). A different light is cast on the GDR in the film *Tomorrow, My Darling* (*I morgen, min elskede*, Finn Karlsson,

Denmark 1971), about an East German woman who escapes to Denmark hidden in a cargo train, but is unable to adjust to her new life. She returns to the GDR, but her Danish friends try to wrest her out to the West. During a dramatic scene of crossing the border by car under cover of night, not unlike the scene in *1989* discussed earlier, the girl is killed by a border guard. The film juxtaposes the carefree hippie times in Denmark with the gloomy reality of the neighbour lying just across the Baltic.

It was not until the final years of the Cold War that narratives about the eastern neighbours, particularly Russia, returned to Nordic cinemas with a power similar to that from before WWII, after an approximately forty-year-long period of caution in depicting these neighbours. The other neighbours across the Baltic also slowly began reappearing in the Nordic consciousness after a period of oblivion and marginalisation in both official and unofficial discourses of Europe.

Nordic Eastern Noir

Although Nordic films that touch directly upon themes related to the Soviet Union and *Norden*'s neighbours across the Baltic were scarce during the Cold War, over its last decade, when the self-censorship became more relaxed due to the transformations in the USSR initiated by Mikhail Gorbachev's reforms (*uskoreniye* – acceleration, *perestroika* – restructuring, *glasnost* – candour, transparency), a number of Hollywood-inspired genre films were produced, expressing a mixture of anti-Russian and anti-Soviet feelings. Mats Helge's martial arts film *The Ninja Mission* (Sweden 1984) instigated this shift and, after its enormous US success, was followed by *Russian Terminator* (Mats Helge, Sweden 1990). In Norway the political conspiracy thriller *Orion's Belt / Orions belte* (Ola Solum, Norway 1985) marked a turn in Norwegian cinema, both as a direct comment on Norway's Cold War politics and as a groundbreaking genre film. The action movie *Born American / Jäätävä polte* (Renny Harlin, Finland, US 1986) achieved a similar status in Finland. However, it is important to note that unlike *Orion's Belt*, distributed both in Norway and internationally,[10] the Swedish films, as well as *Born American*, did not primarily target Nordic audiences. These films employed English dialogue and were principally made for international distribution (*The Ninja Mission* and *Russian Terminator* mainly on VHS). Moreover, despite the political thaw in the USSR, throughout the 1980s Finland remained within the orbit of Soviet-centric appeasement politics, due to which *Born American* was initially banned by the Finnish censorship committee as 'clear propaganda', finally being released in 1986 in a strictly censored version (see Kääpä 2011).

These internationally oriented genre films, in accordance with their commercial intentions, resonated with the intensified and explicit anti-Soviet propaganda of American cinema in the early Reagan era (see Stenport 2015: 171; see Shaw and Youngblood 2010: 32ff.). Moreover, in Sweden a number of James Bond-inspired Swedish language spy films were produced, such as *Codename Coq Rouge / Täcknamn Coq Rouge* (Pelle Berglund, Sweden 1989) and the television miniseries *Enemy's Enemy / Fiendens fiende* (Thomas Borgström, Lars Bill Lundholm, Sweden 1990). These films, whether oriented towards national or international markets, locate the majority of crime and action scenes in Russia and tie them primarily to Russian antagonists. They convey the widespread idea (disseminated in crime and spy fiction, as well as in American anti-communist spy films of the 1950s; see Booth 1991: 147ff.) that representing Russia demands a specific narrative convention – namely, the (widely defined) crime narrative. Indeed, according to the 'master narrative' about Russia and the Soviet Union pervading the popular Nordic imagination, these spaces are inherently related to crime and violence. This narrative finds continuity in the decades following the Cold War, spreading to representations of their neighbours. The evil is now embodied by Russian and Eastern European criminals, former Soviet spies and state security (KGB) agents, who threaten the Nordic idyll. Perhaps the most (in)famous embodiment of this transformation is the shadowy figure of Alexander 'Zala' Zalachenko, father of Lisbeth Salander, the bold female protagonist of the Swedish *Millennium* trilogy (2009), based on Stieg Larsson's crime novels. Zalachenko is a former Soviet agent who started cooperating with SAPO (Swedish Security Service) in the 1970s. In the post-Iron Curtain reality, Zala, still protected by the Swedish authorities, controls the sex-trafficking business.

This dominant narrative, across numerous variations, continues today and is evoked in a number of Nordic crime films and television series, often based on crime fiction, involving Russian and Eastern European villains (for example, *Executive Protection / Livvakterna*, Anders Nilsson, Sweden 2001; *Baba's Cars / Babas bilar*, Rafael Edholm, Sweden 2006; *The Eagle: A Crime Odyssey / Ørnen: En krimi-odyssé*, Denmark 2004–6; *Those Who Kill / Den som dræber*, Denmark 2011; *Look of a Killer / Tappajan näköinen mies*, Lauri Nurkse, Finland 2011, 2016; *Occupied / Okkupert*, Norway 2015–; *Small Town Killers / Dræberne fra Nibe*, Ole Bornedal, Denmark 2016). This hegemonic narrative embodies the pervading stereotype about Russia – and through it, Eastern Europe – as a crime scene. As Homi Bhabha has noted, stereotype is 'a paradoxical mode of representation: it connotes rigidity and an unchanging order as well as disorder, degeneracy and demonic repetition' (Bhabha 2004: 94). This master narrative is what I define in Nordic cinemas as *Eastern noir*.

Eastern noir freezes history, like a stereotype, into one solid block and disseminates ahistorical images irrespective of historical change. Its narrative and audiovisual patterns and tropes share with stereotypes what Mireille Rosello describes as 'the high degree of memorability and iterativity that comes from the transformation of assembled individual units into one apparently solid unique block of meaning' (Rosello 1998: 25). Although stereotypes are reproduced irrespective of the materiality of the medium (Ibid. 23), the impact of cinema in spreading images and influencing the popular imagination is exceptionally strong, as proven by the eager utilisation of cinematic images for propagandist purposes throughout film history.[11] However, a noticeable strategy in recent Nordic Eastern noir films featuring Russian and/or Eastern European characters involves humorous exaggerations of stereotypes, which rather than ridiculing the Eastern neighbours, aim at exposing the stereotypical thinking of Nordic characters and audiences (examples being *Baba's Cars* or *Small Town Killers* mentioned above). Whether humorous and self-exposing or not, mainstream cinematic narratives frequently radicalise and thus consolidate stereotypes in order to produce certain dramatic effects. This concerns both negative and positive stereotypes.

This book does not deny the existence of the Eastern noir (meta)narrative or its accuracy. Instead, it attempts to interrogate and add nuance to the Nordic representation of Russia and Eastern Europe by focusing on a number of Nordic films made in the period from around 1989 (including two mid-1980s films, *Orion's Belt* and *Born American*) till today. While Eastern noir remains the point of reference throughout the analyses, the primary focus is on films that in one or many respects reimagine dominant depictions of *Norden*'s eastern neighbours. These films are as numerous as Eastern noir films, though less popular. To explore the ways in which this master narrative is challenged, it is necessary first to pinpoint its main traits, which I briefly turn to now, elaborating on in more detail in Chapter 1.

It should be emphasised that whereas this master narrative concerns primarily Russia, it spreads to representations of the other eastern neighbours, who are perceived of as 'infested' by Russia's criminality and dubious morality on the one hand and seen as victims of the (former) Soviet oppression on the other. This concerns especially the three Baltic states, which were a part of the USSR, but to a lesser degree Poland, as well. The GDR should be regarded as a separate case. Although lying on the Soviet side of the Iron Curtain, the GDR was seen as a totalitarian state in its own right. This is illustrated by the previously mentioned docudrama *1989*, in which the East German authorities are depicted as the centre of oppression, against which even Soviet rule seems mild. This oppressiveness is embodied by the figures of (former) Stasi agents recurring in Eastern noir films (as in the Swedish film *Executive Protection*, mentioned above) and their depiction, at times, as a continuation of the Nazi-monstrosity. At the same time, the victims of the Stasi police state, ordinary citizens of the GDR, due to the close neighbourliness often depicted in Danish films, are represented not as 'others', but as being close to 'us'. Their familiarity is more pronounced in comparison to Poles, Estonians, Lithuanians or Latvians.

I define as Eastern noir films that in their theme, narrative structure and aesthetics insist on constructing their eastern neighbours as dismal and depict these countries as a specific type of crime scene. From this perspective, Russia and Eastern Europe are represented as gloomy, oppressive and dark places, labyrinthine and not fully intelligible to the Nordic/Western protagonist. Rather than suggesting that these films draw directly upon classical film noir, the adjective 'noir' defines first of all the atmosphere of fear, bleakness and chaos. Nevertheless, the aesthetic and iconographic elements from the American film noir tradition of the 1940s are often evoked, including nocturnal scenes, dismal landscapes and the ambiguous morality of the characters. As in film noir, the distinction between what is right and wrong, lawful and unlawful is disturbed. This blurring of moral and legal borders most typically applies to the 'other' (Russian/Eastern European) side, usually opposed to the (lawful and ordered) Nordic side – the representative example being *Born American*, where the contrast is clearly marked by the black-and-white symbolic division of spaces. The distinction between 'our' and 'the other' side, reinforced by the clear division between 'our' protagonist and 'their' Russian/Eastern European antagonist, is narratively and emotionally emphasised in the depictions of border crossings, which – as in *1989* – are highly loaded events. However, a number of Eastern noir films also defy this contrastive approach and show 'our' side as equally morally dubious as the 'other'. One such example is *Orion's Belt*.

Although the dominant Eastern noir narrative imagining Russia as a crime scene is mainly reproduced by popular fiction cinema (Németh 2015: 44), it is by no means restricted to one specific genre. Rather, it cuts across and combines different genres. A strict division between art cinema and genre cinema cannot be applied to Eastern noir, with *1989* as a case in point. This generic hybridity, increasingly pronounced in more recent Eastern noir productions – for instance, *Occupied* or *Bordertown* (*Sorjonen*,

Finland 2016–)[12] – is only one feature Eastern noir shares with Nordic noir – currently a much favoured term referring to a particular Nordic type of crime fiction, television series and films, characterised by a 'heady mixture of bleak naturalism, disconsolate locations and morose detectives' (Creeber 2015: 21).[13] I do not claim that Nordic noir and Eastern noir are mutually exclusive. They both foreground a sense of place ('Nordic'; 'Eastern') rather than denote one specific genre; in both 'the grey, the gloomy, the cold [. . .] create a kind of an atmosphere where bad things can happen' (Val McDermid in Solum 2016: 136). An Eastern noir film can be classified as Nordic noir at the same time, the case in point being the high-end Finnish television crime series *Bordertown*, a Nordic Eastern noir that both explores the gloomy sides of Finnish society – self-reflexivity being characteristic of Nordic noir – and engages with the unsettling Russian reality on the other side of the border. In *Bordertown* the melancholic mood, considered the distinguishing emotion of Nordic noir (Creeber 2015: 26), is combined with the fear of Russia, a feeling typical of Eastern noir (although also challenged in *Bordertown*). Just as the term 'Nordic noir', coined outside of *Norden*, implies an external perspective on the Nordic region and lumps the Nordic countries together, the notion of Eastern noir is also intended to convey not only the external (Nordic) perspectives on Russia/Eastern Europe, but also the pervading perception of the former Eastern Bloc as one homogeneous area.

Perhaps the crucial difference between Eastern noir and Nordic noir concerns the fact that whereas depictions of the contemporary Nordic societies' gloomy underbelly seem surprising or even shocking, in the case of the Eastern noir narrative on Russia and Eastern Europe, they are expected and taken for granted. In Nordic noir, crime and violence are located in the unspoiled Nordic landscapes and within well-functioning welfare states. As noted by Barry Forshaw, author of the book *Death in a Cold Climate*, Nordic crime fiction offers socio-political insights uncovering 'the cracks that have appeared in the social democratic ideal, an ideal which has been cherished for so long by observers in America, Britain and the rest of Europe' (2012: 2). In Eastern noir, in turn, the gloomy, grey and evil seem a 'natural' part of the place – Russia/Eastern Europe – and come to represent the entire region, its people and society as a whole.

Such representations are not surprising considering that even during the Enlightenment, Eastern Europe was already constructed by Western Europeans as an area filled with savage and violent people, nonsensical disorder, sadness, chaos and darkness. It was 'invented' as an opposition to Western civilisation, although it was also seen as an intermediary space between Europe and the Orient: 'Eastern Europe defined Western Europe by contrast, as the Orient defined the Occident, but was also made to mediate between Europe and the Orient. One might describe the invention of Eastern Europe as an intellectual project of demi-Orientalization' (Wolff 1994: 7). The binarism inherent in this discourse evokes Edward Said's concept of Orientalist discourse producing Western domination and superiority (Said 1978; Ashcroft et al. 1998: 167ff.). It is worth emphasising that eighteenth-century Western travellers attached great significance to the border between Western and Eastern Europe, the crossing of which they described as like leaving the world of civilisation behind (Wolff 1994: 19). Thus, what I designate here as Eastern noir can be seen as a continuation of not only Cold War rhetoric – in many films transformed into 'hot war', latently underpinning the fragile bipolar world balance – but also of tropes much older than Churchill's metaphor of the Iron Curtain.[14]

A salient feature which Eastern noir shares with Nordic noir is the social consciousness and reflection on the dark underside of the Nordic region's prosperous and well-organised welfare states. The disintegration of the Eastern Bloc, as Charity Scribner observed, 'prompted comparisons to the exhausted welfare states of the West' (2003: 64). Precisely because of this, the self-critical reflection in Eastern noir has different incentives when compared to Nordic noir. During the Cold War, the identity of the Nordic countries rested firmly upon the (self-)conception as a 'third way' between communism and capitalism, East and West, due to which *Norden* gained an 'exceptional' status in the international arena. The disruptions in Nordic society addressed in films thematising Russia and Eastern Europe are tied to what many perceived as a crisis of Nordic identity after the political revolution of 1989–91, as well as the growth of global capitalism. With the East suddenly no longer East and the West no longer West, and integration becoming Europe's main agenda, the Nordic model was no longer a better 'alternative' (Wæver 1992: 94). The porousness of borders resulting from the enlargements of the European Union forced the Nordic societies to confront an increasingly transnational reality. The anxieties attached to these processes are often imagined in Eastern noir through criminal plots about (organised) international crime reaching the Nordic countries. Another self-critical emotion expressed in films on Russia and/ or Eastern Europe is the feeling of guilt underpinning encounters with less privileged 'others' from across the border, usually embodied in the trope of the Nordic 'rescuer' and Russian/Eastern European 'victim', the latter of which typically appears in the form of prostitutes or sexually abused women.[15]

While the cinematic master narrative is shaped by a discourse of rigid borders, imagining Russia/Eastern Europe as a place that is dark, criminal and threatening towards *Norden*, numerous films challenge this dominant perception in various ways.

Border and Boundary: Reimagining the Eastern Noir

Beyond Eastern Noir explores, from both a historical and synchronic perspective, how Russia and Eastern Europe are (re)imagined in Nordic cinemas and how these (re)imaginations reflect back on *Norden*. This correlation is inherent in the very idea of the border, pointing to both sides that it divides/connects. The border indicates not only a limit, but also adjacency; not simply the end of 'mine', but also the beginning of the 'other'.

In the current analysis, representations of Eastern European, Russian and Nordic spaces are understood as resonating with one another.[16] Literary scholar Dan Ringgaard convincingly argues that every place 'includes a resonance of other places, and there is interaction between activities, physical space, images and symbolic meanings. No pure, self-enclosed, homogeneous and timeless place exists. Place remains in a constant exchange with the surrounding world' (2010: 31). As such, places cannot be accessed directly because they are always already mediated by cultural 'screens' or 'filters', such as stereotypical tropes and preconceived notions. As cultural theorist Mieke Bal observes, cultural screens 'are largely opaque, not transparent; they hinder rather than help vision'. Yet, they are unavoidable because both vision and language can only be understood and made comprehensible 'if you share at least some of the codes with others' (Bal 1996: 262). Thus, our perception of a place is inseparable from the screens or 'mental imaginations' codified in cultural representations (Beller 2007: 4).

Throughout this book, I focus on what I prefer to call the cultural, rather than mental, imagination, as what I analyse are cultural – cinematic – objects. As mentioned earlier, I argue that the Nordic cultural imagination of Russia and Eastern Europe is shaped by shared geopolitical borders. But the relation between cultural imagination and reality should not be seen as a simple mirrored reflection. Representations do not simply reflect reality, but also generate it, shape it and participate in it. Esther Peeren suggests that the relationship between the cultural imagination and social realm can be neatly grasped by the Bakhtinian term of refraction (rather than reflection), meaning that:

> Artistic works deflect discourses taken from the social realm at particular angles, as does, in turn, the social realm with artistic contents. Through this mutual feedback

loop, cultural representations become part of ongoing social discussions and may
function as a testing ground to imagine and work through their possible permuta-
tions and solutions. (Peeren 2014: 8)

While what lay on the other side of the Iron Curtain was primarily
imagined through the filter of the 'iron' border, after the Cold War this
space was slowly pluralised and reimagined in the Nordic audiovisual
imagination.

At this point, it should be stated clearly that the terms *border* and *boundary* are understood throughout this book not only as thematisations of
(geopolitical) borders, but also as different patterns for imagining Russia
and Eastern Europe. Border and boundary are thus two different, though
interrelated, concepts. As mentioned earlier, my argument is that the
dynamics existing between the adjacent worlds of *Norden* and Russia/
Eastern Europe can be understood by means of these two concepts, which
help distinguish two central strands within representations of Russia and
Eastern Europe in Nordic cinemas: a border discourse and boundary
discourses.

My conceptualisation of the border/boundary discourses is inspired by
philosopher Edward S. Casey's distinction between border and boundary,
as well as by Thomas Nail's approach, arguing for an understanding of
border not as a static membrane dividing two areas, across which movement occurs, but as motion itself. Whereas Casey works with binaries (the
very division of border and boundary is of a 'border' character), Nail proposes thinking of borders as diffuse and in motion, experienced differently
by different subjects.

In his research on various types of edges in human experience, Casey
distinguishes between 'borders' and 'boundaries'. While borders are
established by conventional agreements and emerge as a product of human
history, boundaries are paradigmatically natural and perforated, allowing
for the border to breathe (see Casey 2011: 388). While borders are fixed
and can be measured, boundaries – due to their more fluent nature and lack
of exact positioning – allow negotiation. However, as Casey emphasises,
inherent to borders is their self-undermining potential: '*[B]orders are
always already in the process of becoming boundaries*' (393 [original empha-
sis]). Indeed, the border discourse shaping Eastern noir rarely remains
uncontested by an inner boundary. Binary distinctions between border
and boundary, hard and soft, or artificial and natural borders cannot be
maintained in practice (see also Nail 2016: loc. 199).

Casey sees borders as an expression of state power. Those who claim
the right to delineate the border are usually those who make claims to

power. Hence, the border is hierarchical as such: it divides/connects a centre and a periphery, a core and its margin. Nail compares the act of delineating borders to drawing a geometrical circle, which needs a radius and a centre: 'All the heterogeneous lines radiating outward become equal to one another by virtue of [. . .] the center, from whence they originate' (2016: loc. 1269). Thus, the border always points back towards a centre. In the border discourse on Russia and Eastern Europe, the Nordic self can be seen as the centre delineating the discursive and imagined border, claiming not only 'will to power', but also 'will to truth' (see Foucault 1971: 10–12).

However, as Nail convincingly argues, borders are not reducible to the limits of a state or a centre, but rather they embrace an in-between. 'States approach the limit (border) but never reach it or totalize it once and for all' (2016: loc. 109). Nail suggests that borders should be understood as a means for circulation rather than inclusion or exclusion: '[T]he process of circulation and recirculation performed by borders is not under the sole control of anyone, like the sovereign' (loc. 205). Tourists, visitors, migrants and refugees all contribute to this circulation through their movement.

Nail emphasises that the experience of the border is conditioned socially, culturally and economically, reminding us that some people, like affluent Western travellers, may experience the border as a 'relatively seamless continuity between two areas. For others, such as undocumented migrants, the border may appear as a discontinuous division across which they are forbidden to pass or from which they are redirected' (2016: loc. 121). In the context of borders, Nail distinguishes between two kinds of division: extensive and intensive. Extensive division introduces 'an absolute break – producing two quantitatively separate and discontinuous entities'. Intensive division, in turn, 'adds a new path to the existing one like a fork or bifurcation producing a qualitative change of the whole continuous system' (loc. 109–15). In contrast to the border discourse, boundary discourses promulgate circulation and intensive divisions. These divisions are 'intensive' in the sense that they have the potential to introduce a 'qualitative change' to the whole discursive 'system' and imaginative order.

I view border and boundary as twin poles on the continuum of contemporary Nordic discourses on Russia and Eastern Europe – not necessarily occurring separately and often overlapping, to varying degrees. If narrative can be defined as the 'contents' or story of a film, the way in which a narrative is represented belongs to the level of discourse (narration) – that is, to the treatment of the subject (cf. Bordwell and Thompson 2008: 75–6). However, discourse also encodes ideology. I understand discourse in the Foucauldian sense as a 'system of statements within which the world can be known', and according to which 'the world is not simply "there" to be talked about, rather, it is through discourse itself that the world is brought into being' (Ashcroft et al. 1998: 70–1). Discourse is ruled by exclusions and inclusions that involve 'certain assumptions, prejudices, blindnesses and insights, all of which have a historical provenance, but exclude other, possibly equally valid, statements' (Ibid. 73; see Foucault 1971). The selective perception and partial representations thus come to represent the whole (see Beller 2007: 4–5).

As mentioned earlier, Eastern noir narratives, organised by the discourse of the border, are dominant in the Nordic audiovisual imagination. Their strong position both results from, and is reinforced by, the tendency of the border discourse to organise chaotic realities according to clear-cut categories and thus to contain the fear incited by the potential for chaos. This discourse includes clear divisions between good and evil, claiming to represent Russia/Eastern Europe as a whole.

In contrast, boundary discourses can be seen as attached to weak or weaker narratives, which do not offer easy reassurances by promising to eliminate chaos and threats. Nor do they claim to represent the whole. Whereas border divides vertically, boundary has a horisontal orientation and foregrounds connection. Such discourses are 'weak' not just because they are marginal within the social realm or reflect uncommon perspectives on a hegemonic discourse, but also because they typically find expression outside and beyond the realm of mainstream cinema. However, just as mainstream cinema sometimes offers surprising perspectives on dominant discourses, minor, often independent or art-house productions are also capable of reproducing the Eastern noir narrative. Films that reimagine this hegemonic discourse break its ahistorical solidity into parts and set them in motion by going beyond the pervading stereotypes – though this does not mean they are themselves devoid of stereotypes or that they tell us the 'truth'. Rather, films shaped by the boundary discourses offer competing perspectives on grand narratives and dominant versions of history, often from the perspective of peripheral narratives, which have been marginalised or forgotten.

The scope and strength of the impact – or lack thereof – the films analysed in this book have had on the Nordic popular and cultural imagination of Russia and Eastern Europe is an important issue to be considered. My corpus includes both popular films and television series with the potential to broadly impact the popular imagination, as well as niche documentary productions, art films and student etudes, many of which are made available mainly at film festivals and through narrow distribution canals, with very limited impact on the popular imagination. However, as media scholar Marie Cronqvist emphasises, weak narratives are equally interesting to investigate, as they say at least as much about the community as strong ones. While remaining peripheral to mainstream discourse, they test its limits and have the potential to critique it. They often provide cues to understanding the dominant narratives. A weak narrative, moreover, can be seen as the embryo of a new strong narrative (Cronqvist 2004: 12). Additionally, although I recognise that some of the films are not accessible to broad audiences, and even ephemeral, I wish, following Laura U. Marks' approach, 'to celebrate them at the moment of their brief flowering' (2000: loc. 252). I believe that their perspective should not be neglected, as they constitute a part of the picture of Russia and Eastern Europe in Nordic cinemas and many of them testify to a more nuanced and positive direction in the process of reimagining Eastern Europe. Finally, it should be added that compared to other forms of art, art cinema has a greater ability to address broader audiences and thus to exert an impact on socio-cultural perceptions.

Throughout this book, I will be returning to the above issues and concepts, engaging with them in relation to the films under discussion. Representations or explicit thematisations of borders are not a prerequisite for the inclusion of a film. The border, be it geopolitical, cultural, social, moral and/or economic, can be manifested subtly or implicitly. This book maps out a variety of cinematically rendered relationships between the Nordic subjects and their neighbours across the former Iron Curtain and investigates the diversity of these representations across time. An overview of sixty-five fiction films (including one animation), forty documentaries and seven television series (see the Filmography) – of which thirty-three are closely analysed in this book – leads to the conclusion that the border discourse has not been superseded by multiple boundary discourses, but rather that Eastern noir has come to coexist with other discourses and thus lost its hegemonic status. Nevertheless, due to political developments during recent years, this discourse seems to be returning with full force to the Nordic imagination – though specifically towards Russia.

Research Scope and Structure of the Book

The cinematic imagination of Russia and Eastern Europe in Nordic films remains fairly unexplored. In spite of the frequency of the representations, this subject has not drawn significant scholarly interest in and of itself. That said, a few exceptions should be mentioned, including research referring not only to cinema, but more generally to Nordic cultural narratives. Helena Jerman (2004) and Ágnes Németh (2015) provide an overview of representations of Russians and Estonians in Finnish (mainly television) documentaries. Alexandra N. Leontieva and Karin Sarsenov (2005) explore stereotypical representations of Russian women in the Scandinavian media. A volume devoted to early narratives on Soviet Russia in Sweden investigates Swedish self-reflection in the Russian 'mirror' (Gerner and Karlsson 2008). A Swedish collection of essays addresses historical discourses and cultural narratives on the Baltic Sea (Karlsson and Zander 2000). An analysis of imaginary geographies in Swedish literary narratives of the 1980s and 1990s focuses on the shift to the post-Cold War reality and includes analyses of Swedish travelogues describing the (former) Eastern Bloc countries (Mohnike 2007). 'Eastern European villains' and 'Russian mafia', both of which populate Nordic films in abundance, are mentioned in articles covering transnational issues in Nordic cinemas (Agger 2016a; Marklund 2010). Several Swedish films that represent Russians and Eastern Europeans are analysed by Rochelle Wright (1998). A useful study of Russians represented in Finnish and Scandinavian crime fiction is offered by Paula Arvas (2011); similarly, an examination of the Baltics in Danish and Swedish literature has been undertaken by Sven Hakon Rossel (2009). Mainly, however, other 'others' in Nordic cinemas (Jews and Muslims, for example) have attracted scholarly attention (for example, Wright 1998; 2005; Bakøy 2011; Dancus 2011; Necef and Bech 2013; Mulari 2013; Larsen 2015; see also *Kosmorama* 2007/240).

   Due to the dearth of scholarly material, I was required to pore over a vast number of books and articles in order to establish appropriate films and, indeed, issues for inclusion and discussion. Above all, however, it required me to familiarise myself with a wide selection of films – from the era of silent films to the present day – in order to gain a comprehensive overview of representations of Russia and Eastern Europe in Nordic cinemas, while also allowing for the identification of repeating tropes and themes and discern shifts and nuances in both dominant and marginal discourses. Given the extensive and diverse body of material, it was only with time that I gained insight into the specific nature of this subject. I soon learned, however, that a popular assertion I had frequently encountered among film scholars – namely, that depictions of the eastern neighbours are negligible in Nordic cinematography – proved to be wrong.

   I am aware that this book does not cover the whole range of issues related to this topic, nor does it discuss all Nordic films devoted to Russia or containing Russian and Eastern European themes. Due to the methodology adopted – which is an in-depth analysis of selected films, in order to discern the most important discourses, tropes and problems, as well as determine the specificity of depictions of the eastern neighbours in Nordic cinematography and the changes these have undergone – this book focuses on those aspects I considered to be the most significant and most frequently recurring. However, not all the issues I considered important found their way into the book. Three of these should be mentioned here: the first is the recurring, though not always problematised, theme of the eastern neighbours as predominantly religious countries – mainly in relation to Orthodox Russia and Catholic Poland – often seen as further proof of how they contrast with the highly secularised self-conception of the Nordic societies. One excellent example of the relevance of this theme, which at the same time challenges this self-conception, is Pernille Rose Grønkjær's documentary film *The Monastery: Mr. Vig and the Nun* (*Slottet*, Denmark 2006).[17] Another significant theme omitted here is rooted deeply in Finnish history and cinema – namely, Finland's land lost to the USSR after World War II, in particular, a large part of the historic Karelian Isthmus, which remains a nostalgic subject in Finnish cinema and a setting that has prompted numerous attempts to delve back into the nation's roots and mythical past (see, for example, Oisalo 2016). This theme, because of the complex historical issues and large number of films involved, as well as the sometimes-camouflaged means by which the topic of Karelia is addressed, would require a separate study. Finally, a number of Nordic directors engage with environmental issues related to Russia, an example being Knut Erik Jensen's documentary *Cool and Crazy* (*Heftig og begeistret*, Norway 2001). Whereas the Nordic societies associate themselves – and are associated from the outside – with a high level of ecological consciousness, Russia (and the former Soviet Union) embodies the opposite end of the green spectrum. The explosions in Chernobyl in April 1986, as well as other nuclear power plant catastrophes, prompted numerous representations thematising the fear of pollution and diseases caused by invisible particles and spreading to the neighbouring – also Nordic – countries.[18] This theme is not dealt with in depth in the current book.

Guided by three crucial criteria – the frequency, historical relevance and (re)imaginative potential of recurring themes and tropes – this book focuses on the following issues presented below. In each of the chapters, I maintain a dual perspective – analysing images of Russia and Eastern Europe, while also analysing how these reflect the Nordic self. Due to the strength and frequency of the Nordic cinematic representations of Russia, three out of the book's six chapters are almost exclusively devoted to films foregrounding Russia. Among the neighbours across the Baltic Sea, the largest nation, Poland, with a huge diaspora throughout the three Scandinavian countries, is represented most frequently.[19] Therefore, the cinematic representations of Poles fill a substantial part of Chapter 3 and are the subject of Chapter 6.

My first chapter is concerned with the cinematic narratives of Eastern noir and particularly with the inherent trope of imagining Russia (and thereby often of Eastern Europe) as a crime scene. As I show, this trope essentialises the 'other' place as being permeated by evil. Despite similarities, I point to a crucial difference in how Russia and the Eastern European neighbours are represented: whereas, as I argue, Russia serves as the 'great Other', the centre in whose gaze the Nordic subject is constituted, overseen and controlled, Eastern Europeans function as 'others' with a lowercase 'o', which merely denotes their alleged unfamiliarity. The analytical part of the chapter opens with the Finnish action film *Born American* (1986) and concludes with the Norwegian Nordic noir television series *Occupied* (2015–), thus exploring Eastern noir films over the last thirty years. By juxtaposing a diversity of genres, including two documentaries, I show that the hegemonic narrative, although most persistent in fiction cinema, functions across various modes of cinematic expression. I also demonstrate that although Eastern noir narrates Russia as 'eternal', unchanging over time, the Nordic border discourse on Russia is not unchanging – rather, it is conditioned upon *Norden*'s increasing transnational involvements on a regional and global scale. The border these narratives produce provides the audience with feelings of reassurance and closure in an increasingly globalised world.

Whereas Eastern noir narratives reproduce the 'iron' border between 'us' and 'them' and operate by means of clear-cut national identities, Chapter 2 reconsiders the hard border promulgated by the hegemonic narrative of the Cold War. I focus on iconic figures associated with the Cold War – spies and double agents, whose activities are by definition characterised by crossing borders, although the films analysed do not utilise typical spy film formulas. Using the notion of infiltrated identities, the analysis follows the spies that embody the discourses of boundary. The 'infiltrated infiltrators' demonstrate that isolation and strict division is a fantasy on which power relations feed – and on which they thrived during the Cold War era.

The first two chapters focus on films that are discursively and/or thematically embedded in WWII and the Cold War, although epitomising contemporary perspectives on the past. Chapter 3 investigates films set (primarily) in the 1990s, when Russia had lost its status as an imperial threat. Rather than being positioned as small nations facing a large and dangerous neighbour, the small Nordic countries now find themselves among equally small neighbours that have (re)emerged in the northern consciousness after the disintegration of the Eastern Bloc. The central metaphor encapsulating this change is the Baltic Sea. The sea embodies

Nordic ambiguity towards the changing nature of borders and the anxieties related to the alleged crisis of the Nordic identity after the Cold War. The binary concept of centre/periphery serves as a point of departure for an analysis of the trope of the sea, showing how the border discourse 'bifurcates' (using Nail's term) into boundary discourses, epitomised by the figure of a 'distant neighbour', as well as by narratives of freedom and modernity, replacing the former East/West frame.

While the films analysed in Chapter 3 offer a positive narrative on the Baltic, transforming it from border to boundary, this does not encompass the whole story. In Chapter 4, I explore films addressing the gloomy aspects of mobility and connection across the sea. Two Swedish films, *Lilya 4-ever* and *Buy Bye Beauty*, stage the Baltic as an important economic and moral border/boundary, problematised through the theme of sex trafficking and drawing on the stereotype of the Russian/Eastern European prostitute. I analyse how these films approach the economic inequality and the dichotomy of the Nordic oppressor/Eastern European victim through the concept of guilt. The last section of Chapter 4 is devoted to shame – a feeling often conflated with guilt, but clearly distinguished by its less self-centred approach. Shame is as equally relevant as guilt in the context of transnational disparities. My argument is that whereas guilt draws clear-cut borders between the self and other, shame facilitates boundary discourses. This is neatly illustrated by Pirjo Honkasalo's documentary *The 3 Rooms of Melancholia*. As I also show with brief references to a number of other films, in the Nordic cultural imagination, shame is typically evoked by Russia, whereas the 'weaker' Baltic neighbours tend to stimulate narratives of guilt.

In Chapter 5, using the concept of the militarised body, I explore the pervading image connected to the trope of Russia as a crime scene and inherent in Eastern noir: the Russian soldier. The chapter examines films that attempt to circumvent the fixity of this stereotype and add nuance by addressing not only old conflicts, but also contemporary ones, such as the wars in Chechnya. I argue that rather than simply denying the stereotype – and risking denying irrefutable facts, such as the militarisation of Russian society – the films dissect the figure of the Russian soldier by exposing his constructedness, often serving to define the Nordic body as his disarmed, peaceful and innocent opposite. Whereas the fear of Russia is not completely disavowed – rather, it is historically actualised – other strategies, such as humour and irony, expose *rysskräck* as a Nordic projection. With the concept of the militarised body, Chapter 5 captures what I diagnose as a return of grand narratives in the Nordic cultural imagination of Russia.

In the sixth and final chapter, I return to the neighbours from across the sea – this time, in the context of the substantial post-2004 migrations of Poles to the three Scandinavian countries. I utilise the concept of spectral agency, theorised by Esther Peeren – that is, the agency of the dispossessed, the marginalised, and those made socially invisible by ongoing spectralising processes (the 'living ghosts'), most prominently the processes of neoliberal globalisation. I focus on how Polish 'ghost' workers, cleaning and repairing Scandinavian houses, contribute to reimagining the most ubiquitous political metaphor encapsulating the Scandinavian welfare state – the people's home (Swedish *folkhem*). Looking at the Scandinavian people's 'home' from the ghosts' perspective helps to expose the borders (or walls) implicit in this metaphor, opening up the potential for a reimagining of both the political metaphor and the social reality it reflects and shapes. Although recent films present a particularly unflattering judgement on the capability of Scandinavians to reimagine their home(s), the Polish 'living ghosts' are represented as powerful – though not idealised – figures, resisting spectralisation through their capability to produce a qualitative change in the (discourse of the) home.

As proved by the widespread Eastern noir narratives in Nordic cultural imagination and the limited academic examination of this phenomenon, the Iron Curtain effect is undeniable. With this book, I hope at least partly to mitigate its negative impact on scholarly research – and to encourage further reimaginings of *Norden*'s eastern neighbours within academic discourses.

Notes

1. An example from American Cold War cinema is *The Spy Who Came In From the Cold* (Martin Ritt, 1965). The film ends with a nocturnal death scene at the Berlin Wall, the protagonists (in this case British citizens) escaping to the Western side. Also, on German films about escaping from East Germany, see Brzezińska (2014).
2. In strictly geographical terms, 'Scandinavia' excludes both Finland and Denmark. In terms of linguistic affinity, Finland is excluded from 'Scandinavia'. The term 'Northern Europe', in turn, is too broad, as it tends to include northern Germany, Scotland and other areas.
3. This position forced Finland into a 'friendship agreement' with the USSR, leading to so-called 'Finlandisation' – a term describing Finland's political submissiveness towards Russia during the Cold War in order to sustain sovereignty – formally commenced with the Agreement for Friendship, Cooperation and Mutual Assistance signed in April 1948 (see Meinander 2013: 159–62).
4. For example, Russian military aircraft intruded Swedish air space during

the Easter holiday of 2013; the Russian ambassador to Denmark raised the threat in March 2015 of nuclear war in the event of Denmark's participation in NATO's missile defence system; the Russian ambassador to Norway criticised the television drama *Occupied*, in which Russia conducts a soft occupation of Norway, as a revival of the Cold War; recently, Latvian and Lithuanian authorities announced that fences would be built along the border with Russia, which in the case of Lithuania is the Kaliningrad Oblast.

5. Especially when compared with American Cold War cinema, see Shaw (2007).

6. Translations into English, unless indicated otherwise, are all mine.

7. Danish conservative historian Bent Jensen accused Danish intellectuals of lacking criticism towards Stalinism and the role of terror in the Soviet Union (Jensen [1984] 2002). A similar critique was uttered by Swedish historian Kristian Gerner, who points out the negligence of Swedish intellectuals in regard to the political crimes in the USSR (Gerner 2000).

8. Historian Matthew Kott likewise notes that in Sweden during the Cold War 'military planning and exercises always involved confronting an unnamed "enemy from the east"' (Kott 2015).

9. These events are also depicted in a three-minute-long reportage *The Russians are Leaving Bornholm* (*Russerne forlader Bornholm*, 1946), as well as in the newsreel *The Reconstruction of Rønne and Neksø* (*Rønne og Neksøs genopbygning*, Poul Bang, Denmark 1954), with the screenplay by Carl Theodor Dreyer.

10. *Orion's Belt* was shot in both Norwegian and English (the English-language version features Tristan De Vere Cole as director), and the screenplay, based on Norwegian author Jon Michelet's novel (1977), was adapted by a UK scriptwriter, Richard Harris. The film was distributed in the US and Europe and was also internationally distributed as a TV drama.

11. Mireille Rosello compares the stereotyping process to turning a text into an image, 'because it transforms the symbolic freedom of endless assembling and dissassembling [sic] into a symbolic lack of flexibility' (1998: 23).

12. I am highly grateful to the producers of *Sorjonen/Bordertown* (Fisher King Production) for granting me online access to the first season of the series (discussed briefly in Chapter 2).

13. I coined the term 'Eastern noir' in 2009 in my research project (financed by The Danish Council of Independent Research, FKK) entitled *Østblok noir. Forestillinger om 'Østeuropa' i dansk litteratur, essayistik, film og billedkunst ca. 1980–2009* (*Eastern Bloc Noir. Imaginations of 'Eastern Europe' in Danish Literature, Film and Visual Arts 1980–2009*). The term 'Nordic noir' was first used by the American journalist Laura Miller in *The Wall Street Journal* in January 2010.

14. Interestingly, the negative stereotypes of Russia(ns) and Eastern Europe(ans) persist in Nordic cinemas to a much greater degree than depictions of other ethnic 'others', represented primarily as agreeable characters who wish to integrate and who expose racist structures in society, especially in Sweden (Hedling 2007; Tigervall 2005). It seems that because depictions of Russians

and Eastern Europeans are not a question of race and integration, their cinematic representations are less influenced by what Carina Tigervall described
as 'antiracist' official Swedish rhetoric (2005: 45). My tentative thesis is that
negative images of Eastern European others are considered more 'permissi-
ble' than in the case of ethnic others, especially in Swedish film. In Norwegian
cinema (see Larsen 2015: 181–3), as well as in Danish cinema (see Necef and
Bech 2013), there is a stronger tendency to depict ethnic otherness beyond
the politically correct frame.

15. Guilt and social responsibility are also salient features of Nordic noir (see
    Solum 2016).
16. I use the notions of space and place interchangeably. Some scholars dis-
    tinguish between 'space' as an abstract notion opposed to the concrete and
    bodily experienced 'place' (see Ringgaard 2010: 94).
17. Another noteworthy documentary film focusing on religion is Pirjo Honkasalo
    and Eira Mollberg's *Mysterion* (1991) about an Estonian Orthodox monastery.
18. Documentaries thematising environmental issues related to Russia include
    Marja Pensala's *The Eclipse of the Soul* (*Sielunpimennys*, Finland 2000) and
    Volga – a Russian River (*Volga – venäläinen joki*, Finland 2009). Documentaries
    by Danish director Boris Bertram: *Tank City* (*Tankograd*, Denmark 2010),
    Swedish journalist Gunnar Bergdahl: *The Voice of Ljudmila* (*Ljudmilas röst*,
    Sweden 2001), inspired by the Belorussian writer Svetlana Alexievich's book
    Chernobylskaya molitva. Hronika buduschego (*Chernobyl Prayer*) and its fol-
    low-up *Ljudmila & Anatolij* (Sweden 2006), as well as the short fiction film
    Berik (Daniel Joseph Borgman, Denmark, Russia 2010), all examine nuclear
    disasters in the former Soviet Union and their longer-term effects on citizens.
19. Polish migrants are not a significant minority in Finland (see Bartram 2007).

CHAPTER 1

Borders: Russia and Eastern Europe as a Crime Scene

Borders and border crossings constitute a powerful trope in Nordic narratives on Russia and neighbouring Eastern Europe. This chapter investigates films that not only (explicitly or implicitly) thematise borders, but, more importantly, adopt a border discourse on Russia and Eastern Europe – a cinematic pattern that I define as *Eastern noir*. As emphasised in the Introduction, the term 'border' is understood as distinct from 'boundary'. Unlike boundary, which problematises the very idea of border and is porous in character, border is hierarchical and vertical as such: delineated from the centre, it designates both a core and its margin.

The Nordic border discourse that structures Eastern noir narratives represents Russia and/or Eastern Europe in terms of *extensive* division: it produces two discontinuous entities, two separated 'sides' (see Nail 2016: loc. 109–15). However, even the most hierarchical cinematic approaches to Russia and Eastern Europe reveal ruptures in this oppositional discourse. As we shall see, while Eastern noir expresses Nordic cultural superiority and aims to discursively subordinate Russia, this relation of superiority versus inferiority is often charged with ambivalence: the Nordic discursive power may serve to hide the deep-seated anxiety of the small (both demographically and in terms of political control) Nordic nations regarding their position as neighbours with the great Soviet Empire/Russia.

Negative representations of Russia, especially from the last years of the Cold War, often reflect, both thematically and in terms of genre (notably, the popular choice of the Hollywood inspired action film genre), *Norden*'s ideological alliance with the US and a desire to draw a distinction between Nordic society and the USSR. At the same time, there exists a tendency in Eastern noir to express ambivalence towards any alliances with the two superpowers. Marking clear distinctions towards both the West and East may serve to emphasise the idea of *Norden*'s uniqueness. During the Cold War, this uniqueness (characteristic of so-called Nordic exceptionalism) denoted, among other things, the construction of the Nordic identity as a 'better' region compared to the rest of ('warlike') Europe and generally the West. The Nordic region represented a third way between communism and capitalism and 'a model of the enlightened, anti-militaristic society' (Wæver 1992: 77; see also Browning 2007). Yet, such a clear distinction may also be seen as an attempt by small nations who feel threatened by larger international players to defend their sovereign position and identity, while also making an effort to compete with the larger powers – in the vein of what Mette Hjort (in the context of film founding and production) has denoted 'reactive globalisation' (2005: 162).

In Eastern noir films, the 'peacefulness' of the Nordic countries, combined with a desire to demonstrate superiority, is emphasised by a contrastive strategy: the border discourse imagines Russia as a crime scene, which helps to foreground in high relief one's own nationally specific elements. However, the crime scene that Russia represents in Eastern noir is not a crime scene as we would understand it in the traditional sense. Over the course of this chapter, I will pinpoint the main features of the Eastern noir renderings of Russia as a crime scene, in order to add nuance to this discourse and to investigate how this narrative has been structured at different times (from mid-1980s till 2015). I will also ask in what ways the shifts in this hegemonic narrative have been conditioned by the cultural and political specificities and developments of the individual Nordic countries (if such specificities are relevant to the films discussed).

Eastern noir imagines Russia not simply as a place where crimes occur ('there' as opposed to 'here'), disturbing an otherwise 'normal' order; rather, crime is depicted as inherent to the Russian national character. In discussing a traditionally understood crime scene – that is, a physically delineated space where a crime has been committed – Kjetil Sandvik observes:

> The crime scene is a place that [. . .] constituted the scene for some kind of physical activity, which has changed its nature. As such, the place has been encoded so that the particular actions and events [. . .] have left a variety of marks and traces, which may be read and interpreted. (2010: 291)

While Sandvik is speaking here about traces of blood, hair, nails and the general physical disposition of a particular crime scene (like a locked room), the traces of a crime in Eastern noir comprise evidence of an omnipresent evil emanating from the centre of Soviet/Russian power. In discussing the meanings and functions of the 'locked room' in crime fiction, David Schmid observes that the room only appears to be locked; in fact, it is connected to other spaces and other social, political and existential dimensions – the crime scene is an entity that 'connects with multiplicities' (2012: 10). This is clearly the case with Eastern noir, where the relation between the actual scene of a crime and this all-encompassing evil is centrifugal, not centripetal. In other words, a crime is not an isolated event, but is collective and social, leading back to the centre, from which it emanates. Interestingly, if in the Soviet tradition of the detective story the focus was on the harm the individual brought to society (Vatulescu 2010: 32–3), in Nordic Eastern noir it is the reverse: the emphasis is on the harm the state (the centre of evil) inflicts upon individuals, especially its own citizens.

In the quoted excerpt, Sandvik describes a crime scene as the product of a temporary change introduced to a certain place, thus recognising the possibility of distinguishing between the place itself and the crime scene. In Eastern noir, however, the crime scene is not a temporary condition, but a permanent state, part of a place's eternal ontology. Moreover, while 'the detective's ability to perform logical reasoning and deductive thinking [. . .] is crucial to how the crime scene is first deconstructed and then reconstructed as the setting for the story' (Sandvik 2010: 292), in Eastern noir the methods the Nordic detective would apply in his own country, associated with logical reasoning, rationalism and visibility, prove insufficient; what is required is the ability to orient oneself within the Eastern 'labyrinth', learning its specific rules, normally unintelligible to someone from the West.

In terms of narrative patterns, it is illuminating to relate the border discourse that frames Russia as a crime scene to a differentiation made in the 1960s by anthropologist Gilbert Durand between diurnal and nocturnal orders, or 'regimes' of representation. The border discourse typical of Eastern noir can be thought of as 'diurnal' to use Durand's term – that is, belonging to the day in the sense of being ruled by the rational, the solid and the rigid, and characterised by antithesis, oppositions and subject-object divisions (Falicka 2002: 11). Boundary discourses, in contrast, belong to the 'nocturnal regime', characterised by features associated with the night: fluidity, elusiveness and a porous structure, inviting disturbing and subversive elements and, as such, tending toward synthesis and the annihilation of vertical and binary structures (Ibid. 7). Whereas the nocturnal order (or boundary discourse) offers plots featuring 'descending, exploring, wandering, engagement, and involvement; [. . .] rhythms [. . .] of repetition and return', the plots of the diurnal 'entail combat and separation, the dynamics of polemic; its trajectories would include ascensional movement and falling, but also dividing, departing, separating, leavetaking, making new beginnings etc.' (Chambers 2001: 104–5). Although in Eastern noir films the symbolic endowment of black and white, darkness and light is conventional, with darkness (and thus negativity) associated with Russia and whiteness (and thus positivity) associated with *Norden*, Durand's 'diurnal regime' aptly describes the border discourse representing Russia as an opposition to the Nordic self. However, as we shall see, even the most 'diurnal' films entail 'nocturnal' elements undermining the border from within.

While discussing cinematic renderings essentialising Russia as a crime scene, it is important to emphasise that a crucial distinction emerges in representations of Russia and the neighbouring countries across the Baltic. Typically, in Eastern noir both Russia and Eastern Europe function as crime scenes or places from which crime originates. There are plentiful examples of both Russian and Eastern European villains in Nordic films and television series, which by conflating Russia and Eastern Europe repeat the absorbing gesture of the Soviet coloniser (see Mazierska et al. 2014: 7).[1] However, depictions of Eastern European countries indicate Russia's oppressive influence as the reason behind the crime, rather than suggesting that crime belongs to the essential and eternal 'nature' of these nations. After the dissolution of the Soviet Union, Eastern European countries became increasingly perceived through the 'filter' of Russia, rather than simply conflated with it. As a consequence, whereas Nordic perceptions of Russia can be described in binary terms (us *versus* the Russian/Soviet Other), the perception of the Baltic countries and Poland tends to have a triadic structure: rather than conflating Russia and Eastern Europe and thus rendering them indistinguishable, Russia serves as the primary filter through which the eastern neighbours are viewed (especially in the 1990s) by Nordic subjects.

Consequently, I suggest that Russia can be defined as the 'great Other', while the Eastern European neighbours are others with a lowercase 'o' – not only in Eastern noir, but more generally in Nordic films which thematise Russia/Eastern Europe. The notion of the great Other, which I borrow from postcolonial studies (which adopted this distinction from Jacques Lacan's psychoanalysis), is meant here to convey the perception of Russia as superior: the great Other acts as 'the imperial centre, imperial discourse, or the empire itself', because 'it provides the terms in which the colonized subject gains a sense of his or her identity as somehow "other", dependent' (Ashcroft et al. 1998: 170–1). I do not mean to argue that Eastern European subjects were colonised by Soviet Russia, which they undoubtedly were in several respects and to varying degrees (see Mazierska et al. 2014: 3–12), but instead aim to capture Nordic feelings of dependency on, and fear of, Russia, especially in the context of the Cold War. Although Russia tends to be orientalised, which typically serves to enhance the idea of *Norden*'s cultural superiority, it is also seen as a threatening colonising power. Thus, the distinction between the 'great Other' and Eastern European 'others' helps to describe a contrast which emerges in Nordic cinemas between Russia and Eastern Europeans. Rather than being seen as threatening, Eastern European neighbours are imagined as 'others' because they are different, distant and stigmatised by the great Other; in many ways, they resemble the Nordic self. This distinguishes them from the Russian Other, imagined as essentially different, barbaric, despotic and culturally inferior – both when compared to the Nordic self and to the Eastern European others.[2]

The films analysed in this chapter span three decades. The first two, *Orion's Belt* (*Orions belte*, Ola Solum, Norway 1985) and *Born American* (*Jäätävä polte*, Renny Harlin, Finland, US 1986), serve as early Eastern noir examples of a strictly binary approach to Russia. The next two, *The Russian Singer* (*Den russiske sangerinde*, Morten Arnfred, Denmark 1993) and *The Dogs of Riga* (*Hundarna i Riga*, Pelle Berglund, Sweden 1995), signal a gradual shift towards a transnational perspective, recognising connections, especially with the Eastern European neighbours, in spite of the overarching divisions. The features, themes and narratives of Eastern noir are found not only in genre cinema, but also in other cinematic modes, examples being the Danish documentaries *Maximum Penalty* (*Den højeste straf*, Tómas Gislason, Denmark 2000) and Lise Birk Pedersen's *Putin's Kiss* (*Putins kys*, Denmark 2012). This chapter concludes with an analysis of the Norwegian television series *Occupied* (*Okkupert*, TV2 Norway, 2015–), representing both a continuation of, and a unique take on, how Norwegians imagine themselves in relation to the Russian Other. As I will show, although Eastern noir narrates Russia as eternal and unchangeable across time, the Nordic border discourse on Russia is not unchangeable. Although Eastern noir has a tendency to endlessly repeat stereotypes, it is also determined by *Norden*'s increasing transnational involvement and changing position globally.

Darkness and Snow: *Born American* and *Orion's Belt* as Early Eastern Noir

Popular genre films, in particular, depict Russia and neighbouring Eastern Europe as a crime scene, employing rich patterns of the 'diurnal regime' as conceptualised by Durand. The Iron Curtain, dividing and separating, provided an imaginary structure for the diurnal order *par excellence*. Although a symbol of the 'Cold' War – as opposed to 'hot' – the Iron Curtain also signified the latent, constant threat of combat and 'hot' confrontation. This latent dimension of the 'Cold' War found explicit expression in two early Nordic genre films. Even though the negative representations they contain can be perceived as a continuation of pre-WWII depreciative depictions of Russians in Nordic cinemas, the films are deeply embedded in the Cold War order – both in terms of plot and their ideological structures. Made in the mid-1980s, they are the first cinematic examples in Nordic cinemas of controversial political content directly related to the entanglement of the Nordic countries in the Cold War; at the same time, they represent attempts to create domestic action films influenced by American examples of the same (Gustafsson and Kääpä 2015: 11; Iversen and Solum 2010: 62). Both films incorporate the binary black-and-white imagery typical of the Cold War master narrative. However, whereas *Orion's Belt* blurs distinctions and concludes with an omnipresent bleak malaise, *Born American* maintains control over the darkness and continues to confirm the binary structure of this narrative's oppositions. Therefore, I will first discuss *Born American* as embodying a more pronounced binary discourse, then proceed to *Orion's Belt*.

Born American is a Finnish-American action drama, released in 1986. The historical moment that coincided with its release – Gorbachev's economic reforms and the resulting political thaw – is one of the reasons why a film so depreciative of Russia was at all possible in Finland. Nevertheless, as mentioned in the Introduction, the film was initially banned and later censored because of its anti-Soviet sentiment (see Kääpä 2012: 184), which demonstrates the strength of Finland's submissive foreign policy towards the Soviet Union at this time.[3] *Born American* tells the story of three young American tourists who arrive in Helsinki and drive to the north of Finland. When they come within the vicinity of the border with the Soviet Union, they make a snap decision to cross the border just for fun. This turns out to be a foolish act of recklessness, which changes their lives entirely. After being forced to flee from Soviet border guards, they arrive at a small Russian village, where they are subsequently accused of murdering a girl (who was killed by a local priest), as a result of which they become involved in a bloody firefight. Soon, they are being chased by Soviet military forces; they are captured, brutally interrogated and thrown into prison, where they are kept in inhuman conditions. Two of them die. Only Savoy, with the help of another American prisoner and a Russian girl, Nadia, manages to escape after dramatic combat with Soviet troops and ultimately cross the border back to Finland.

This first Finnish Hollywood-style action movie was 'consciously moulded after the then-popular action genre, featuring a muscular war veteran fighting an ideologically motivated inhuman enemy' (Kääpä 2011:

57). Notably, before the tourists cross the border, the film mobilises the conventions of another essentially American genre – the road movie. As David Laderman observes, in road movies the road frequently 'provides an outlet for our excesses, enticing our desire for thrill and mystery. [. . .] Exceeding the borders of the culture it makes possible, for better or for worse, the road represents the unknown' (2002: 2). The 'unknown' and the excess promised by the young Americans' travel are found on the other side of the Russian–Finnish border. However, where the protagonists are heading is not 'unknown', because they already have a specific image of it. Their preconceptions – or 'knowledge' – of Russia are merely confirmed. The viewer is persuaded into holding a similar preconception through a prologue scene, showing the brutal murder of the girl in the Russian village.

Indeed, all the action and crime scenes are set on the Soviet side of the border. The structure of the Soviet prison has several 'circles', reminding one of Dante's hell – a not uncommon trope in depictions of Russia and/ or Eastern Europe.[4] Almost everyone in Russia is depicted as corrupt and capable of committing crime – priests, soldiers and even ordinary villagers. Russians are represented as brutal, primitive, repulsive and deceptive and are divided into two main groups: soldiers (of various ranks) and prisoners, who follow 'the law of the jungle'. On the Finnish side, in turn, everything is safe, the sun is shining and the three travellers, before they cross the border, engage in carefree activities. Furthermore, the Finnish part of their trip and the final scenes in Finland are shot during the day, whereas once the men enter the border zone, night falls. From that point on, combat scenes take place at night or in prison cells without windows. Tellingly, when Savoy and Nadia cross the border back into Finland, the dawn promises a 'new day'. While the Soviet part of the plot unfolds in destitute industrial areas, Helsinki is represented by the Cathedral and Senate Square. Thus, the binary logic of black and white, night and day, crime and safety, hell and heaven and so on is firmly established in the film. The 'whiteness' of Finland is intensified by sunlit snowy landscapes, which can be seen as symbolically referring to the White forces, who during the Finnish Civil War of 1918 fought the Reds – the Bolsheviks.

The crossing of the border into the Soviet Union is endowed with a large affective load, emphasising the distance between the two sides and playing a crucial dramatic function as a point of no return. It is a process entailing danger and obstacles (such as barbed wire) and, expanding the notion of the border from a line on a map to a bodily experience, eliciting tension, fear and pain. The border between Finland and Russia, East and West, is not 'a zone of interaction where people on one side of the border share values, beliefs, feelings and expectations with people on the other side of the border' (Rumford 2012: 895). Narratively, the border marks discontinuity and extensive division – an absolute break.

It is important that the border appears in the film as if it were a construct imposed by the Soviets. On the Finnish side, there is no border control, thus implying the peacefulness of 'our' side. The Iron Curtain is embodied by Soviet soldiers, who – as soldiers – 'physically constitute the border itself as they march forward in the military extension of the city or state' (Nail 2016: loc. 1321). During the Cold War, all traditional divisions between war, peace and neutrality, as well as politics and economy, the military and civil society, combatants and non-combatants became undermined, 'mocked'. The only valid and unshaken division that remained was between friend and enemy, which constituted the source and essence of the Cold War (see Stjernfelt 2003). In Eastern noir, the 'friend', with whom viewers are encouraged to sympathise, is the non-militarised protagonist, whereas the 'enemies' are the militarised Russian bodies. However, even if not militarised in a professional manner, the American trespassers in *Born American* do have weapons: a hunting rifle and a crossbow. These props are justified by the conventions of the action genre and the plot's development, but they also reflect mutual antagonism. While the men are essentially innocent tourists, this innocence only serves to neutralise the fact that they are armed trespassers, and as such, they also mark the border as they move along and across it, thus making the two 'competing' sides of the border (and the two competing powers) visible as they clash in dramatic firefights. The border here brings to mind a military trench more than anything else.

Thus, in *Born American*, the Finnish–Russian border denotes not only national edges, but also the split between two halves of the world. This carries important implications for Finland. First of all, Finland is clearly inscribed into the West, not least because the film is a Finnish-American co-production, draws on American genres, features American actors and contains English dialogue, all of which results from the international orientation of its producers. Aiming to 'flag up Cold War-era ideological solidarity with the United States and situate Finland in the geopolitical sphere of the West' (Kääpä 2011: 58), the strategy of inscribing Finland into the West can also be seen as an operation of erasing the Russian 'layer' from Finland. However, Russia cannot be erased: the Finnish and Russian spaces are not merely sharply divided, they also overlap. As one of the American tourists reads in a guide, 'the Senate Square was built by Russians', thus evoking Finland's historical past as a part of the Russian Empire. On the other hand, it is striking that *Born American* reduces

Finland to a passive, silent landscape, subordinated to larger powers: the USSR and the US. Not a single word of Finnish is uttered, not even by the only (supposedly) Finnish character in the film – a man who sells his car to the three travellers. Apart from the purely practical reasons behind the 'erasing' of Finland (international production and distribution), this might be seen as a comment on Finland's submissive post-war foreign policy, known as Finlandisation, under the ambit of which political compromises were made with the USSR in order to secure Finnish sovereignty, which also suppressed the widespread Russophobia (see Meinander 2013: 159–62). The devastating censorship of the film, which left its producers destitute, only confirms this submissiveness. The overtly negative depictions of Russians in *Born American* can be seen as an objection to this self-imposed censorship and collective suppression of negative sentiment towards Russia. At the same time, the scene where the protagonists trespass over the border into the Soviet Union evokes the two most famous Finnish war films, from 1955 and 1985, both entitled *The Unknown Soldier* (adaptations of Väinö Linna's novel from 1954), about the Continuation War (1941–4), when Finland was allied with Germany. Both films feature scenes in which Finnish soldiers cross the border into the Soviet Union, thus embodying the expansive side. These implicit references allude to the complexity of the border and the inner fissures, fears and desires of the Finnish national subject, one such desire being to conquer and subordinate (at least parts of) Russia – depicted as Finland's eternal oppressor according to the dominant Finnish national narrative – whereas the same narrative represents Finland as innocent and forced to defend itself (see Sundholm 2013a: 36; see Chapter 5 in this book).

As *Born American* suggests in its penultimate scene, the Soviets, embodied as KGB agents and spies, are to be feared, and not only literally at the Soviet crime scene: this evil spreads its tentacles and radiates out from the centre, far beyond the official line of power. In *Born American*, however, in accordance with the film's binary logic and the American superiority it conveys, evil is controlled and annihilated – and the agent killed. Although the position of Finland is ambivalent, the ideological structure is unambiguously hierarchical – the film produces a language of domination, according to which Russia is inferior to the West and, more specifically, to the US.[5]

A quite different conclusion is reached in *Orion's Belt* (1985), the first Norwegian Hollywood-inspired genre film, combining action drama and political thriller. Unlike *Born American*, the film was not censored, but in 1983 the production gave rise to official protests from the Soviet authorities at the embassy in Oslo, who described it as an 'unfriendly act against the USSR' (Iversen and Solum 2010: 66). Much more openly than *Born American*, the film deals with the problematic entanglements of the Nordic countries – in this case, Norway – between the West, represented by the North Atlantic Treaty Organization (NATO), and the USSR.

The film opens with dazzling shots of the magnificent snow-covered mountains and animal life of Spitzbergen. The images evoke the gaze of a tourist, confirmed in the first scene, which is set onboard a boat, the *Sandy Hook*. Two local Norwegians, Tom and Sverre, take American and German tourists on a boat tour of the area. While on the tour, the tourists spend their time obsessively taking photographs of their surroundings and attempting to (illegally) shoot a polar bear. The tourist gaze, to draw on sociologist John Urry's notion, connotes a reifying, idealised, disembodied and thoroughly visual experience of a place (Urry and Larsen 2011: 14). This gaze is commercially motivated and detached from everyday practices (Näripea et al. 2016: 50). Here, it serves to ridicule the tourists, who (somewhat stereotypically) are depicted as foolishly naïve. At the same time, the images that open the film invoke the Norwegians' national self-conception. Norwegian nature – or, rather, a 'constructed nature mythology, based on real nature (dark forests, fjords and high mountains)' – is 'a recurrent symbol equated with Norwegianness in the rhetoric of the nation' (Henlin-Stromme 2012: 1). This official national discourse is undermined in the film's very first shots through its overlap with the detached tourist – outsider – gaze. Later, the national discourse encoded in the enhanced nature shots becomes increasingly challenged, finally reaching its opposite – its own dark underside, hidden within the white magnificence of the seemingly unspoiled landscape. The Western tourists' attempt to shoot the bear from the deck of the *Sandy Hook* anticipates the threat posed to Norwegian sovereignty by the West. Another threat is signalled by the Russian mining village of Barentsburg on Svalbard, which is safely viewed and discussed from onboard the boat. In the opening scene, these threats seem manageable: the gun can be taken from the insubordinate tourists, and Barentsburg is a limited space seen from a distance.[6]

Orion's Belt tells the story of three inhabitants of Svalbard, Tom, Sverre and Lars, who take various jobs to make a living. Tom has a girlfriend, Eva, who is politically involved and criticises Norwegian foreign policy for 'serving two masters' – by both being a NATO member and allowing Soviet military bases on its soil (even though Svalbard is a demilitarised zone). Eva's political discussion introduces the theme of Norway's difficult geopolitical position. The action begins when Lars convinces his two friends to commit insurance fraud. The plan is to accept payment for transporting a bulldozer from Greenland and to 'lose' it in the sea, so as to

Figure 1.1 The black cable leading to the Soviet military installation visualises the border, whereas the knife represents combat, separation and the dynamics of polemic. *Orion's Belt*. Photograph by Harald Paalgard. Courtesy of Petter J. Borgli.

claim for the insurance loss. On their way back, the three friends are forced to seek safety on shore due to bad weather. Sverre ventures onto the shore and finds a thick cable hidden in the rocks. From this moment onwards, as in *Born American*, their trip evolves into an acutely embodied experience that changes the lives of the three men completely.

As the men come ashore, they are not yet aware that they are trespassing, crossing a forbidden, invisible border, marked by the black cable shown in close-ups, 'crossed' by Sverre's knife (which he uses to check how much copper is contained within the cable) and anticipating a bloody confrontation.

From this point on, sharp angles, frog perspectives and a limited field of vision dominate visually. Following the cable, the men are led to a cave, where they stumble across an illegal Soviet military installation. A Soviet soldier enters the cave, registers the hunting rifle that one of the men is carrying and, perceiving the three men as a threat, starts shooting at them. Lars kills him, and the terrified Norwegians escape, but shortly thereafter, a helicopter approaches the *Sandy Hook*. A war-like firefight begins. The noisy orange helicopter provides an aggressive contrast to the boat and its peaceful surroundings. As a destructive force, the helicopter symbolically threatens the Norwegian national self, encoded in the shots of nature. Both visually and narratively, it introduces verticality and division, ascensional movement and falling, replacing the horizontal unity of the ship and the sea. The Soviets remain faceless, anonymous enemies, representing the violent spectacle, terror and irrational destruction embodied by the helicopter. In the end, Tom is the only one to survive. In what follows, he is doomed to loneliness.

The atmosphere becomes dense as Tom realises that he is being drawn into a macropolitical power game. In Oslo, he is interrogated by American NATO officers. Neither the Soviets nor the Norwegians want the incident to see daylight, fearing that the risk of war is too great. Set at night, in desolate, dark waterfront areas of Oslo, the final scenes evoke the genre of paranoid political thriller in which the individual becomes the victim of broader and unclear political operations (Iversen and Solum 2010: 68–9; see Booth 1991: 152). These scenes have strong film noir undertones, elicited directly through a close-up of an iconic film noir object – a black telephone ringing. Here, however, unlike in classical film noir, the telephone does not carry a message of death. In the context of the Cold War, it signifies total surveillance, from which there is no escape. It rings on the desk of a Norwegian officer, who has received a message about Tom's location. Having discovered he is being followed, Tom is forced to flee. He soon finds himself in a gloomy industrial area on the waterfront. The frames are dark, with low-key lighting, and the area is labyrinthine, while expressionist light-and-shadow interplay and unsettling music elicit an atmosphere of fear. Shortly afterwards, Tom is dead. It is not clear who shot him, but it can be inferred that Norwegian and/or American, rather than Soviet, agents were following Tom. Unlike in *Born American*, the ending of *Orion's Belt* remains open.[7] The final shot is a panorama of Svalbard at night, seen from the perspective of a helicopter. Contrasting with the previous frog perspectives evoking Tom's entrapment, the final shot confirms the unsettling feeling of surveillance, suggesting that any escape from the omnipresent controlling gaze is impossible.

The tourist gaze that opens *Orion's Belt* overlaps with the Norwegian national self-conception encapsulated in the nature shots, while also connoting distance and detachment. This detachment is displaced by a painful confrontation at close range with the 'dark side' of the 'Norwegian' landscape. At the end of the film, another type of gaze is introduced: the panoptical surveillance of a fixed space, assumed from the perspective of a Soviet helicopter. Panoptic power is based on the asymmetry of the gaze: a tiny group of people observes the majority, and although the observed cannot see the observer, they begin to behave as if they were under constant observation (see Foucault 1995). Indeed, in *Orion's Belt*, Norway emerges as a self-controlling state fully submitted to the gaze of the Russian Other, going as far as to sacrifice one of its own citizens for a larger political cause. As in the panoptical prisons described by Michel Foucault, crossing forbidden borders within the hardened space means punishment or death. Thus, in *Orion's Belt* the border not only divides two countries and two opposite sides in a global conflict (as in *Born American*), but is also multiplied within Norway itself. Unlike *Born American*, *Orion's Belt* directly criticises the Norwegian authorities. As in American paranoid thrillers and film noir-inspired spy dramas of the 1960s and 1970s, the film shows that in terms of methods and morality, there is no essential difference between East and West (see Booth 1991: 151–2).[8] The peaceful, sunlit landscape covered in bright, white snow in the opening scenes is revealed to be a mere façade. In the omnipresent darkness of the final shot, there is no 'white' place for an individual to hide, no border to cross back into another territory.[9]

While *Born American* represents a discourse of Western cultural and political superiority over Russia, Solum's film focuses on the specifically Norwegian experience and disrupts the certainty of this self-perception as superior. Rather, it shows the inferiority and subordination of the small Norwegian nation to the powerful Russian neighbour and to the East/West political game in which its own national identity is reduced to feebleness, withdrawal and geopolitical loneliness. These highly dramatic Eastern noir plots, expressing the Cold War master narrative of friend *versus* enemy, are complemented in the 1990s by narratives of early transnational involvement, although the 'other' side continues to be narrated as a crime scene, ultimately different than *Norden*.

Division and Involvement

Such a shift in depictions of both Russia and Eastern Europe can be seen in two films that thematise connections as well as divisions. *The Russian Singer* (1993) and *The Dogs of Riga* (1995) are both adaptations of novels by well-known Scandinavian crime fiction writers, the most popular being Henning Mankell, Swedish author of the famous Kurt Wallander series, who published *The Dogs of Riga* in 1992 (Mankell 2012). The action of both the novel and the film is set in Ystad, a small town in southern Sweden, and in Riga, the Latvian capital, in early 1991, before the proclamation of Latvia's independence from the USSR, during a time of sweeping political change in the Baltic countries. *The Russian Singer*, by the Danish author of political/spy thrillers Leif Davidsen, was released in 1988 (Davidsen 1988). The plot, set in both Moscow and Copenhagen, takes place in the turbulent period in Russia's history surrounding the dissolution of the USSR. Although the novels differ crucially in their approach to the border/boundary dialectic (see Mrozewicz 2013b), the two adaptations demonstrate a number of similarities. For instance, both films assume an overall binary approach, but unlike the discourse represented by *Born American*, the protagonists of the two adaptations become involved with the 'other' side, even though many of the usual binaries remain unquestioned and problematic.

The Dogs of Riga opens with Inspector Kurt Wallander finding a life raft washed up on a beach close to Ystad with two dead men inside, identified as Russians with connections to the mafia operating in Latvia. If in *Born American* the Russian crime scene is a fixed and localisable space on the 'other' side of the border, and in *Orion's Belt* it is multiplied within Norway, here the raft is a tiny mobile crime scene, detached from Latvia and spreading to Sweden simply by means of the tides, rather than due to some intentional actions of the 'enemy'. As such, the raft signifies the post-1989 destabilisation of a previously fixed space and the international threat resulting from the growing openness of the borders. The connection between Sweden and the 'other' shore across the Baltic Sea provokes anxiety in Wallander, who can be seen as embodying a more general 'Swedish anxiety' (Agger 2016b: 137). As he realises, the sea enables infiltration by evil from the 'other' shore, which suddenly lies much closer than during the Cold War.

Soon, however, a more promising cross-border encounter occurs in the film, when a Latvian major and dissident, Liepa, arrives to help with the investigation, during which Wallander and Liepa establish a friendship. Shortly after his return to Riga, Liepa is murdered. Inspector Kurt Wallander then travels to Riga to help solve the murder. The political situation in Latvia proves to be tense. Wallander returns to Sweden, with the murder remaining unsolved and the case formally closed. Later, he travels to Latvia unofficially, urged by a group of Latvian dissidents led by Baiba, the wife of the murdered Liepa, who claims to need Wallander's support. The dissidents' aim is to get hold of, with Wallander's help, Major Liepa's secret report – the existence of which explains his murder – detailing felonies carried out by the pro-Soviet police in Latvia. Wallander first refuses to travel illegally, but finally agrees. His motivation is, however, not entirely idealistic – he has fallen in love with Baiba and is now driven by a desire to rescue himself, rather than Latvia.

The plot of *The Russian Singer* begins in Moscow. Jack Andersen, a diplomat at the Danish Embassy, is asked to take care of some formalities related to the murder of his secretary. The Soviet authorities are quick to close the case as a suicide, but Andersen and the Russian police investigator Gavrilin refuse to believe their version of events, especially after a nightclub singer of Estonian origin, who later becomes Jack's lover, Lilli, suggests that they are mistaken and that the truth is far more sinister. Their investigation leads straight to the highest ranks of the Soviet military. Jack reports this to the Danish authorities, which leads to his expulsion from the embassy. After a Danish intermezzo, he travels back to Moscow and finds the city in a state of chaos and political turmoil. He manages to find a secret report written by Gavrilin (who in the meantime has been murdered), and the case is transferred to a democratic court. Jack reconciles with Lilli and travels back to Denmark with her, though not without obstacles. At the Russian–Finnish border a dramatic scene takes place, and the couple barely manage to escape from Soviet soldiers, who attempt to kill them.

The construction of the two plots is similar. The Nordic protagonist serves as a helper in establishing democratic values on the 'other' side and as a rescuer of the system's victims (usually embodied by women), whereas the other characters are divided into two groups: pro-Soviet and anti-Soviet, according to a binary structure. The crime centres around the oppressive Soviet authorities, embodied in both films by high-ranked soldiers – the agents of death. When Jack Andersen wonders who the murderer might be, his Russian friend says: 'You can't catch the system: it has too many heads like a monster in a nightmare'. However, as if to fulfil the desire to localise the crime and find the perpetrators, in Eastern noir the agents of death are always identified in the end. Victims, in turn, are depicted as dissidents, artists, liberals and, in Arnfred's film, prostitutes. Importantly, *The Dogs of Riga* introduces another, third figure disrupting this binary constellation: the (distant) neighbour, emerging through evocations of the historical relations between Sweden and Latvia.

A male Western protagonist becoming emotionally involved with a Russian or Eastern European woman is a common trope in spy and crime thrillers. However, less typically, *The Dogs of Riga* comprises a meaningful reversal in terms of the dynamics of nationality and gender: the Latvian widow, Baiba, becomes the driving force behind the events in the second part of the film (when Wallander travels illegally to Latvia), and, in contrast to the usually objectified women (like Lilli in *The Russian Singer*), she acts as a powerful subject and agent. At the same time, Wallander is briefly turned into an object of play between Latvian dissidents and pro-Soviet authorities. Thus, not only in terms of nationality but also gender, the Latvian other becomes Wallander's superior, which casts doubt on the discourse of superiority of the Swedish self. Moreover, Baiba most evidently embodies the Swedish protagonist's 'neighbour' – she can speak Danish and is played by a Danish actress, which due to the geographical and cultural closeness of Sweden and Denmark accentuates the kinship between Sweden/Scandinavia and Latvia.

In both films, the Nordic protagonist's emotional involvement translates into their political involvement in local conflicts. However, *The Russian Singer* (similarly to *Born American*) stages Russia and the Nordic countries as two separate systems with no interconnections. In this respect, the final scene is symbolic: the crossing of the border from Russia to Finland is a turbulent event, with Jack and Lilli's car being shot at by Soviet authorities. As soon as they cross the borderline into Finland – even though it is only an arbitrary line and not a physical barrier protecting them from bullets – they are depicted as beyond the reach of the evil. As an example of the opposite, Kurt Wallander tries to separate Sweden and Latvia as two mutually isolated spaces (for instance, by first refusing to help the Latvian dissidents), but realises that their interconnectedness is impossible to ignore. As the plot unfolds, the 'other' space becomes increasingly manifest in Wallander's consciousness. This involves evocations of a common history in the film's narrative, emphasising the closeness of the Baltic country to Sweden. As if to illustrate that the end of the Cold War made it possible to see that 'different "other" territories and subjects are reciprocally connected' (Sundholm 2013a: 32), Wallander learns that parts of today's Latvia were ruled by the Swedes in the seventeenth century – a time when the Russian Empire was the principal enemy of the Swedish Kingdom. This indirectly suggests that Sweden and Latvia share (both in the past and present) a common enemy.

The figure of a Nordic rescuer of Russian, and especially Baltic, victims can be seen as appealing to a guilty conscience resulting from the non-involvement of the Nordic nations – particularly Sweden and Finland – towards their Baltic neighbours during the Cold War (see Lundén and Nilsson 2006; Lauridsen et al. 2011: 115–16).[10] However, an opposition between the (male) Nordic rescuer and (female) Russian or Baltic victim is problematic: it is hierarchical, tends to victimise the other and invokes colonial tropes. Yet, both *The Dogs of Riga* and *The Russian Singer*, rather than simply assuming such an approach, make it an object of reflection. In Berglund's film, this is achieved by reminding viewers about Sweden's colonial past in the neighbouring region and endowing Latvians with agency while turning Wallander into an object of their political gameplay. In *The Russian Singer*, the discourse of superiority towards Russia is represented by the initial attitude of Andersen, who tends to patronise the Russians, rather than by the film's ideological structure.

Nonetheless, both films, but especially *The Russian Singer*, adhere to the tradition of Western discourses on Russia. According to American historian Martin Malia, Western perceptions of Russia have developed along a twofold path: on the one hand, there exists a tradition of belief in the progress of Russian society towards what Western commentators take to be 'normal' development – that is, liberal democracy and capitalism of the Western cut. On the other hand, there is a romantic-essentialist view, according to which Russia's national character is unchangeable and fundamentally different from Western values and civilisation – inherently 'barbaric' and violent. The latter view is manifested in the trope of 'oriental despotism', as opposed to 'enlightened despotism' (Malia 1999; Naarden and Leerssen: 227–9). According to Malia, positive perceptions tend to dominate when Russia's development is considered to be convergent with the West (as in the 1990s), while the romantic-essentialist view prevails when it is seen as divergent from the (Western) 'norm' and threatening democratic values (see Alm 2008: 140). In particular, the

> Soviet 'experiment' loomed as the great Other [. . .]. To the hopeful, it represented the socialist antithesis to capitalism, and the future as against the past. To the fearful, it became the totalitarian menace to the free world of the West, and the enemy of civilization. (Malia 1999: 3)

In both films, *The Russian Singer* and *The Dogs of Riga*, the Soviet system (rather than Russia) incarnates the threatening source of the evil. The positive Russian and Latvian characters are opposed to the Soviet authorities, representing the enlightened fraction adhering to Western norms and associated with civilisation (in polar opposition to barbarity). Barbaric domain and divergence from 'normal' civil society, in turn, is strongly represented by the militarised Soviet authorities. The Soviet soldier – whether a high-ranking police officer (*The Dogs of Riga*) or a general (*The Russian Singer*) – represents the ultimate deviation. In both films, the civilised forces, together with assistance from the Nordic protagonist, win in the end. Thus, the plots fulfil the classical Western desire for the victory of the West's own values. The oppositional discourse is especially strong in *The Russian Singer*. This has to do with political thrillers as an international genre and with Denmark (equalled with its capital, Copenhagen) being depicted as a secure place located far away from the Russian turmoil. Berglund's adaptation of Mankell's novel, in turn, seeks to avoid an oppositional perspective of Latvia. This is due to Latvia, rather than Russia, being the place of Wallander's engagement, as well as with the common past between Latvia and Sweden, and with the setting of Ystad, which is a peripheral Swedish location (as opposed to Stockholm, which cooperates with Soviet authorities). It is emphasised that Ystad is connected to Latvia by the Baltic Sea. In *The Russian Singer*, the fact that Lilli is Estonian implies that establishing a connection with a Baltic country is more probable than forging one with Russia. The possibility of a connection with the Baltic states can be seen as an act of sympathy from the small Nordic nations towards the neighbours on the other side of the Baltic.

Both films (and the novels) should be seen as firmly rooted in the moment of their making, when the situation in Eastern Europe and Russia was changing radically. *The Dogs of Riga*, in particular, represents a remarkable shift: even if it draws on the fundamental East/West division, it problematises the border as porous and historically contingent and introduces the figure of the Baltic neighbour – a trope that recurs throughout the 1990s, as elaborated on in Chapter 3. The division is intensive rather than extensive, meaning that it introduces a qualitative change to the whole 'continuous system' (Nail 2016: loc. 109–15): Wallander not only initiates change on the 'other' side by becoming involved in a local conflict, his worldview is also affected by 'others'. In this narrative, the Baltic country becomes detached from the, until recently, unquestionable centre – Russia. Whereas the Cold War prevented transnational exchange across time and space, in the post-Cold War narratives, forgotten connections make a return – the encounter with 'others' is possible, if not necessary.

Transnational Memory and Eternal Russia

A case in point in the transnational re-evaluation of mutual connections and one's own national history is Tómas Gislason's documentary *Maximum Penalty* (Denmark 2000). The film tells the story of Arne Munch-Petersen, a Danish communist and secretary of the Communist Party of Denmark (DKP), who was arrested in Moscow in 1937 during Stalin's purges, accused of counter-revolutionary espionage and died of tuberculosis in Butyrka prison in Moscow in 1940. Munch-Petersen's fate remained unknown to the general Danish public until 1989, when his file was found in Soviet archives by Danish journalist and historian Kurt Jacobsen. The DKP party leader from 1987 to 1991, Ole Sohn, wrote a biography about Munch-Petersen (Sohn 1992; see Sohn 1999). In Gislason's documentary, Sohn acts as an expert and researcher guiding viewers through Munch-Petersen's story. The documentary casts a critical light on the DKP, as it discloses the fact that its leader, Axel Larsen, hid the truth about Munch-Petersen's tragic fate, not only from the public, but also from Petersen's wife. Munch-Petersen's and Larsen's lack of critical engagement as regards the significance of the Moscow trials (1936–8) is exposed as naïve. According to Sohn, Munch-Petersen's faith in Stalin remained unshaken even after brutal interrogations, during which he was forced to sign a document 'admitting' that he was a spy.

As Aleida Assmann and Sebastian Conrad observe, in the post-1989 (digital) age 'the globalization process has placed a question mark over the nation state as the seemingly natural container of memory debates'; 'synchronic interactions and entanglements are of increasing importance [. . .]. This implies, essentially, a spatial turn in our understanding of memory dynamics' (2010: 5, 6). Such spatial re-evaluation of the national memory resonates in *Maximum Penalty*. Gislason's documentary disrupts the linear national logic by means of a transnational perspective on past events and by contrasting two spaces: Denmark and Russia. The film depicts historical facts that could not be discussed openly before 1989. With the help of an interpreter, Sohn explores the Soviet archives, which provide proof not only of the authenticity of historical facts, but also of the memory that cuts through borders and was suppressed during the Cold War. Richly utilised excerpts from famous Soviet avant-garde films (including those of Dziga Vertov, Sergej Eisenstein and Vsevolod Pudovkin) perform a similar function of activating viewers' transnational memory, while they also evoke fear, pathos and irony.

Gislason's documentary is an important voice in the historical re-evaluation of Danish politicians' and intellectuals' 'fascination with Stalinism', to quote the conservative historian Bent Jensen ([1984] 2002). The entanglement of the two spaces – Denmark and Russia – is conceived through a complex visuality created using digital means, including split screens and fragmented frames that combine images into collage-like mosaics. This strategy emphasises the film's spatial/transnational and synchronic dynamics, adding complexity to Ole Sohn's generally linear narrative. Its complex visual and aural component, evoking a strong emotional response in the viewer, conveys the idea of a labyrinthine reality with many unanswered historical questions (Bondebjerg 2012: 438–9). Through the figure of Sohn as narrator, who was once a leading member of the DKP, the film establishes a reflexive connection between the past and the present, and implicitly interrogates the legacy of the communist movement in Denmark, as well as Ole Sohn's personal stance towards the Soviet Union – not least by frequently juxtaposing his face with that of Munch-Petersen or Stalin. At the same time, the use of montage techniques and film excerpts that evoke the great era in Soviet cinema of the 1920s, before Stalin stopped its development, partly explains this fascination with communism.

At the same time, the documentary employs a series of aesthetic and narrative strategies that convey the idea of Russia as unchangeable and inherently 'barbaric'. The split screen technique and complex visual

Figure 1.2 Synchronic dynamics and collage-like visuality. *Maximum Penalty*.
Courtesy of Angel Films.

side can be seen as conveying not only historical complexities, but also
the idea of Russia as labyrinthine and unintelligible – if seen from the
implicit Western perspective. The border between Denmark and Russia
emerges as one of extensive division, emphasised by a division of the
film frame through split screens. The film does not subscribe to the stereotype wherein ordinary Russian citizens possess aspirations convergent
with those of the authorities (see Czapliński 2016: 22) – on the contrary, it
focuses on the oppression of citizens by the state, similarly to *The Russian
Singer* or *The Dogs of Riga*. Nevertheless, it suggests that the relation
between the authorities and the powerless citizens remains unchangeable in Russia. For instance, when Sohn talks about Munch-Petersen's
detention, his words are intercut with an authentic scene in contemporary
Moscow: two Russian policemen, filmed from their marching feet to their
uniformed heads, arrest a man they have randomly stopped, who turns
out to have no residence permit (see Gislason in Sohn 2002: 49). Through
the use of parallel editing, the prison in which Munch-Petersen was held
is juxtaposed with the two policemen interrogating the random man in an
unnamed detention centre. The arrest of an innocent man not only serves
as visualisation of Munch-Petersen's tragic fate, the montage also suggests
continuity between past and contemporary methods. In a central scene
in the documentary, when Sohn and the interpreter visit the archives of

the former NKVD (the People's Commissariat for Internal Affairs, an agency of the Communist Party, associated with Soviet secret police and Stalinist repressions), they encounter resistance to their request for access to Munch-Petersen's file. Through fleeting close-ups of the inaccessible documents and the repetitive admonitions of the staff, it is emphasised that the truth about the past is still highly protected. The hostile atmosphere is intensified through the added sounds of a typewriter's keys tapping furiously and a phone that keeps ringing. Furthermore, when Munch-Petersen is depicted for the first time in the film, his photograph is juxtaposed with Russian soldiers marching in a line. The final shot in the documentary, taken from contemporary Russia, shows a row of soldiers shooting into the air. Although the latter image actually depicts a military parade commemorating the victims of Stalinism (Ibid. 51), this information is not shared in the film. Rather, the viewer is left to deduce that today's Russia is the same militarised state as in the past.

One of the interviewees, a writer and former victim of Stalinist rule, says that contemporary Russia 'regrets nothing'. His words are illustrated by a cemetery, followed by a panorama of Moscow with concrete blocks of flats and a cloudy sky. The final images showing today's Russia are gloomy, shot at night and in winter, and the accompanying sounds enhance this dreary atmosphere. The conclusion seems to be that Russia is immutable, unable to reform itself (see Malia 1999: 6; Gislason in Sohn 2002: 48).

Creating a highly suggestive depiction of Stalin's repressive state, and opening up a historical case which was not accessible during the Cold War, while implicitly confronting the naivety of Danish communists and the fatal consequences this approach had for the lives of people like Munch-Petersen, the documentary at the same time constructs a truly Eastern noir atmosphere. Gislason's documentaries can, indeed, be seen as both aesthetically and narratively inspired by film noir and are often organised around a person searching for the truth, sifting through many contradictory clues (Bondebjerg 2005: 87). However, *Maximum Penalty* is not only about a search for the truth, it also essentialises Russia as a crime scene in the sense discussed earlier: the crime is omnipresent, inherent to Russian 'nature' and emanates from the centre of power. Through a number of scenes staged in prisons, as well as accounts by previous detainees, the panoptic gaze, mentioned previously in connection with *Orion's Belt*, is here made tangibly material and stands not only for Stalin's totalitarian regime, but also for the current societal conditions. At the same time, Ole Sohn functions as a Western detective, representing knowledge and rationality (not unlike Jack Anderson in *The Russian Singer*). Importantly, his knowledge is supported by the accounts of Russian witnesses. Drawing

richly on the memories of victims of Stalinist repression, the film neutral-
ises the Western perspective and emphasises a universally human dimension as a contrast to Stalinist terror; this universality is highlighted by
a generous use of close-ups and extreme close-ups, which remove the
specific people focused on from their time and place (Sohn 2002: 59).
As a former prisoner says, Munch-Petersen came from one civilisation
and landed in another, one that was so completely different from his own
democratic world as to be unintelligible. Although this unintelligibility is
stressed by the complex graphic construction of the frames, the essence
of Russia, its logic, seems fully legible to Sohn, who 'explains' Soviet/
Russian reality from a 'universal' and implicitly Western viewpoint. Thus,
Maximum Penalty conveys the idea that not only the Soviet Union, but
also contemporary Russia is a crime scene, and as such, it needs a certain
narrative: that of a crime/detective story, 'like Dashiell Hammett's novels
from the 1930s', as Gislason himself put it (Sohn 2002: 49).

A similar anxiety with contemporary Russia as an authoritarian state
accepting criminal methods, and likewise resonating with the common
Western narratives, is the Danish documentary *Putin's Kiss* (2012) directed
by Lise Birk Pedersen. It portrays the political youth movement Nashi,
incarnating strongly nationalistic and xenophobic tendencies in Russian
society. The film consists mainly of interviews, and its rhetoric, in the vein
of documentary journalism, claims objectivity and neutrality. The documentary has a clearly developed 'plot': the leading person and prominent
Nashi member at the beginning of the film, Masha Drokova, 'unfolds'
according to a certain 'character arc', literally growing from her 'character
flaws'. Apart from Masha, portrayed between the ages of sixteen and nine-
teen, the documentary also follows journalist Oleg Kashin, who belongs to
the milieu of oppositional journalists and social activists known for their
critique of Nashi, as well as of Putin and the Kremlin. Masha's and Oleg's
stories interweave, and the two are frequently asked to comment on each
other's experiences and views. The final scene, which depicts them having
a friendly conversation in a café, reflects Masha's gradual shift in her
political views, which finally leads her to leave the ranks of Nashi.

The structure of the film relies on a binary division between the 'bad
ones' (Nashi, Putin and Putin's people) and the 'good ones' (the milieu of
liberal journalists criticising the authorities). Such a depiction of Russia
adheres to the well-established Western discourse used to describe the
Soviet Union, especially during the Cold War: the oppressive authoritarian system on one side, and the oppressed dissidents fighting for their
rights and democratic values on the other. Masha is the only 'element' in
the film representing a position and movement between these two poles, as

she gradually moves from her top post in Nashi towards expressing open public support for Oleg Kashin after he is almost beaten to death for his political activism.

In Pedersen's documentary, Nashi represent a divergence from 'normal' civil society, towards the barbaric, 'oriental' end of the spectrum in Russian society. At the same time, Kashin's and his friends' views display a convergence with Western values – the democratic, non-violent and non-militarist body, similar to the self-perceived Western/Nordic body. Thus, the Western 'norm' is implicitly established as a stable point of reference, towards which Masha gradually moves. This 'double' portrait of contemporary Russia leaves no space for ambiguities: the film states clearly that the society, split between 'black' and 'white' forces, is ruled by a nationalistic and highly oppressive regime. The oppositional commentators representing the 'enlightened' perspective make up a tiny group. The violence of the state is most explicitly exemplified by the brutal attack on Oleg Kashin – a scene which is set at night, utilising low-quality footage taken from a surveillance camera. Russia is depicted as a dark hotbed of xenophobia, savage mass movements and overall oppression.

In scenes showing a Nashi demonstration on National Unity Day, the participants hold banners displaying the portraits and names of Russia's 'enemies'. They are told to throw them on the ground – it is 'here they belong', a woman yells. Through the use of close-ups exposing shoes treading on the faces of the photographed people, the documentary conveys the division and hatred involved in the demonstration. As Kashin communicates in a voice-over: the aim of the demonstration was to explicitly identify the enemies of Russia. In one scene, a banner features a photograph of Boris Nemtsov, the well-known criticiser of Putin. This image makes a strong impression today, after Nemtsov's murder in Moscow in February 2015. In her most critical Nashi utterance in the film, serving as the culmination point in the documentary and proof of her positive development, Masha states: 'The idea of the enemies of Russia is associated with Stalinism and his death lists. Nashi do not suggest shooting these people or using violence. But their practice of pointing at enemies and showing their pictures is not the best style'. However, the brutal beating of Kashin undermines Masha's naïve belief in the non-violence of Nashi – but also points to Masha's apprehension about expressing more forceful opinions publicly.

Thus, the story of Masha, who in the beginning admires Putin and his strong, patriotic masculinity and over the course of the film becomes increasingly sceptical, is narrated as a story of Western democratic values winning over anti-democratic tendencies – if not in wider society, then

Figure 1.3 Trampling the 'enemies of Russia'. *Putin's Kiss*. Photograph by Lars Skree. Courtesy of Monday Danmark and Lars Skree.

at least in respect to the main protagonist portrayed in the documentary. Typically for Eastern noir, the fear of (Putin's) Russia is both enhanced by cinematic means and also contained by a clearly depicted border between good and evil.

Both in *Maximum Penalty* and *Putin's Kiss* Russia is essentially different from the Western world and therefore incites fear. Thus, although Russia is narrated in relation to changing historical circumstances, its 'nature' seems unchangeable. This is convincingly proved by the recent television series analysed below, which nevertheless introduces profoundly novel elements to the Eastern noir palette of the cinematic border discourse on Russia.

Eco Eastern Noir in a Global World

The use of the detective formula in films such as *The Russian Singer*, *The Dogs of Riga* and *Maximum Penalty* implies that there is a mystery and thus a truth about Russia, hidden in the archives or elsewhere; it can be either uncovered or not, but it is there. The Nordic Eastern noir television series *Occupied* (2015–) places Norway's relation with Russia in the context of current global challenges.[11] In this narrative, Russia emerges as a state in which no truth exists beyond the ones Russians themselves create, along the thesis advanced by Peter Pomerantsev, a British-Russian journalist and filmmaker, who wrote that today's Russia is a hypermodern state, whose power rests in its ability to construct reality through simulations. Russia is

a society of simulacra – that is, of signs detached from their referent, generating 'models of a real without origin or reality: a hyperreal' (Baudrillard
1983: 2). Accordingly, Russia is a 'postmodern dictatorship that uses the
language and institutions of democratic capitalism for authoritarian ends'
(Pomerantsev 2014a: 42) and which 'reinvents reality, creating mass hal-
lucinations that then translate into political action' (Pomerantsev 2014b).
A similar view structures the depiction of Russia in *Occupied*, which has
consequences for a reformulation of the Nordic/Norwegian self when
compared to the earlier discussed films – *Orion's Belt* in particular.

The first action scene in the series features Norway's prime minister,
Jesper Berg, being kidnapped and swept away in a Russian helicopter,
following which he is blackmailed into accepting an unusual agreement
with Russia. The agreement, backed by the European Union, states that
Russia can take control of Norway's oil platforms and secure a continuous
energy supply to Europe after Norway's left-wing government, following a natural disaster, cuts all oil and gas production in order to fight
climate change. At the end of the last episode of season one, Berg is
kidnapped again – this time, being taken away in a helicopter operated
by Norwegians, who bring the prime minister to the headquarters of a
resistance movement, Free Norway, formed in response to Russia's 'soft'
occupation of Norway. Thus, what was not possible in *Orion's Belt* in 1985
– resistance against Russian power on Norwegian ground – can be fulfilled
in 2015. *Occupied* can be seen as a continuation of a particular Norwegian
self-narration against the Russian Other that can be traced back to Ola
Solum's groundbreaking film, while also adding a new component to the
Eastern noir representations of Russia, implying that Russia is no longer
the source of all evil.

The series, based on an idea by the acclaimed crime fiction writer Jo
Nesbø, combines the genres of political drama and conspiracy thriller.
It is a quality television drama, possessing high artistic values and given
a prominent position in the prime-time schedule. As such, its plot needs
to be 'newsworthy by its suggested immediacy to real-life events' and/or
to 'an already existing grand-scale narrative' (Engelstad 2016). Indeed,
Occupied triggers several established grand-scale narratives, from both
the past and present. First, it is an Eastern noir *par excellence*: it assumes
a binary border discourse reminiscent of the Cold War master narrative.
Second, it includes plentiful references to a national narrative of the heroic
past: that of the Norwegian resistance movement against Nazi occupation.
The references to the Cold War and WWII are 'newsworthy' in that they
remind the viewer of the current tensions in Europe and imply that the
menace of war lurks apocalyptically in the near future, at which point

neither US nor Norway are NATO members, and the environmental and energy crisis has become a reality. Due to these circumstances, Russia re-emerges as a threat with new and acute actuality.

As in *Orion's Belt*, nature plays a crucial role as a symbol of the Norwegian nation, with the Russian helicopter signifying a threat to national independence. The narrative opens in April – the month associated with the occupation of Norway (and Denmark) by Nazi Germany in 1940. There is still snow in the woods where Jesper Berg is released from the helicopter after he has agreed to both Russia's and the EU's conditions. A close-up of his face cuts to traces of blood on the snow. The blood is that of a witness to the kidnapping, killed by the Russians. Thus, even if the occupation is 'soft' – that is, without bloodshed – it is nevertheless blood that marks the first traces left by Russians on Norwegian soil, transforming it into a crime scene. A similar bloody line is later seen in the snow at the Russian–Norwegian border in Finnmark, left by reindeer that were killed by Russian military vehicles. Thus, the blood incarnates the border, which is both imposed and violated by the Russians. Violence is committed not only against people, but also against nature and animal life, and thus against Norwegian national sovereignty.

However, *Occupied* does not reduce Russia to a crime scene from which evil spreads to 'our' Nordic side. The threat posed by Russians is combined with the modern national discourse that shapes Norwegian identity in relation to ecological threats. In recent decades, protection of the environment has grown to become 'a key concern at the center of *Norwegianness*' (Henlin-Stromme 2012: 54 [original emphasis]). *Occupied* critically evokes the self-perception of Norway as 'the "green Samaritan" on the planet' (Ibid. 54–5). Norwegians' environmental concerns are depicted as having global aspirations that they believe 'Europe and the whole world' should also embrace. The series exposes this discourse as ridden with self-complacency. Norwegians are convinced about the righteousness of their green policy, which they believe all of Europe should accommodate. Their universalising approach – and hence the negligence of borders and cultural and economic differences – embodies exceptionalism, understood as a self-image 'resting on a notion of ethical and moral superiority', justifying 'well-intentioned Nordic intervention in the crisis areas' (Volquardsen 2014: 40). These aspirations are incapacitated by the Russians (in cooperation with the EU). Adhering to the stereotype of Russia as a polluted and anti-environmentalist state, Russia is seen as threatening the Nordic natural world and obstructs Norway's environmentalist activities. Nevertheless, it is suggested by the narrative that ecological concerns should give way to the apparently more important cause – the need to defend Norway's national borders. The message in *Occupied* is thus ambivalent: its anti-environmentalist discourse may be seen as succumbing to the 'Russian way', despite the theme of Norwegian military resistance.

In contrast to several films discussed earlier in this chapter, the distinction between the 'enlightened' and 'barbaric' Russians does not hold in *Occupied*. Even if some Russian characters – especially the highly cultured Western-cosmopolitan types – evoke sympathy, all of them are a multiplication of the central corrupting power. Russians not only delineate but also multiply the border, as they begin controlling Norwegian institutions and move into Norwegian houses. This multiplication of power is strongly invoked – similarly to *Orion's Belt* – by an emphasis on surveillance: irrespective of legal regulations, Russians make use of drones and cameras anywhere they wish throughout Norway. But in contrast to *Orion's Belt*, Russia is no longer represented exclusively as a faceless 'barbaric' power materialised by the helicopter. Russia also has a highly civilised face in the ambassador, Irina Sidorova, whose main characteristics are that she perfectly imitates the Western self-complacent rhetoric of being democratic, civilised and a model for others to follow.

Importantly, Russians do not simply simulate but also ridicule Western and specifically Nordic discourses and patterns of behaviour. For instance, imitating Nordic exceptionalism, Russia forces Norway into a position in which usually only remote, crisis-ridden, poverty-stricken countries are depicted: it is Norway who, according to the more influential and resourceful Russians, needs intervention; therefore, Norway is offered 'generous help'. Moreover, this strategy appropriates the idea of the Nordic rescuer of Russian victims, discussed earlier. Now, it is the Russians who think that Norwegians should be rescued from their own environmentalist government. Commenting on the results of a referendum held by Berg, Sidorova says that it 'did not meet international standards' and that there were 'irregularities in the counting procedures' – which echoes real-life comments in the Western media frequently accompanying Russian elections. Hence, the depiction of Russia as a dictatorship where the truth is irrelevant is double-edged: the simulations created by Russia mimic Western and Nordic discourses, but they also question the idea of the truth and righteousness to which these discourses make claims.

A way to oppose Russia – a postmodern dictatorship with no graspable truth behind the façade – is, according to *Occupied*, a return to its own 'truth' and grand-scale narrative, a pre-postmodern understanding of nationality rooted in a territory with strong borders. However, protecting one's sovereignty against the hypermodern Russia requires not only an organised military defence, but, above all, an image of the self which others – and the Russian Other – will believe is real (see Czapliński 2016: 173). This is exactly what happens in *Occupied*. The female head of the Norwegian Police Security Service (PST) consolidates the resistance movement by creating a simulacrum of herself as the leader. Suffering from a terminal disease, she makes a video in which she tells the world that she has become the leader of Free Norway. With the help of a priest, the video is uploaded onto the Internet after she commits suicide; however, her death remains a secret. Thus, the image of the leader is a created one; afterward, it becomes a reality everyone believes in. This strategy is a perfect simulation of the Russian strategy, used against the Russians themselves.

Contrary to *Orion's Belt*, where the national self proves to be weak, *Occupied* takes a strong Norwegian position against the Russian Other.[12] However, there are significant breaches in this oppositional discourse. On the one hand, Russia can ultimately be mastered and subordinated to Norway precisely because Norway is capable of recognising Russia's methods. On the other hand, Russia's position as the centre is confirmed by the suggestion that Russia can only be defeated by its own means.

Moreover, although *Occupied* expresses the perception of Russia as a menace to Norwegian sovereignty, it also contradicts the previous narratives of Russia as the centre of evil. By taking control of Norway's oil platforms, Russia emerges as a threat to nature and the environment in a literal sense. But *Occupied* indicates that the 'threat' – that is, fossil fuel – has been generated by the Norwegians themselves. Oil is their 'sin' and their ecological bad conscience (Henlin-Stromme 2012: 52), which they seek to erase by implementing green policies. Russia only 'takes control of' the threat that already emerges from the centre of the Norwegian self. Furthermore, if nature is seen as a symbol of the Norwegian nation, then the threat to 'Norwegianness' can be interpreted as the oil boom that started in the 1970s; the resulting societal affluence is often perceived as having proved destructive for the values that earlier defined the Norwegian society (see Dancus 2011: 247). Such an understanding is supported by the nostalgic discourse of the national pre-oil past (WWII and the resistance movement). Moreover, by the implicit references to *Orion's Belt*, this 'threat' can also be related to the Cold War. In *Orion's Belt*, the Norwegian authorities are complicit in Tom's death. Notably, in *Occupied*, Thomas, an independent journalist critical of the government, is murdered in Finnmark on the Norwegian–Russian border before he manages to uncover Russian conspiracy and exploitation. However, *Occupied* recuperates the sin of submission to Russia – represented by Jesper Berg – by establishing a strong national discourse from before the Cold War, which is utilised against the Russian enemy. Another Norwegian sin the series exposes is the appropriation of nature by national discourses and for the purpose of branding one's own identity, rather than truly prioritising nature. Thus, even more radically than *Orion's Belt*, *Occupied* suggests that the crime scene is not simply on the 'other' side: the blood contaminating the whiteness of the Norwegian snow is a result of Norway's own misdeeds, signalled in the initial juxtaposition of Berg's face with the traces of blood in the opening shot of episode one.

To conclude, whereas it represents a continuation of certain tropes and narratives on Russia, *Occupied* also represents a fresh approach when compared to the Eastern noir films discussed above, as well as to the anti-Russian pre-World War II films mentioned in the Introduction. There is no 'truth' about Russia – Russia's image cannot be fixed and narrated by means of one definitive discourse. The image of Russia as the source of evil ricochets back on Norway: the evil originates in Norway's own political and ecological sins. At the same time, the series involves a playful twist on the meta-narrative level: the theme of the Russian occupation of Norway can be seen as a simulation of a probable reality which – according to the principle ventured by Pomerantsev – can create the reality it simulates. Hence, the production of the series may suggest the lack of fear towards Russia in contemporary Norwegian society.

The context of globalisation in *Occupied*, understood as the globalisation of conflict and risk, instigates conservative narratives of nationhood, rather than facilitating reciprocal involvement across borders. The distinction between the local and the global is dichotomous and mutually exclusive. The local (Norway) is opposed to the global (Russia, EU and the US), and the Norwegian national identity rests on firmly territorialised borders – against both Russia and the West. In the end, the series produces a nostalgic national discourse, as self-enclosed as the initial eco-exceptionalism it criticises.

Conclusion: Border as Reassurance

From metaphors of strict East/West division to omnipresent darkness, from a position of superiority through submissiveness to self-critical evaluations, from a self-elevating rescuing of the other to the re-emergence of common histories, from escapist conflation with the West to Nordic exceptionalism, Nordic Eastern noir seizes upon some of the essential local, regional and global issues emerging from transnational encounters over the past three decades. The fiction films, documentaries and television series discussed in this chapter tie the relation between the Nordic countries and Russia or Eastern Europe to the current political and cultural discourses. At the same time, all these films present a distinctly Nordic perspective on the Soviet Union/Russia – whether in relation to the monolithic Cold War order or the post-1989/91 contexts – influenced by the countries' geopolitical location at the edge of the Iron Curtain, as well as by the difficult position of small nations, as opposed to the physically substantial, competitive superpowers. However, a noticeable line of division runs between Denmark and the other countries: whereas Danish Eastern noir discourse closely adheres to Western discourses on Russia (as identified by Malia), Norway, Finland and Sweden express more emphatically their strenuous oscillation between East and West.

The diversity of genres included in this chapter proves that Eastern noir cuts across various cinematic modes of expression. Irrespective of genre or changing political discourses, Russia is consistently represented over time as a crime scene and as a source of evil power. However, if Russia remains unchangeable, the Nordic border discourse on Russia is not immutable: the implication that while Russia may be the eternal evil, 'we' are no innocents either breaches the dichotomy. This insight, conveyed in the films discussed here and especially by *Occupied*, is central to a number of Nordic films on Russia and/or Eastern Europe, as we shall see in the following chapters. What distinguishes Eastern noir is that the hegemonic narrative, defined here as the border discourse, avoids ambivalence and seeks closure. Even if it reveals breaches, it strives, above all, to offer viewers the comforting reassurance that there is safety and justice on 'our' side.

Notes

1. The Estonian Mafia rules the criminal underground in Helsinki in the Finnish television series *Look of a Killer* (2011). In the Danish television series *The Eagle* (*Ørnen*, 2004–6), Eastern Europe is depicted as a source of organised crime reaching to Denmark. The conflation of Russians with East Europeans is often expressed by casting Eastern European actors as Russians. In the television series *Occupied*, a Polish actor, Krzysztof Pieczyński, plays a vicious Russian character. Nonetheless, in Kathrine Windfeld's spy action film *Hamilton – In the Interest of the Nation* (*Hamilton – I nationens intresse*, Sweden, 2012), a clear distinction is drawn between Russians (embodied by arms dealers) and Poles (embodied by Hamilton's girlfriend, a Swedish-speaking physician played by a Swedish actress).
2. This echoes the perception of the Russo-Soviet colonisation as 'reverse-cultural colonization': the colonising Russo-Soviets were seen by the Baltic and Central European countries as culturally inferior 'Asiatics', "'Orientals'" (Mazierska et al. 2014: 10).
3. This analysis is based on the original (non-censored) version of the film.

4. In Henning Mankell's novel *The Dogs of Riga*, a direct reference to Dante's *Inferno* in *The Divine Comedy* stages Latvia as an absolute dystopia (Mankell 2012: 251). This recalls a novel by the Danish writer Ole Sarvig, *De rejsende* (*The Travellers*, 1978), where the protagonist, named Dan T., travels to the Soviet Union, Riga included, participating in a symbolic fight between good and evil (Rossel 2009: 299).
5. A similar oppositional narrative and employment of black-and-white imagery is found in the Swedish martial arts action film *The Ninja Mission* (Mats Helge, 1984). As *Born American*, the film is closely modelled upon American genres.
6. According to the Svalbard Treaty of 1920, the signatory countries have equal rights to explore natural resources on the Norwegian archipelago. USSR joined the treaty in 1924.
7. The film had two endings. Since the original ending did not meet with the audience's approval, the film had a new premiere with a different finale (see Iversen and Solum 2010: 56). I am referring here to the second ending.
8. Booth discusses here *The Spy Who Came In From the Cold* (Martin Ritt, 1965) – 'the classic Cold War allegory' (1991: 151). The penultimate scenes in *Orion's Belt*, just before Tom is murdered, evoke the film noir atmosphere in the final sequence of Ritt's drama.
9. The political thriller *After Rubicon* (*Etter Rubicon*, Leidulv Risan, Norway 1987), inspired by *Orion's Belt*, similarly problematises the cynicism of Norwegian authorities towards individuals in view of larger political Cold War interests. Paul Bjerke remarks that a switch of paradigm in the Norwegian press occurred in the 1970s from 'commitment to support the [. . .] NATO membership' to 'a *right to criticise* government and other powerful institutions and to defend individuals against abuse or negligence from authorities and other powerful agencies' (Bjerke 2015: 195 [original emphasis]). *Orion's Belt* and *After Rubicon* represent this last approach within Norwegian cinema.
10. Unlike Sweden and Finland, Denmark never recognised the annexation of the Baltic countries by the USSR in 1940. Denmark was also the frontrunner in supporting the Baltic countries' independence in 1990/1 (Lauridsen et al. 2011: 116).
11. I analyse season one of the series.
12. *Occupied* was compared to Michel Houellebecq's novel *Submission* (*Soumission*, 2015), see https://www.bloomberg.com/view/articles/2015-08-28/norwegian-tv-taps-into-fear-of-russia (accessed 10 October 2016). This comparison implies that Norway's greatest fear is encapsulated by the fantasy of Russia, rather than Islam, as an invader, while the juxtaposition of Russia and Islamic countries evokes the trope of Russia's 'oriental despotism'.

CHAPTER 2

Boundaries: Infiltrated Identities

The films examined in Chapter 1 placed Nordic and Russian/Eastern European encounters in an international rather than a transnational frame. Clear-cut and homogeneous nationalities are inherent in the border discourse. This distinction between international and transnational follows from the definition of internationalisation provided by political scientist Peter Katzenstein, who differentiates between internationalisation and globalisation – the two processes that dominated public discourse after the end of the Cold War. Whereas internationalisation is 'a process that refers to territorially based exchanges across borders', which 'permit continued differences in national practices', global processes are defined by Katzenstein as transcending space and compressing time, producing a move toward a 'convergence of national differences and also toward a wide variety of local processes of specific adaptation to global changes' (2005: 13). In transnationality, which I understand here in the vein of Katzenstein's definition of globalisation and as different from internationality, the border itself becomes negotiated and blurred; rather than a communication or exchange between two different destinations/nations/cultures, the transnational forges the inseparability of the actors, who also become transformed by the very process in question. This inseparability is emphasised by the metaphor of transnationality as a single coin with two sides (Weissmann in Agger 2016a: 86). Even when the plots analysed earlier in Chapter 1 led to exchanges across borders – rather than conflict and division – the distinct national identities of the characters (Norwegian/Russian, Swedish/Latvian) remained unaffected by these interactions.

I shift my focus in the present chapter to figures that embody transnational entanglements *par excellence*: spies and double agents. Espionage activities are, by definition, about crossing borders in ways that should remain unnoticed by the infiltrated group. Yet, the films explored in this chapter are not typical 'James Bond' spy narratives – represented in Nordic cinemas by numerous adaptations of the Swedish writer Jan Guillou's novels about Commander Hamilton, alias Coq Rouge[1] – but rather, they assume complex perspectives on the spy's entanglement with the 'other' (or 'enemy') side. Neither do these films adhere to the Cold War spy master narrative casting the foreign spy as the unquestioned antagonist of 'our' protagonist. Rather, the spies here embody discourses of the boundary: their ability to perform the 'other' identity and cross borders seamlessly questions and even threatens narratives of national purity and cohesion, undermining what I have defined earlier as the border discourse. What I explore here are such infiltrated identities and the 'nocturnal' plots they instigate, shaped by repetition and return, exploration, wandering and involvement (Durand in Falicka 2002).

In order to investigate how these figures work in relation to particular national discourses and representational conventions, I will utilise the notion of infiltration as conceptualised by Mireille Rosello, who distinguishes between two basic ways of telling a spy story: one, the 'spy-as-star' story, is about 'the visible heroes of detective fiction', preserving 'the difference between the spy and the infiltrated structure'; the other is about the 'ambivalence of the spy as infiltrated, or contaminated by, the culture he or she supposedly wanted to endanger' (1996: 184). The 'James Bond stories', or in the Nordic context, the 'Coq Rouge stories', presuppose the fixed identity of the spy as one of 'ours', and imagine the system in terms of an inside and an outside – a closure, its safety based on the assumption that the infiltrator is an exception. What is essential to Rosello's concept is that infiltration can be understood in another sense: as a process in which it is impossible to sustain distinctions between the infiltrator and infiltrated. The infiltrator is an ambivalent figure, 'one who penetrates a closed territory only to expose the fantasy upon which power relations are founded' (1996: nonpaginated). Rosello argues that the relation between the infiltrator and the infiltrated rests not upon distinctions but on interdependence: 'The infiltrating element itself, especially if it is a subject with agency, is part of the process and becomes an infiltrated element too' (182). Thus, the idea of a pure system and the mutual isolation of the two sides is only imagined. Whereas 'James Bond stories' provide safety and closure, not least because they indicate very specifically when the process of infiltration begins and when it ends, the other kind of knowledge is 'politically disturbing' (186). The 'infiltrated infiltrator' does not reassure the ruling system. Rather, (s)he

exposes the fact that each structure is built on sand and infested by termites. The infiltrator [. . .] does not disappear in the midst of a cloud of smoke, but he or she leaves a subtle trail of slow disintegration, fissures, slippages, movements in a turbulent flow. (Rosello 1996: 191)

Thus, the infiltrated infiltrator (as opposed to the spy-as-star) offers a challenge not only to the Eastern noir border discourse, which narrates Russia in strict opposition to the Nordic self, but also to hegemonic national narratives that imagine the (national) community as pure, homogeneous and non-infiltrated, and the border as totalised by the centre. Even if embedded in the realities of WWII or the Cold War, in which national and political divisions were relatively clear-cut, the infiltrated infiltrator embodies a transnational connection 'contaminating' an assumedly clear national identity. Nevertheless, we should also remember that 'by positioning his [sic] or herself or by being positioned as the new other', the infiltrator also confirms the existence of the border (Ibid. 190).

It should be emphasised that infiltrated identities are featured not only in documentary or art-house films, which commonly defy genre conventions (such as those utilised by Eastern noir), but can also be found at the heart of the Eastern noir genre. This is true in the case of an eight-episode Finnish television series released in 2011, *Look of a Killer* (*Tappajan näköinen mies*), directed by Lauri Nurkse, and later followed by a feature-length film of the same title (Nurkse 2016). The film and series are based on Finnish crime fiction writer Matti Rönkä's novels about Viktor Kärppä, who is ethnically Finnish, but who grew up in the Soviet Union in the previously Finnish Karelian town of Sortavala. Although he brings to mind a stereotypical Russian 'agent of death' (Arvas 2011: 124), he also embodies the infiltrated infiltrator, who exposes both systems as porous and 'built on sand' (Rosello 1996: 191). Kärppä, a Finnish citizen living in Finland, works as a spy for 'Mother Russia'; at the same time, he cooperates – against Russia – with the Finnish police, who cannot progress in their investigations of Russian and Estonian organised crime without the information Kärppä is able to provide.

An even more disruptive attitude to the infiltrator/infiltrated binary is represented by another Nordic Eastern noir television series, *Bordertown* (*Sorjonen*, Finland 2016–), set in the Finnish town of Lappeenranta, situated close to the border with Russia. Two of the series' female protagonists, Lena and her daughter Katia, come from St Petersburg and are initially portrayed as stereotypical Russian figures: Lena, a former member of the mafia and later FSB agent (Russian security service, the successor to the KGB), resembles a Russian agent of death; Katia, in turn, seems nothing more than another Russian prostitute and victim of Finnish men, who benefit from being neighbours with the much poorer Russia. However,

as the series develops, the women unfold as psychologically complex characters representing nationally fluent identities: they speak both Russian
and Finnish and feel as much at home in Finland as in Russia. They both
embody the fluid boundary that structures the 'bordertown', where connections to Russia underlie both business and crime. Lena and the main
protagonist, Finnish police detective Kari Sorjonen, start cooperating as
two policemen of similar rank, their collaboration incarnating the boundary across nationalities, genders and social status.[2] The border is never
visualised explicitly – in the universe of the series, it does not exist, and the
protagonists' travels to Russia are always easy and effortless. Both areas are
infiltrated by each other and mutually dependent.[3]

Both the typical framing of spies as anti-national traitors and the 'spy-
as-star' convention are bypassed in a number of recent non-genre Nordic
films, which critically confront past and present hegemonic national narratives. Although all films analysed in this chapter relate to past historical
events (Finnish Civil War, WWII, Cold War), they are far from nostalgic;
rather, they question the assumed coherence of national discourses. All
of these films were produced between the mid-1990s and today, representing a post-Cold War take on spies and double agents. According to
media scholar Paul Bjerke, alternative perspectives on spies were not possible earlier: 'The overall framing of the espionage matter was the Cold
War, in which *our* spies were heroes, while the enemy's spies were villains'
(Bjerke 2015: 206 [original emphasis]).[4] Moreover, as ethnographer
Stein Mathisen explains about the case of the Norwegian border region
Finnmark, the period of the Cold War was characterised by a lack of narratives about Russia, a result of both fear and a lack of personal interaction:
'The area was as closed and invisible as the many submarines which were
active by the nearest coast on a daily basis' (1998: 17). Also, limited access
to archival materials (in Finland, for instance, national archives were first
opened to the public in the 1990s) made it difficult to narrate historical
events in a way that deviated from the hegemonic master narrative of the
Cold War.

Strikingly, if in Eastern noir narratives the focus is on male protagonists,[5] films foregrounding infiltrated identities tend to highlight female
protagonists. Hegemonic – and homogeneous – national narratives are
typically represented by male characters, while their contesters, the infiltrated infiltrators, are female. In other words, men usually embody the
border, whereas women represent boundary. As I will show, such a distribution of gender roles by no means relegates women to the 'soft', 'fluent'
or marginal domains.

My exploration of the complexities embodied by infiltrated infiltrators begins with an analysis of three recent Finnish films: a documentary by Ville Suhonen *Seamstress* (*Ompelijatar*, 2015), Lauri Törhönen's *The Border* (*Raja 1918*, 2007) and Jörn Donner's *The Interrogation* (*Kuulustelu*, 2009). All three films feature Finnish-born women with communist beliefs, sentenced to death for national treason. In depicting the system as infiltrated from the beginning, they all challenge the pure national Finnish identity embodied by the male militarised protagonists and constructed in opposition to Russia. Next, I discuss the German-Norwegian drama *Two Lives* (*Zwei Leben*, Georg Mass, 2012), which also focuses on a female spy – a Stasi agent in Norway, whose infiltration of a Norwegian family is portrayed as the return of a suppressed dark chapter in the country's past. Finally, I analyse Knut Erik Jensen's fiction films about two well-known Norwegian spies, a male in *Burnt by Frost* (*Brent av frost*, 1997) and a female in *Ice Kiss* (*Iskyss*, 2008). The two films depict infiltrated identities as undermining the Cold War fantasy of mutual isolation. Here, the complex trajectories and emotional involvement of the infiltrators produce – in line with David Harvey's notion – relational spaces, alternatives to arbitrary maps marked by red lines of division (Harvey 2009). All of the films above treat controversial historical spy figures,[6] represented as tragic heroes rather than as triumphant 'spies-as-stars'.

'Tinged' From the Beginning

In the Finnish films *Seamstress*, *The Border* and *The Interrogation*, the distinction between the 'Finnish' and 'Soviet' layers – and thus between friend and foe, infiltrator and the infiltrated – is depicted as unclear and difficult to make. This obscurity challenges the clean-cut borders discursively produced by those in power and implemented, sometimes by force, in social reality. All three films are symptomatic of the recent tendency in Finnish cinema to critically examine WWII and dominant national narratives on war (see Csoma 2012: 85–8). If in Eastern noir the border is usually depicted as designated by the Russian side, here the Finnish side is the centre, claiming the right to totalise borders.

Through the figures of infiltrated infiltrators, the films question the typical male gendering of the dominant narrative of Finnish national identity (see Nestingen 2013: 125), deriving from the nineteenth century, when Finland was part of the Russian Empire, and when, inspired by Romanticism, the idea of the Finnish nation started taking shape. This Romantic national self-conception frames the Finnish people as an ethnically pure and culturally homogeneous group, as well as an oppressed nation 'that has always existed, first under Swedish, later under Russian

rule'. This 'anti-colonialist' perspective, narrating the Finnish self in contrast to both Russia and Sweden, has been 'reiterated again and again in
the 20th century in the darkest hours of Finland' (Østergård 1997: 55). As
revisionist historians emphasise, Finland was never colonised by Sweden,
but 'constituted a Finnish-speaking half of the original Sweden', and as a
separate entity 'first emerged in 1809, when Tsar Alexander I established
the Grand Duchy of Finland' (Ibid. 56). The idea of strong cultural, historical and linguistic traditions and the heroic nature of the Finnish people
was consolidated by nineteenth-century national literary epics, such as
Kalevala – a collection of folklore poetry gathered by Elias Lönnrot –
and the *oeuvre* of the national poet Johan Ludvig Runeberg, who laid
the groundwork for Finnish nationalism (Mrozewicz 2004: 25–33). This
national narrative was cultivated by the so-called White forces during the
Finnish Civil War, which broke out in early 1918, following internal political splits after the declaration of Finland's independence in December
1917. The leftist forces – the so-called Reds – consisting of Finnish
workers and the Finnish Social Democratic Party's radical left wing, and
supported in part by the Soviets, opted to sustain Finland's political unity
with Russia. After four months of fighting, the Reds were defeated by the
non-socialist Whites (recruited from the middle classes and backed by
German troops), who aimed at establishing a Finnish democracy shaped
after Western models – and independent of Russia. The deep political split
of the Civil War returned with double force at the end of the Continuation
War (1941–4), during which Finland fought against the Soviet Union and,
as Germany's ally, ultimately lost. The White national narrative was the
dominant narrative for decades. The Red narrative remained suppressed
until the post-war period and especially the 1960s and 1970s, when a
new radicalised generation rediscovered an alternative history of Finnish
society – and when Finlandisation (that is, Finland's far-reaching political compromise with the USSR during the Cold War decades) was most
oppressive (Salokangas 2015: 77).[7] Today the White version of Finnish
history is again the hegemonic national narrative, though no longer the
exclusive one (Sundholm 2013b: 220ff.).

An inspection of Finnish–Soviet entanglements is offered by Ville
Suhonen's documentary *Seamstress* (2015), which tells the story of a
Finnish communist activist, Martta Koskinen (1897–1943), who was the
last woman executed in Finland. During her lifetime, she was deemed a
communist spy and traitor to the nation; however, by the 1970s the leftist
generation cherished her as a martyr and heroine. In the documentary she
is depicted, above all, as a human driven by idealism and a heroic martyr
who died for her beliefs.

The documentary narrates Koskinen's fate and the history of the communist movement in Finland from the 'Red' point of view. The voice-over narrator never refers directly to spies and espionage when referring to Koskinen's activities. When the military court sentence is quoted, viewers learn only the sentence Koskinen received (death and loss of civil rights), but never what she was sentenced for (high treason and espionage). Similarly, the men who refused to participate in the Continuation War, supported by Koskinen, are never described as 'deserters', but rather as 'opponents' of the war. The many socialists and communists arrested by the Finnish State Police are denoted in the voice-over as 'resistance members' or 'political prisoners'. Although the crimes committed by the Red forces during the Civil War are mentioned, the emphasis is on the crimes of the Whites. Similarly, the fact that the Winter War (1939–40) started as a result of Soviet invasion (on which there is consensus among historians, see Salokangas 2015: 78) is not mentioned in the documentary. Nor is it stated clearly that members of the Finnish communist movement cooperated with the Soviet Union and were perceived as a threat to Finnish sovereignty. Furthermore, viewers learn from the voice-over that during the anti-communist crusade that began with the Civil War and continued towards the end of WWII, 'informants, infiltrators and traitors' were 'recruited' by the Finnish Investigative Police. The notion of traitors is used here to denote those who were originally members of the communist movement and later shifted to the White side. Similarly, the notion of infiltrators denotes not the Reds, but White infiltrators of the Red movement. This reverse rhetoric – if compared to the hegemonic, White discourse – is assumed to be self-evident: viewers are supposed to discover for themselves that the Red viewpoint is the film's perspective. This reversal of perspective is initially somewhat confusing, but this confusion serves to displace (especially Finnish) viewers from what they are accustomed to.

Upon closer inspection, it becomes clear that rather than simply assuming the Red point of view, the documentary examines the mechanisms producing traitors and spies by the ruling power (the White, anti-Soviet side). Martta Koskinen's letters to friends and family, as well as the short stories she published in a magazine before the war, read by a female voice-over, introduce viewers to her thoughts and paint a picture of her personality as sensitive and multidimensional. This portrait is fleshed out further through a number of staged scenes, in which 'Martta' is shown sewing, writing or bringing food to those evading recruitment. This heterogeneous portrait of Martta's life is interwoven with documents from the files on Koskinen put together by police investigators.

Ironically, these files can be said to epitomise what Cristina Vatulescu defines as 'secret police aesthetics', typical of Soviet police files. Analysing the Soviet secret police files of innocent citizens, fabricated by the Soviet secret services, Vatulescu shows that what distinguishes the Soviet personal file from a traditional (Western) police file is that the standard starting point of any secret police interrogation was (auto)biography: 'Whereas criminal records are usually limited to the investigation of one crime, the Soviet personal file is typically concerned with the extensive biography of the suspect' (2010: 32). Another important trait of the Soviet secret police file is that it was required to provide a 'negative biographical pattern' (33) – that is, an account of the life of the accused that would prove him or her to be an enemy. Moreover, whereas the documentation collected in a surveillance file offered a 'cacophony of voices', this heteroglossia was strongly constrained by selection and interpretation. From the collection of voices of various informers, denouncers, interrogation depositions, censored mail, personal letters and other documents, the file

> ended with a 'general synthesis' written by the chief investigator. [. . .] The heterogeneous portrait was here reduced to a cliché from an infamous stock of characters: the spy, the saboteur, the counter-revolutionary, the terrorist, and so on. [. . .] The surveillance file collated and then cut the synthetic portrait of the state enemy. (Vatulescu 2010: 38)

In view of the above, the fact that Suhonen's documentary opens with a letter written by Koskinen at the end of her life, followed by pictures of the young Koskinen and a voice-over narration that details her initial sparks of interest in joining the Red Guard, reveals a subversive take on the secret police file: the nuanced biographical part constitutes the film's guiding thread, whereas the 'negative biographical pattern' provided by police files emerges as a severe reduction of the heterogeneous portrait of Koskinen. This negative pattern emerges from components strongly reminiscent of the typical Soviet secret police file (see Vatulescu 2010: 32): mug shots identifying Martta (and 'half a million Finns') as a criminal, interrogation depositions with sentences underlined by the investigator, informers' reports, identifying photographs, censored letters, letters to the government, house search warrants, a 'verbal portrait', a 'record of peculiar characteristics' (about Koskinen: '8 mm skin button on the right cheek; hard of hearing') and so on.

This secret police aesthetics is supported by cinematic devices such as the surveying camera, illicitly gained snapshots taken from various hiding places and the camera panning closer and closer on the documents from Koskinen's file. These devices in part overlap with the patterns of Eastern noir. An atmosphere of constant threat is evoked by oft-used components of Eastern noir, such as the depiction of a black telephone with a bugging device used to listen in on Koskinen's phone conversations, the sound of a typewriter's keys, an unanswered phone ringing, dark streets and suspicious male silhouettes (complete with trench coat and fedora) observing their targets and barbed wire topping a prison wall in a low-angle shot. However, the utilisation of such devices – as well as of Soviet secret police aesthetics – is in this case unusual, because it does not serve to describe 'Russia as a crime scene', but to characterise White Finland. The repressive apparatus, violence, terror, surveillance, brutal interrogations sometimes ending in death, censorship, denunciations, widespread arrests, the government passing legislation in order to achieve more control and the prohibition of previously legal organisations – all this occurs not in the oppressive Soviet Union, as in Eastern noir films and the predominant narrative about Russia/the Soviet Union – and as Russia and the Soviet Union were narrated by the Whites – but 'here', in Finland. Just as the rhetoric is reversed from a typical White to a Red perspective in the voice-over, likewise typical depictions of the atrocities of the Soviet Union are utilised to describe the atmosphere of political terror in Finland. Hence, both the rhetoric and iconography usually used against the Soviets (and not least, Soviet spies) is adopted to describe the White Finnish authorities, especially the Investigative Police, which later became the State Police, Finland's secret police.

Contradicting the 'negative pattern' narrative of Martta's life, the documentary suggests that rather than be 'identified' as the enemy, the enemies are constructed – similar to the narrative and subsequent fate of Arne Munch-Petersen, depicted in the documentary *Maximum Penalty*. Striking in this respect is a shot of one of 'tens of thousands' of identifying photographs, showing a large group of people. The photograph is covered with a thin sheet of transparent paper, on which numbers have been added next to each person's head. The camera shifts focus from the photograph to a macro close-up of the surface of the paper, which now looks like a spider web covered with the aforementioned numbers. Cinematic means are used to focus on the paper's structure, thereby undermining the inseparability of the *signifiant* (the number, the 'enemy') and the *signifié* (the person depicted). The 'spider web' connotes being captured like flies, but it also visualises a complex web of interdependencies, rather than a simple black-and-white reality.

The hegemonic White national narrative is established by the use of various archival materials, such as the recording of the Finnish Foreign Minister delivering a speech after the Winter War, saying: 'Now that the war has ended, we should bear in mind this achieved experience, the power

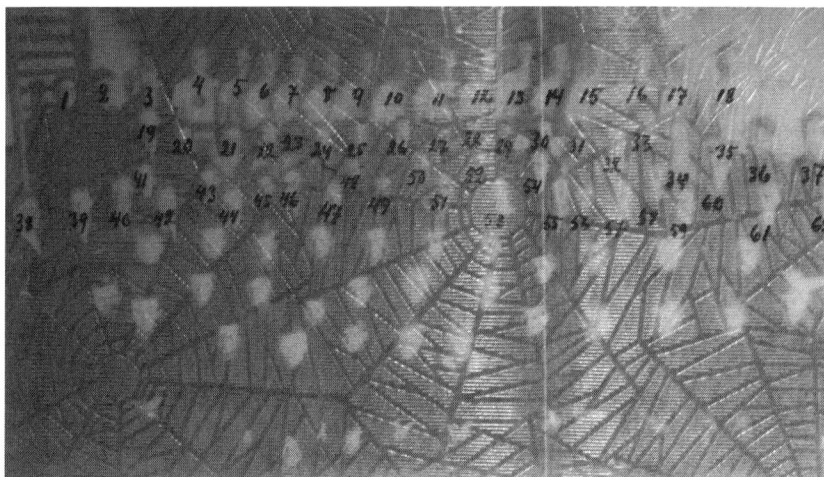

Figure 2.1 An identifying photograph. The focus on the paper's structure disrupts the unity between the 'spy' and the depicted person. *Seamstress*. Photo from the National Archives of Finland. Courtesy of Ville Suhonen.

of unity. It can [. . .] secure the life and livelihood of our nation'. Indeed, the unity of the nation, mobilised in the face of invasion from the east, is a common cognitive frame applied to the Winter War (see Mrozewicz 2004: 72). However, the documentary argues that this national unity is a rhetorical construction, rather than an ultimate truth. Similarly, the White point of view is illustrated by a fragment from a Finnish propaganda thriller (*The Secret Weapon/Salainen ase*, Theodor Luts, Erkki Uotila, 1943) incorporated in the documentary, in which a State Police detective was one of the screenwriters. In a scene included in the film, two investigators catch a communist *in flagrante*. Confiscating the activist's leaflets, the detective declares: 'Blatant lies by unscrupulous foreigners. But the Finnish people are too enlightened to believe this'. However, Suhonen's documentary demonstrates that it was not 'foreigners', as the hegemonic narrative has it, but large parts of Finnish society that were involved in the communist movement – they were a part of 'us'. Thus, Soviet-mindedness is not in opposition to the Finnish national self, but rather a part of its identity and history.

In other words, the documentary challenges the deep-rooted White narrative that framed the development of Finland as a nation. It shows how the 'enemy' – or the infiltrators coming from the 'outside' – are fabricated by the ruling power, which itself establishes widespread organs and mechanisms of infiltration. However, rather than disrupting the binary order, the documentary reverses positions within the same system of oppositions. The Reds are 'us' in the film's narrative, while the Whites are the corrupt and dangerous ones. Rather than disavowing the border, the documentary shows that the border is internal rather than external. That said, it should be emphasised that the historical figures portrayed – Martta Koskinen and other Finns involved in the Finnish communist movement – testify to the fact that a homogeneous national unity and a binary Finnish/Russian division is only one way of framing Finnishness, a one-sided narrative cultivated for specific political purposes. As a part of the Russian Empire for over 100 years, Finland has been infiltrated from the 'beginning' of its existence as a separate entity. Indeed, '[n]o system is ever pure of strangeness, of foreignness' (Rosello 1996: 12). If seen from the White perspective, Finland has been 'tinged' Red; if seen from the Red perspective, it has been infiltrated White.

An examination of hegemonic national self-conceptions which disrupt the us/them opposition is found in Lauri Törhönen's *The Border* (2007), which explores the Finnish Civil War from both sides of the conflict and, more precisely, focuses on the aftermath of the Civil War on Finland's eastern frontier in Karelia.[8] The theme is the establishment of the first Finnish state border between Finland and Soviet Russia in the post-Civil War period. The concept of infiltration should be here understood metaphorically, denoting not literal spies, but people of divergent political beliefs who infiltrate one another. The narrative can be described as being organised around a struggle between border and boundary. Shortly after the war, the young Captain Carl von Munck, who fought on the White side, arrives in a small village in the Karelian Isthmus to carry out an order issued by the central authorities in Helsinki: he is to establish a border between the newly emerged independent Finland and Soviet Russia. As he soon realises, the Russian-speaking and Finnish-speaking people here cohabit on a friendly basis, shape families and speak both languages, comprising a transnational 'collective fluid identity' in terms of political, economic, social and cultural cooperation (Kaskinen 2012: 125). Trying to convince von Munck that closing the border crossing at the local bridge is not a good idea, they explain that 'people have wandered this way back and forth for 600 years'. Thus, both sides have been seamlessly infiltrating one another for hundreds of years. Suddenly, free passage is blocked and the inhabitants are required to provide documents confirming their identity as either Russian or Finnish. The community is abruptly reorganised by the abstract idea of the border, which the people do not fully comprehend.

Von Munck warns his deputies that Russians should not be allowed entrance to the Finnish side, because spies may be among them. Soon, however, he himself delegates spies, in order to be informed about what is happening in Russia (where the bloody Bolshevik revolution is gathering its harvest). Von Munck also realises that he is addicted to Russian tea and befriends a Russian major stationed on the other side of the river. Moreover, the White captain falls in love with a local woman, Maaria Lintu, who is neither Red nor White, but is engaged to a wanted Red revolutionary leader, depicted as being brutal and relentless. Maaria criticises von Munck for 'believing in his borders'. He explains, 'I believe in Finland'. Indeed, the process of establishing Finnish national identity by delineating borders around the Finnish self against all 'others' is depicted as being based on the violent enforcement of the border and on the exclusion of those who do not belong to the community according to the centre.[9] After the border is closed, people find alternative ways of crossing the river by night. But the illegal crossing of the border, which is guarded by soldiers, is punishable by death. Von Munck personally experiences the deadly consequences of imposing the border when his friend – the Russian major – is shot, and even more acutely when Maaria is killed leading a revolt against the imposition of the border.

The message of the film is clearly anti-border, though it promulgates multiple forms of boundary. In the final scenes, Maaria, wearing a red dress, is sentenced to death for hiding her Red fiancée in her home – in other words, she does not obey the law imposed by the border. When she leads refugees kept in quarantine to revolt, her appearance and zeal evoke the painting 'Liberty Leading the People' by Eugène Delacroix (1830); like the French national allegory, she embodies the ideal of (unattainable) absolute freedom, which for Maaria is synonymous with a world without borders. The attraction between the White von Munck and the Red-leaning – but above all idealistic – Maaria proves that emotional trajectories complicate and resist political borders. Although Maaria rejects von Munck, the two infiltrate each other, despite the binary political master narrative originating from the central authorities and embodied by the soldiers. In the end, von Munck, who is promoted to a major for his merits in the border zone, abandons his military career and becomes a scientist.

The figure of Maaria – who dies for her ideals of freedom and a borderless world – is in many respects evoked by the protagonist in Jörn Donner's *The Interrogation* (2009) (the choice of the same actress, Minna Haapkylä, suggests that the similarity is not incidental). The film focuses on a Finnish-born Soviet citizen and one of the many spies sent from the USSR to Finland, Kerttu Nuorteva, who was dropped by parachute near Helsinki in February 1942, during the Continuation War – that is, at a time when Finland was allied with Germany. The action begins in

September 1942, when Finland held an advantage over Soviet troops. The film concludes with the end of the Continuation War (September 1944), the breakthrough point coming in February 1943, when German troops were badly defeated at the Battle of Stalingrad, and the Finnish alliance with Germany became increasingly problematic.

The Interrogation is theatrical in style: it is set in enclosed interiors, with the use of point lighting and a limited number of props, and the narrative propelled by rich dialogues between two or three persons. The dialogues comprise the interrogations of Nuorteva, who is arrested after she forgets her espionage equipment in a laundry. The theatricality is not merely a stylistic device. The film uses visual and narrative means to underscore the difficulty in defining Nuorteva's identity as either Soviet or Finnish. In the first interrogation scene, Nuorteva is wearing heavy make-up and a wig and claims her name is Elina Hämäläinen. This is clearly a performance. Although she speaks fluent Finnish, her unfamiliar accent is noticed by the interrogator. Nuorteva's theatrical image – implying that she is not who she claims to be – is contrasted with the police interrogators in Helsinki – soldiers of various military ranks, who see themselves as representing the truth.

The relation between theatricality, associated with Nuorteva, and the truth, represented by the interrogators, is increasingly challenged as the plot develops, just as the balance of power seems to gradually change. In the first interrogation scene, Nuorteva sits at the table and bursts into tears, the interrogator coldly presenting the consequences of acting as a spy (death penalty) and raising his voice while trying to extort Nuorteva's confession. The domineering position of the interrogating side is emphasised when a mug shot of Nuorteva is taken, and her make-up is forcibly removed – as if to uncover the 'real' Nuorteva. However, in the next interrogation scene, with a new investigator, the power relations have already begun to shift. Nuorteva does not accept the cigarette offered her by the captain and remains standing while he sits. Most importantly, when her new interrogator says that he hopes she will tell the truth, she replies: 'Likewise'. When he expresses surprise at her response, Nuorteva demands: 'Am I the only guilty party here?' She persists in putting probing questions to her interrogator, such as: 'Is honesty held against the interrogated?' The clear division between the interrogator and the interrogated becomes less evident. When she admits that her real name is Kerttu Nuorteva and explains her devotion to the Soviet Union, the captain responds by saying that he does not believe in dictatorship, to which Nuorteva straightforwardly counters: 'Dictatorship? And what sign do you have on your arm? SS. You are Hitler's thugs'. The evoked cooperation between Finland and

Figure 2.2 Mutual infiltration: the interrogator and the interrogated. *The Interrogation.* Photograph by Pirjo Honkasalo. Courtesy of Donner Productions.

Hitler's Germany calls into question the captain's humanist claims, such as, for example, a refusal to use violence during interrogations. Nuorteva questions the truth and righteousness the interrogator steadfastly maintains that he represents.

Because Nuorteva, a strong and independent woman, obstinately refuses to confess, causing the interrogators to give up, a third interrogator is assigned to her case – a lower-ranking soldier, Second Lieutenant Kastari. In scenes that take place in February 1943, Kastari – who has assured his colleagues that he will find a way to get Nuorteva's full confession – uses a tactic aimed at infiltrating Nuorteva's mind with ideas about Finnish national identity and cultural heritage. Kastari encourages Nuorteva to read books about Finnish democracy and the Finnish literary canon. The relationship between the interrogator and the interrogated changes from one of hostility to friendly conversations concerning political issues and views on literature, and the cold, dark and impersonal interrogation cell is replaced by Kastari's cosy and bright office. Nuorteva remains a devout believer in Stalin and the bright future of global communism, while Kastari tries to convince her about the right of the Finnish nation to independence. Despite these differences, they are no longer depicted as unequal, but are seen sitting next to each other, like peers. Although he wears a military uniform in every scene, Kastari declares himself to be a humanist and not a devoted soldier; appealing to Nuorteva's Finnish origins, he seems primarily interested in her as a human and in her 'view on Finnishness'.

The film becomes particularly interesting when interrogations trans-form into an exchange of ideas between the two sides that infiltrate one another, which, as in *The Border*, also includes erotic fascination (especially Kastari's for Nuorteva). A crucial scene expresses this mutual infiltration. Kastari arranges a romantic dinner, complete with candles, during which he offers Nuorteva the chance to flee abroad with a false passport if she agrees to confess. Interestingly, this scene creates the impression that Kastari intended to propose to Nuorteva – which she, for a brief moment, suspects. This demonstrates the shift in power distribution on the mili-tary front (the victory of the Red Army at Stalingrad), but also between the two characters, Kastari succumbing to Nuorteva. However, the scene can also be seen as Kastari using theatrical methods (initially associated with Nuorteva) in order to seduce Nuorteva into making a confession. Kastari suggests that she call him by his first name, Paavo. In response, Nuorteva quotes a line about Paavo, the peasant character from *Farmer Paavo* (1829) – a poem by Runeberg, the national poet cherished especially by the Whites. She comments: 'There is a little socialist in Paavo, isn't there?' The ironic remark indicates that Nuorteva seems to have become acquainted with 'Finnishness'. On the other hand, Kastari's fascination with Nuorteva questions the purity of the White narrative. Kastari, the infiltrator, and Nuorteva, the spy, become 'contaminated' by each other, even if subtly. They drink to peace.

The next step in Kastari's interrogation method – or infiltration of Nuorteva – is to arrange a meeting between Nuorteva and a former com-munist, an old friend of Nuorteva's father. He tells her the truth about Stalin's purges, including that her own father was among Stalin's victims. After this conversation, Nuorteva suffers a mental breakdown and is hos-pitalised. In the end, she confesses – which, at least in the film's narrative, does not seem to provide the Finns with any crucial details about Soviet espionage. Kastari's victory over her is not particularly triumphant. Importantly, Nuorteva now seems to have gained insight into the blindness of the dogmatic ideology, fear and terror on which the USSR thrives. In a letter to old friends, she writes that she feels 'Finnish-minded'. It seems as if Kastari's infiltration has been successful – the infiltrator, Nuorteva, becomes infiltrated by the culture she initially wanted to endanger, but which – she comes to realise – makes up a significant part of who she is. It is not, however, clarified whether her 'Finnish-mindedness' means that she has internalised Kastari's lessons or whether she recognises that her own life and worldview is a part of 'Finnishness'.

In the end, despite her confession, Nuorteva is sentenced to death. In her last conversation with Kastari, she expresses her bitter disappointment with his unfulfilled promises. The freedom he promised and the deep humanism he proclaimed turn out to have been merely a strategy to make her confess and uncover her status as a spy. Considered retrospectively, the interrogation did not differ much from the Soviet methods, which, as Vatulescu observes, relied on a mix of theatricality and reality – although, unlike the Soviet methods, documents were not fabricated against Nuorteva (see Vatulescu 2010: 141).

The last scene depicts Nuorteva outdoors for the very first time in the film, when she is released from prison after the Finnish–Soviet Moscow Armistice is signed in September 1944. Also, for the very first time, a male voice-over in Finnish is heard, explaining: 'She returned to the Soviet Union in October. We do not know the reason'. The pronoun 'we' should not be neglected: the male voice stands for the collective Finnish self, or at least the White idea of Finnishness, represented throughout the film by the militarised men, who, unlike the women (such as a silent female witness during interrogations and a female doctor who supports Nuorteva), cannot understand Nuorteva. Indeed, Kastari continues to pester her about her reasons for agreeing to serve as a spy. From this particular point of view, Nuorteva remains incomprehensible and her motivations unintelligible. But while the voice-over, although non-diegetic, still works at the level of plot, the overall message of the film offers a critical scrutiny – rather than condemnation – of both the White national self-conception and the Red 'infiltrator'. Whether Nuorteva is a real infiltrator – meaning someone from the outside – is questioned. After all, as Kastari says, Nuorteva 'was born Finnish'. She is a part of Finnishness, even if this part is strangled or suppressed by opposite forces within the national battlefield.

In the three films discussed above, non-White Finnish nationality is represented by strong female protagonists, as opposed to (militarised) men embodying the hegemonic White Finnishness, which corresponds with the typical coding of nationality as male in Finland. Even if women are not ultimately the winners, they are equipped with agency, enabling them not only to question the powerful position of male national subjects, but also to infiltrate communities narrated from the male centre as coherent wholes and expose this coherence as a construction. In the following, I further explore primarily female infiltrators who problematise communities, proving that '[i]f the infiltrator's insertion into a structure that imagines itself solid is relatively successful, then the identity of all the other members of the supposedly natural community is brought into question' (Rosello 1996: 17).

Infiltrating Biographies: *Two Lives*

In the films discussed so far, the figure of the infiltrated infiltrator, such as Kerttu Nuorteva in Donner's *The Interrogation*, served to blur the borders between 'us' and 'them', between those belonging to 'our' community and those falling outside of it. Community, as both *Seamstress* and *The Border* have shown, is a muddled category: it can denote abstract notions and ideological agendas imposed from top-down, or real communal feelings and interconnections, with the two dimensions not necessarily overlapping. Creating a community based on sameness, as the films demonstrated, entails first designating all those who do not belong and then expelling them.

The secret police file, as *Seamstress* showed, was concerned with constructing an extensive biography of the accused, in order to provide reasons to pass sentence and thus exclude those who are meant to be excluded. Another 'secret' activity closely linked with (auto)biography is the process of creating spies, who are provided with thorough training and often recruited from groups susceptible to infiltration, such as children in orphanages.

Two Lives (2012) was directed by Georg Mass, a German director, and is a German-Norwegian co-production. The film tackles an important subject which concerns Norway: its ongoing toxic entanglements with (first Nazi and later GDR) Germany. It features Norwegian actors and Norwegian is spoken on an equal basis with German. The film tells the story of a Norwegian family which gradually collapses after the fall of the Berlin Wall and the reunification of Germany.[10]

The plot is set in October 1990, just after German reunification. The protagonist is a middle-aged woman, Katrine, who lives a comfortable life in an idyllic Norwegian town. She has a daughter and a granddaughter and is happily married to a maritime officer. It soon turns out, however, that Katrine hides a dark secret: she is a Stasi agent, sent to Norway in 1969. She claims to have escaped from the GDR and to be one of the so-called *Lebensborn* children, which leads to her being reunited with her Norwegian 'mother', Åse (played by Liv Ullmann). The *Lebensborn* children were conceived during the German occupation, the progeny of women from the occupied countries and German soldiers, and therefore called 'children of war' or 'children of shame'. *Lebensborn*, established by Heinrich Himmler in 1935 and meaning 'well of life', was a Nazi organisation for furthering Germany's racial policy and the birth of 'Aryan' children (Olsen 2005). The organisation was set up in several occupied countries during the war. The Norwegian population was counted among the most qualified and seen as 'racially precious' (Ibid. 20). After the capitulation of Germany in 1945, the mothers of such children were ostracised within Norwegian society and often placed in labour camps with the consent of the Norwegian government. Some of the children had been sent to Germany during the war, and the Norwegian authorities did little to find them and bring them back home (Ibid. 29).

In *Two Lives*, Åse's real daughter was adopted by a German family living in Saxony (East Germany). She manages to escape from the GDR via the Baltic Sea and is rescued on the Danish coast. She arrives at Åse's house to find Katrine waiting for her, alone. Katrine plans to betray the girl, but changes her mind and decides to help. It is, however, too late. Two male Stasi agents, one of whom was Katrine's 'mentor' before she was sent to Norway, arrive and pursue the girl, who has fled, finally overtaking and killing her. Following the reunification of Germany, the truth slowly surfaces after an intrusive human rights lawyer asks Katrine and Åse to join a lawsuit against the Norwegian government in the *Lebensborn* case. Katrine attempts to prevent the truth from coming out, travelling to the orphanage in Saxony where Åse's daughter lived and removing records from the archives. But her attempts to retain control of the past proves unsuccessful as the borders become increasingly porous and the reappearance of archival footage – a television interview with Åse's real daughter – destroys Katrine's hope for continuing her current life.

The film does not condemn Katrine – rather, she is depicted as both a part of the oppressive system and its victim. She is an infiltrator, but she was also infiltrated by the Stasi (represented by men), who showed her 'loving' care while she was growing up in an orphanage. They infiltrated her life first by enlisting her and then by sending her to Norway, which she saw as a chance to establish a family and a new start. Through Katrine, the Stasi infiltrate the Norwegian family, which metaphorically stands for the Norwegian nation. What is more, the Stasi create the nation's biography: the family is not simply recreated by the reunification of mother and daughter, but rather constructed in an artificial manner. Nevertheless, Katrine and Åse develop a loving mother-daughter relationship. The East German Katrine infiltrates Norway seamlessly – which epitomises her familiarity, rather than otherness – and becomes herself infiltrated when she falls in love and marries the man who was the subject of her invigilation, later having a child with him. Thus, the Norwegian family is the result of turbulent and complicated historical events, reaching back to acts committed by the Norwegians themselves – first, by being complicit in the deportation of children to Germany by the Nazis, and later by doing very little to try to bring these children home. The excluded return in the lurid form of Stasi invigilation. Katrine is not simply the 'enemy' from the outside; rather, her 'return' is a consequence of Norwegian society's own suppressed past. At the same time, Katrine proves that community is not necessarily based on natural bonds. Just as the spy's (auto)biography is to be written and memorised in the process of training and indoctrination, the community is likewise produced by repetitive performance of certain identities, codes and discourses.

When her family falls apart after Katrine confesses the truth, they remain a family – at least in the narrowest sense of the biological bond between Katrine, her daughter and her granddaughter. It is telling that female bonds shape the future of the Norwegian family – in contrast to the past which has been shaped by men (Nazis, Stasi agents and the pushy human rights lawyer). The spy does not disappear in a cloud of smoke, but leaves 'a subtle trail of slow disintegration' (Rosello 1996: 91). The disintegration triggered by Katrine's actions brings to the surface a dark chapter in Norway's past. Who is entitled to belong to the Norwegian family? As the example of the *Lebensborn* children and their mothers demonstrates, community is indeed based on exclusion. The re-exclusion and murder of Åse's biological daughter by the Stasi is a symbolic repetition of the nightmarish gesture of exclusion made earlier by Norwegian society. But the disintegration also concerns Katrine, as her identity rested firmly upon the old world order. This is epitomised by her death, her 'departure' or *départenance* to use Rosello's term – that is, 'a multiple movement away from the very concept of belonging'. Rosello speaks about 'an always defeated attempt not to belong', as inscribed in the figure of the spy (Ibid. 17). Katrine is aware that a performance of belonging is the only possible way that she can continue to exist, and this demands that others are excluded. Indeed, her impulse to defy belonging has to be defeated: even as she tries to help Åse's daughter, Katrine knows that only the girl's disappearance can provide her with a chance to belong – and survive. But this death becomes Katrine's worst nightmare, which never lets her fully belong.

As mentioned in Chapter 1, the crumbling of the Cold War order activated transnational memory work that was impossible earlier due to rigid spatial divisions. Although Norway was geographically far away from the epicentre of the events, the fall of the Berlin Wall ushered in rapid changes in the Norwegian family depicted in the film. The unblocking of transnational flows redefines the family/community through a renegotiation of the concept of belonging. With the borders becoming porous, allowing excluded (past) others 'in' (as demonstrated by the video recording with Åse's daughter), the borders delineating Katrine's identity and keeping the 'ideal' Norwegian family whole can no longer remain unaffected. However, the porousness of borders is not specific to the post-1989 period. As the films discussed below demonstrate, expanding borders was a necessary condition for the binary Cold War order to exist – and to uphold the fantasy of the two sides' mutual isolation.

Relational Spaces and No Other Side

All the films analysed in this chapter question the belief spread and consolidated by the Eastern noir narratives that narrating Russia requires the conventions of the crime or spy thriller film genre. Such conventions are equally challenged by the Norwegian director Knut Erik Jensen in his two feature films, *Burnt by Frost* (1997) and *Ice Kiss* (2008). Both films, based on famous espionage cases in Norway's Cold War history, deal with Norwegian citizens forced by historical circumstances to work for the Soviet intelligence services, and both '[differ] significantly from the standard formula spy movie, providing a background that transgresses the simple black-and-white rhetoric of the Cold War' (Sørenssen 2015: 336). *Ice Kiss*, depicting Norway's most famous spy (love) story, that of Gunvor Galtung Haavik, who worked for twenty-eight years as an agent for the KGB, was met with harsh criticism. A critic at the leading Norwegian newspaper *Dagbladet* expressed very directly his disappointment at the fact that Jensen's film was 'art cinema' and not a spy thriller with classical dramaturgy (see Ibid. 342–3). Indeed, rather than fulfilling expectations for a spy thriller or a 'mainstream historical film' (biopic), Jensen's films '[opt] instead for a subjective insight in complicated personal and historical situation, demanding an effort of the audience to interpret and re-interpret the images, words and sounds' (Ibid. 344–5). Both films resort to a fragmentary narrative woven of tableaus, poetic use of images and sounds, Steadicam, slow motion, non-linear chronology with flashbacks and flashforwards, all of which comprise the aesthetics typical of Jensen's experimental approach to cinema.

Both films are partly set in northern Norway, which, especially in regard to Finnmark and its post-war history, is a central, significant location as regards Jensen's cinematic *oeuvre*. Although situated far from the geographical, political and cultural centres of Norway, Finnmark – the extreme northeastern Norwegian county that shares a border with Russia – has been a geopolitically strategic location not only during the Cold War, but throughout the twentieth century until the present (Aas and Vestgården 2014: 188). Since 1949, it has been the border between NATO and Russia. In 1944, German troops retreating from Finland destroyed the villages of Finnmark using scorched earth tactics, burning and razing everything of use to the Soviets. East Finnmark was liberated by the Red Army in the autumn of 1944. During the war, the resistance against Nazi occupation was one of the strongest in northern Norway, and many Norwegians cooperated with Russian partisans. Faced with a new reality after the war, old friends were often redefined as enemies.[11]

The prototype of the male protagonist in *Burnt by Frost* is the Norwegian spy Selmer Nilsen, whose family was pressured into sending him to the USSR at seventeen years old. There, he receives training as an intelligence agent, after which he serves as a spy in Finnmark, where NATO bases were installed in 1949 (Sørenssen 2015: 338). The non-linear and dream-like narrative can be summarised as follows: Simon is a young man, who fights in the resistance movement against the Nazis alongside a Soviet partisan, Lasov. Befriending Simon's family, Lasov returns to their village after the war to recruit Simon to the KGB intelligence services. Lasov is an agreeable and cultivated man and soldier, who serves as a teacher and father figure for Simon – and who shapes his biography. Simon's espionage activities are not unknown to the villagers, whose growing hostility makes him feel increasingly isolated from the local community. Finally, Simon is sentenced for espionage and treason, but after his release from prison he returns to the village. In the end, only his lover, Lillian, remains on his side. Lillian also acts as the subjective narrator of large parts of the film.

The film never depicts the physical border between Finnmark and Russia apart from two arbitrary visualisations: a line on a map in a NATO base and a similar red line on a map when Simon is being trained in spycraft by Lasov. Rather than being a theme in the film, the border is construed by means of contrasting editing, which juxtaposes the rural maritime areas of a fishing village in Finnmark – Simon's home – with various places in Russia, where Simon has been trained, surrounded by art, magnificent architecture and military elites.

Whereas the typical (Cold War) framing of espionage presupposes two enemy sides, Simon proves that this relation is not one of disconnection and opposition, but instead of interdependence, introducing qualitative change to the whole continuous (rather than discontinuous) system. Simon's activities incorporate this change – he is not just a fisherman from Finnmark, but also a former partisan and 'Soviet hero', who proudly bears the Soviet uniform and clearly enjoys both of his roles. In Russia, the narrative of 'spy-as-star' is fulfilled: Simon (in reality, Selmer Nilsen) discovers the route of the American U2 spy aircraft, which leads to its famous shooting down. Thus, in Russia, like a true agent, Simon enjoys

Figure 2.3 Lasov (left) and Simon (right), with the latter as the 'Soviet hero'. *Burnt by Frost*. Photograph by Svein Krøvel. Courtesy of Barentsfilm.

reward and success, and like a true agent, he has a Russian lover. Tellingly, when Lillian begs him to give up his activities, Simon answers: 'I have one more thing to do. Then I will be free'. In response, Lillian says: 'There is no other side'. What her words convey is the impossibility, for Simon, of crossing the border 'back' – his identity comprises both the Soviet spy and Finnmark fisherman, and as such, it reflects the boundary.

Rosello observes that part of the job of a spy is to 'perform' with little to no ambiguity apparent in his/her actions, in order to 'pass' for a member of a group (1996: 17). However, Simon does not seem to 'perform' his different roles – rather, he is a natural part of both worlds. While the juxtapositions (through editing) of Finnmark and Russia are governed by the principle of contrast, Simon's body serves as an entity where these two spaces find continuity. Only the local community of Finnmark cannot accept Simon's identity. Although Simon himself fully identifies with Finnmark – and embodies the complexities of the region produced by its closeness to Russia – the villagers treat him as an outsider and a threat to their peaceful existence, conditioned upon adaptation to centrally imposed cooperation with NATO and the isolation of Norway from USSR – the 'Red threat'. Simon does not adhere to this imagined – and desired – isolation, on which power relations were officially founded during the Cold War.

On the contrary, Simon's infiltrated identity results from a specific external situation. Using the critical geographer David Harvey's notion, Simon can be seen as embodying the 'relational space' created between the individual and the contextual. This space has its origins in the map, but it exceeds the map by its relational infrastructure. Simon's infiltrated identity can be seen as reflecting Finnmark's entanglement in the macropolitical order, with emphasis on the relational dimension of his entanglement. It is thus worth taking a closer look at the relationality embodied by Simon.

In an article on space and affect, Frederik Tygstrup draws on the distinction introduced by Harvey between absolute space, relative space and relational space (Harvey 2009: 131ff.). Absolute space is objective and immovable, designated by a map. Relative space relates to time, showing that history and geography coexist: it includes histories, traditions, rituals and narratives connected to a specific place. As Tygstrup observes, these two types of spaces rest upon an old 'architecture', conceiving of space as either objective (absolute) or subjective (relative). Relational space surpasses this binary subject/object or inside/outside division. This concept of space involves dimensions that cannot fit into the other categories: it is flexible and expandable, shaped by memories and dreams that are personal and yet culturally produced. Relational space embraces the social and cultural distribution of things and ideas, emotions and fantasies, which all 'delineate a very real historical space that cannot be mapped in a satisfactory way as either absolute or relative' (Tygstrup 2013: 26).

Simon's infiltrated identity cannot be grasped by geopolitical maps or by the relative space represented by the inhabitants of his home village in Finnmark. He embodies relational space, which results from a suspension of the division between inside and outside (Finnmark). When one of Simon's relatives warns him against his espionage activities and cautions: 'Remember where you come from', Simon answers: 'I'm from Korsfjord. And the ocean outside'. While the phrase 'and the ocean outside' repeats like an echo, rhythmically fluctuating water fills the frame in one long, undivided take. For Simon, there is no clear division between 'here' and 'outside', nor between being a fisherman from Korsfjord and a Russian spy and hero. The sea, photographed as one smooth body, is like Simon's body: it signifies the indivisible connection with, and hence infiltration by, the global reality. This connection is illustrated in a scene that depicts Simon's boat and a Soviet submarine meeting in clandestine fashion on the open sea to exchange intelligence and money. While both the maps and the villagers represent the isolation of spaces and times from one another (Norway from Russia, West from East, present from past), the sea and Simon incarnate the relational spaces that expose this isolation as a fantasy. Moreover, relationality is implemented on the level of formal solutions in *Burnt by Frost*: interconnections across both space and time are created by weaving fiction and archival footage together, as well as by evocations of the Russian director Andrei Tarkovsky's cinematic aesthetics. The spatio-temporal complexity in *Burnt by Frost*, conveyed through dream-like sequences, slow-motion tracking and rhythmically structured long takes, is here connected, as in Tarkovsky's films, to memory and consciousness and expressed through nature and its flowing forces, such as wind or water (see Totaro 1992: 21, 23).

Because Simon embodies relationality, his character problematises the borders of the national community. It is, however, important to emphasise that he identifies with Finnmark and not with Norway as such. The dominant national narrative, based on post-war cooperation with the US, is represented by a maritime officer working for NATO, who travels to Finnmark from the 'south' – that is, from Oslo. Simon confronts him aggressively in a scene in which he emphasises his identification with Finnmark, rather than with the whole nation. Simon's activities are a way of undermining the hegemonic narrative from the centre/south, which he sees as having been imposed on Finnmark, without understanding the region's relational involvement with the 'outside', including Russia.

The rich use of archival footage, intercut with the film's fictional elements, emphasises Finnmark's entanglement in global politics. The essence of montage as such is to create relational meanings (one shot relating to the other and producing a 'third' meaning in the viewer's mind). The archival materials used in the film place Finnmark in direct relation with crucial events from the 'outer' world, such as the Cuban crisis, the trial of the U2 aircraft pilot Francis Gary Powers, the victory of the Soviet Union in WWII, Stalin's death, the liberation of Finnmark by the Red Army, Ronald Reagan's famous utterance in Berlin in 1987: 'Mr. Gorbachev, tear down that wall', and finally the fall of the Berlin Wall. The archival footage and the storyline are sometimes combined to accentuate the contrast between the two, but most often the fiction and the archival material interweave in ways that emphasise the infiltration of Finnmark's history by world history – for instance, by means of match cuts, analogy (such as Powers' trial being followed by Simon's trial) or sound. At the same time, whereas the complex plot is fragmentary and guided by personal memory, emotions, dreams and experience, and the scenes and images combined by free association rather than a linear logic, the archives introduce the master narrative of History – the absolute space of the historical map.

Likewise, in *Ice Kiss*, the female protagonist, Vera, who ends up working as a double agent, embodies an infiltrated identity that exceeds binary oppositions and the extensive divisions of an absolute space. In the opening sequence, the Cold War is metaphorically evoked by an ice-covered river, and the images shown are saturated with intense blue, conventionally associated with cold (Antunes 2016: 160). Coldness makes also itself visible through the red cheeks of the smiling woman, Vera, who, wearing a traditional Norwegian sweater, is framed by the impressive Kremlin towers in the background (see the cover of the book). Despite the cold, she does not seem to be freezing. Throughout the film, Vera's body crosses back and forth over the cold border, regardless of political temperatures – until it becomes appropriated by the border.

As in *Burnt by Frost*, the cinematic means utilised in *Ice Kiss* produce a relational space that results from the interactions between characters, their emotions, dreams and the political realities they confront. In the opening sequence of the film, Vera faces the viewer, saying: 'Do you remember our dreams? Do you remember my joy simply because you existed in this world?' In *Ice Kiss*, the emphasis is on affect, understood as a corporeal reaction to impulses from the outside (other persons, objects, art, environment), which in turn affect others, and thus denote a not purely individual response to the external world, but a relational synergy, where the inner and outer realities interweave (see Tygstrup 2013: 23). The relational space in *Ice Kiss* is an affective space embodied by Vera bypassing the 'cold' divisions. The film emphasises Vera's affective reactions to the surrounding reality, her subjective memory and emotional experiences of Russia. Vera's affective responses to Russian culture remembered from her youth spent in Finnmark are expressed through close-ups of her face – the gleam in her eyes, her blushing cheeks – and the joy articulated with her whole body through music and folk dancing, her energy connoting a warmth that contradicts the political coldness. Her intense reactions are ironically juxtaposed with an official Russian voice expressing hope for the strengthening of friendship between Norway and the Soviet Union. Affect and political reality interweave in ways that will define Vera's whole life. Her love for Russian culture and a Russian man – that is, the fact that she is already infiltrated by Russia – will position her as a potential infiltrator, whom she becomes against her will. After being forced to sign a cooperation agreement with the KGB, and threatened that her Russian lover will be sent to Siberia, Vera unflinchingly retorts: 'My own country I could betray. But not you'. Significantly, this is the only instance when she physically freezes on the spot in the film. Unlike Simon in *Burnt by Frost*, she abhors working in espionage.

The narrative backbone of *Ice Kiss* is established by a female voice-over,

Figure 2.4 Affective embodiment of political reality: Vera (freezing) and Vladimir (overpowered by the regime's persecutions). *Ice Kiss.* Photograph by Mona Haug. Courtesy of Filmhuset AS and Knut Erik Jensen.

based on letters written by Gunvor Galtung Haavik to her Russian lover, Vladimir Kozlov. During the war, Haavik was a nurse stationed at a hospital in northern Norway, where she met Kozlov, a prisoner-of-war. Due to her excellent skills in Russian, she acted as an interpreter during the repatriation of Russian prisoners. Later, Haavik worked at the Norwegian Foreign Ministry and was involved as an interpreter with the establishment of the Norwegian/USSR border in Finnmark. In 1947, she was employed at the Norwegian Embassy in Moscow and was highly trusted by the Norwegian authorities. In 1950, Haavik was pressured into service by the KGB. After returning to Norway in 1956, she served as an agent until her activities were disclosed in 1977, and she was put into prison, where she died six months later (see Sørenssen 2015: 341). In 1993, Knut Erik Jensen and Alf R. Jacobsen, author of the novel *Iskyss* (1991) and co-author of the resulting film's script respectively, travelled to Russia, where they met Kozlov, who shared Haavik's letters with them (Jensen made a documentary based on the letters: *My Dear Friend / Min kjære venn*, 1994). Ten years later, encouraged by Jensen, Kozlov shared the story of their affair. The screenplay for *Ice Kiss* is based on Kozlov's account and

Haavik's passionate letters (Sørenssen 2015: 341–2). In a similar manner to how letters function in Suhonen's *Seamstress*, the female voice-over provides viewers with an insight into the protagonist's thoughts and paints a picture of her personality. As in *Seamstress*, Vera's sensitivity remains in opposition to the brutal political reality, imposed on her after her enlistment as a spy.

In contrast to *Burnt by Frost*, *Ice Kiss* includes no archival footage. Nevertheless, authentic documents – that is, Haavik's letters and Kozlov's memories – are incorporated in the narrative and constitute its foundation. It is here that 'fact' and 'fiction' interweave seamlessly. It is significant that Haavik's name was changed to Vera Våge, whereas Kozlov's name remains authentic. This change was interpreted as Jensen's strategy to allow himself artistic freedom while approaching a subject considered to be '*The Great Norwegian Epic Drama*' (Sørenssen 2015: 342 [original emphasis]). However, the fictional name can be seen as emphasising the director's choice to conflate facts with the woman's affective experience of the facts. 'Vera Våge' is a playful choice in this respect: the name Vera, from the Latin 'truth' (*veritas*) and the Norwegian verb *våge*, meaning 'to dare', imply no fear of the truth. But rather than a naive faith in historical truth, the focus is on Haavik's truthfulness to the intensity of her experience and feelings, and on her tragic choice between her motherland and the man she loved. At the same time, the Russian name Vera together with her Norwegian surname express the two aspects of her infiltrated identity – two sides of one coin. This is also conveyed through the use of montage, depicting Vera once in Norway, once in Russia. Because Vera works for central political institutions, the fact that she comes from Finnmark does not play such a large role as it does in *Burnt by Frost*. Nevertheless, similarly to Simon, Vera's origins in northern Norway, where she becomes 'infiltrated' by Russian culture as a young woman, and most importantly her identity together embody the boundary.

If Norway and Russia smoothly interweave to make up Vera's identity, there is no symmetry between the two states in reality – Norway is only a small nation bordering the newly emerged Soviet Empire, and it is Norway, not Russia, that is the infiltrated side. Vera experiences this asymmetry of power in relation to her own body when she is forced into cooperating through physical abuse – a sort of rite of passage, including poisoning, vomiting, fainting, being forced naked into a bathtub filled with freezing water while spectators look on, and blackmail. This asymmetry of power is similarly emphasised in a scene early on in the film, set on the newly established Norwegian/USSR border in Finnmark.[12] A Russian officer steadfastly claims: 'Norway has nothing to fear, and if you need

Figure 2.5 Becoming an infiltrated infiltrator: the interpreter's in-between status at the Norwegian/USSR border in Finnmark. *Ice Kiss*. Photograph by Svein Krøvel. Courtesy of Filmhuset AS and Knut Erik Jensen.

our help again, we are prepared, as your good neighbour'. Unlike in other scenes when Vera acts as interpreter, this sentence is uttered twice, once in Russian and once in Norwegian – a strategy conveying the centrality, as well as the ambiguity, of the scene, which expresses Norway's precarious position as Russia's neighbour. The asymmetry is made clear when the Norwegian ambassador answers: 'The USSR has nothing to fear from us either', at which the Soviet officer bursts out laughing. He asserts: 'The border between our two countries stands firm', thus pointing back to the USSR as the centre delineating the border. In this scene, Vera's role as interpreter can be seen as a first step toward becoming an infiltrated infiltrator: an interpreter is always in-between ideas, able to switch smoothly from one cultural code to the other, an insider and outsider at the same time.

Both *Ice Kiss* and *Burnt by Frost* diverge from Eastern noir narratives not only because of their experimental and 'experiental' aesthetics (see Antunes 2016: 156ff.), but also because they depict the Norwegian infiltrated infiltrators in a positive light and elicit not only sympathy from viewers, but also – especially in the case of Vera – force them to become affectively involved.[13] For Vera and Simon, Russia is not an unknown, strange and threatening place, but a beloved nation – although one with an oppressive, Soviet system (this distinction is especially clear in *Ice Kiss*) – whose language they speak. Power, incarnated by Soviet rule, uses infiltration for its own purposes – but as Vera and especially Simon show, infiltration is also power, by means of which the hegemonic (national) narrative and the national cohesive community imagined by the centre can be undermined. The imagined whole of the community is challenged not only thematically, but also by the fragmentary narrative and complex aesthetics of the films. Nonetheless, both in *Ice Kiss* and *Burnt by Frost*, the infiltration of the protagonists' bodies and lives by the power apparatus (rather than their own active infiltration of the system) gradually takes over, their tragic fates indicating that there is no other side to the dominating Cold War order.

Conclusion: Powerful Infiltrators

The cinematic portraits of infiltrated infiltrators demonstrate that what hegemonic narratives present as opposition proves to be 'two sides of one coin', to use a metaphor evoked earlier. However, although the duality inscribed in this metaphor aptly reflects the dual order within which the infiltrators exist, as well as the inseparability of the two sides, the coin provides an inaccurate image of transnational entanglements: what it does not capture is the imbalance of power between the two sides. The infiltrated infiltrators are tragic heroes, quite unlike the 'spies-as-stars'. They embody the asymmetry of power, using infiltration either to expose hegemonic national narratives as exclusionary or to disclose the vulnerability of their own in-betweenness. Although the term 'transnational' might not seem adequate in the context of the rigidly divided realities of (Cold) war, from a contemporary perspective the infiltrated infiltrators can be seen as embodying transnational entanglements; their identities would most likely be denoted as hybrid, hyphenated or transnational in other (contemporary) cultural, political and/or historical circumstances.

By staging Russia not as an unknown and distant other, or as a negative projection of the Nordic self, but rather as heterogeneous and connected to *Norden* in multiple ways, the films discussed in this chapter embrace the complex neighbourliness between the Eastern empire and the small Nordic nations. Although the films portray an atmosphere of fear regarding the 'Red threat' in the Nordic societies over the course of various historical periods (from the Finnish Civil War to the end of the Cold War), the plots focus on protagonists who display no fear of Russia, but who do not necessarily support Soviet rule either. Rather than by fear, they are driven by the opposite – a fascination with, and love for, Russia. The films break with the overarching frame of friend *versus* enemy, East *versus* West. They rehabilitate previously condemned spies as having the power to challenge narratives on homogeneous communities. The border is always already a boundary, and as such, it does not provide comforting reassurance.

The next chapter explores cinematic narratives built around a large and important boundary in Nordic cinemas, connecting *Norden* and the former Eastern Bloc – the Baltic Sea. Unlike the majority of films discussed thus far, these narratives are set in a time when Russia is no longer an imperial threat, and rather than facing their large and dangerous neighbour, the small Nordic nations shift to narrate themselves in relation to the similarly small, neighbouring nations that (re)emerged in the northern consciousness after the disintegration of the Eastern Bloc.

Notes

1. To name a few examples: *Codename Coq Rouge* (*Täcknamn Coq Rouge*, Pelle Berglund 1989); television miniseries *Enemy's Enemy* (*Fiendens fiende*, Thomas Borgström, Lars Bill Lundholm 1990); *Hamilton – In the Interest of the Nation* (*Hamilton – I nationens intresse*, Kathrine Windfeld 2012).
2. This pair reminds one of the famous Nordic noir detective partners, Sarah Lund and Jan Meyer (*The Killing/Forbrydelsen*, DR, Denmark 2007–12) and Saga Norén and Martin Rohde (*The Bridge/Bron/Broen*, DR/SVT, Sweden, Denmark 2011–15).
3. A different take on the figure of the double agent/spy within genre cinema is offered by the Norwegian action comedy *Norwegian Ninja* (*Kommandør Treholt & Ninja troppen*, Thomas Cappelen Malling 2010), which tells the story of Arne Treholt, a former Norwegian minister convicted in 1984 of high treason and espionage on behalf of the Soviet Union. Treholt is depicted as a covert spy, working for the king and protecting Norway from foreign threats (see Kääpä 2015).
4. This narrative tends to be reiterated in post-Cold War scholarship, not questioning the overall binary frame of spy narratives (for example, see Cronqvist 2004: 39, 313).
5. A pattern contested in *Occupied*, where a Norwegian woman is a collaborator, and another woman becomes the leader of resistance movement; moreover, Russia is embodied by a female ambassador.
6. The exceptions are *The Border* and *Two Lives*, both about fictitious 'infiltrated infiltrators'.
7. See Jouko Aaltonen's documentary *Revolution* (*Kenen joukoissa seisot*, Finland 2006), about the left-wing cultural movement in Finland during the 1960s and 1970s. I am grateful to Jouko Aaltonen and Ville Suhonen for inspiring conversations which helped me to improve this chapter.
8. As Bolesław Mrozewicz notes, critical examinations of the Civil War were already present in Finnish literature shortly after the war – for example, Frans Eemil Sillanpää's novel *Hurskas kurjuus* (1919) (2004: 75–6).
9. These ethnic 'others' in *The Border* are primarily Russians, but also Jews. The

trope of anti-Semitism in *The Border*, combined with anti-Russian and anti-Soviet sentiment in Finland after the Civil War, can be seen as an implicit reference to Finnish films of the 1920s and 1930s that expressed similar sentiment, such as *The Highest Victory* (1929) and *Soldier's Bride* (1938), mentioned in the Introduction.

10. The title may be a reference to an early Norwegian occupation drama, *Two Lives* (*To liv*, Titus Vibe-Müller 1946), where the father of a young Norwegian anti-Nazi resistance fighter attempts to revenge his son's death, but is unable to pull the trigger. Instead, the mother kills the traitor (see Iversen 2012: 240).

11. Knut Erik Jensen, born in Finnmark in 1940, experienced the war as a child. Jensen's documentary television series *Finnmark between East and West* (*Finnmark mellom øst og vest*, 1985) depicts Finnmark's history from the frog perspective of those who experienced the evacuations of 1944 (see Iversen 2001).

12. Norway and Russia shared the border from 1533 until the area of Petsamo was ceded to Finland in 1920. Petsamo was ceded to USSR in 1944.

13. In *Burnt by Frost*, the viewer is affectively involved with Lillian rather than Simon, who remains a self-enclosed and emotionally distant character.

CHAPTER 3

The Baltic Boundary

The Baltic Sea, which features centrally in two of the films discussed in previous chapters, can be located, alongside geopolitically strategic spaces such as Svalbard or Finnmark, within the Nordic continuum of environments central to the Cold War imagery. Whereas Svalbard and Finnmark are associated with extreme northern environments, occupying 'a liminal space in the ecological and geographical spatiality of earth' (Stenport 2015: 162), the Baltic Sea, which together with the Finnish and Norwegian eastern borders comprised the northern part of the Iron Curtain, signified a liminal space to the south-east during the Cold War. This utmost limit connoted the end of the Western world, not least because connections across the Baltic, which made travel possible, now ceased to exist. At the same time, the Baltic aroused ambivalence: on the one hand, it induced fear of infiltration by the Soviets (proven justified by the intrusion of a Soviet submarine that ran aground on the Swedish coast near Karlskrona in 1981); on the other, a (rather optimistic) perception of the Baltic framed it as a '"moat protecting the Swedish fortress"' from Soviet military invasion (Malmborg 2001: 159).

Over the centuries, the Baltic often froze completely during severe winters (the last time being over the winter of 1946–7), due to which it was used as a land route between the distant shores (Marusek 2010). Whereas earlier in history the Baltic facilitated connections, with the Iron Curtain it became a wall rather than a passage. Despite multiple instances of successful escape involving GDR citizens fleeing to southern Denmark (Clemmensen 2012) or the inhabitants of communist Poland fleeing to the Danish 'island of freedom', Bornholm (Karaś 2017), the south-eastern shore of the Baltic became marginalised within both official and unofficial Nordic discourses. The existence of the eastern countries across the sea 'faded from the consciousness of their northern neighbours' (Kirby 1995: 378).

In view of these facts, it is not surprising that movement across the Baltic did not become a noteworthy theme in Nordic cinemas until after the Cold

War. The political changes around 1989 enabled a revival of (old) routes and made it possible to establish new ties (Karlsson and Zander 2000: 7). Some even believed that 'Norden can be rearticulated as a Baltic project' (Wæver 1992: 100). However, the post-Cold War imagination of the Baltic was dominated by a new kind of ambivalence: the Baltic Sea now promised a reconnection, a return of long-suppressed interaction and exchange; yet, despite physically connecting the different shores, it also represented an ocean of cultural distance and, at the same time, the possibility of infiltration by undesirable elements from the east. As Swedish scholars Yvonne Sandberg-Fries and Peter Althini observe: 'The changes in the Baltic Sea region after the fall of the Berlin Wall did not progress as fast as many hoped in the beginning of the 1990s'. The earlier bonds, broken during the fifty years of closed borders, were difficult to re-establish. Additionally, '[p]rejudice and lack of knowledge erected barriers' (Sandberg-Fries and Althini 2000: 5).

Like the Iron Curtain and the Berlin Wall, the Baltic Sea became a symbol, although a less widespread one, of the division and distance between the Nordic world and the Eastern Bloc countries. But unlike the spectacular metaphor of the wall, which could 'collapse' or 'fall', thereby denoting the end of an epoch, a system or even the 'end of history', the Baltic Sea could not simply dry up or disappear, and thus did not offer easy imagery for framing the social and political developments of that time as an absolute break between two eras and an opening or beginning of a new way of life and reality. As the philosopher Bronisław Baczko suggests: '[E]vents are less important than the imaginary representations they create and which they are framed by' (1994: 44). Indeed, as an imaginary representation, the Baltic Sea produces meanings different from those created by the Iron Curtain or the Berlin Wall: as a fluid, mutable and unpredictable body, the sea does not easily organise the chaotic dynamics of reality into a manageable structure. This unpredictability is illustrated by historian David Kirby's metaphor of the Baltic's spring thaw:

> The period in which the icebound waters of the Baltic begin to break up is always dangerous. We are living through such a period at the present moment, and there are many who look back with longing to the winter which is now over. (1995: 438)

The symbolic 'ice' of the Cold War guaranteed the threatening chaos represented by the now stormy waters would be kept under control.[1] The threat of military invasion was replaced by the threat posed by the unpredictable consequences of opening up the borders – of the new life and changes that would follow the 'thaw'.

The films under discussion in this chapter, which address the uneasy return of the eastern neighbours to the northern consciousness and reflect upon the complexities of establishing bonds across the 'thawing' sea, include *The Birthday Trip* (*Kajs fødselsdag*, Lone Scherfig, Denmark 1990), *Screwed in Tallinn* (*Torsk på Tallinn*, Tomas Alfredson, Sweden 1999), *Take Care of Your Scarf, Tatjana* (*Pidä huivista kiinni, Tatjana*, Aki Kaurismäki, Finland 1994), the documentary *The Escape* (*Flugten fra DDR*, Jesper Clemmensen, Denmark 2014) and the short feature films *Coffee in Gdańsk* (*Kaffe i Gdańsk*, Per-Anders Ring, Sweden 2008), *You Can't Eat Fishing* (Kathrine Windfeld, Denmark 1999) and *In Transit* (Lisa Aschan, Denmark 2005). In addition, I refer to other relevant cinematic examples oriented around the Baltic (*Dresser/Kredens*, Jacob Dammas 2007; *Stateless/Statsløs*, Jacob Kofler 2004; *The Ship/Skibet*, Marian Marzyński 1970–2010). These films span three decades, during which the discourse surrounding the Baltic Sea evolves from explorations of the 'other' shore as a distant and somewhat threatening, but also promising, periphery to a replacement of the centre/periphery metaphor incarnating the border discourse with boundary discourses, epitomised by the figure of the 'distant neighbour', as well as narratives of freedom and modernity manifested by the 'other' shore.

Questioning the Baltic Periphery

In many of the films discussed thus far, the binary notion of centre/ periphery has functioned as an implicit cognitive structure framing Nordic/Eastern relations. With regard to Russia and Cold War contexts, the films expressed the position of the Nordic countries as peripheral to the imperial neighbour to the east. At the same time, it is important to remember that during the Cold War *Norden* enjoyed a stable position as a 'better' socio-political option in relation to both East and West, combining the 'ideal' type of state – the welfare state – with the security model defined as 'Nordic balance', based on both cooperation with, and distance towards, the superpowers. After the political changes of 1989/91, *Norden* was threatened with becoming a mere peripheral region, rather than being a role model for the rest of Europe (see Wæver 1992).

These anxieties are indirectly articulated in a number of films made in the 1990s. In relation to the 'newly emerged' Eastern European neighbours across the Baltic, the metaphor of centre/periphery takes on a new dimension: in the post-Cold War order, Nordic protagonists eagerly imagine the 'other' shore as a periphery, in this way assigning the position of the centre to themselves. However, although in the 1990s, Eastern

Europeans were indeed portrayed in the Nordic media as Europe's periphery – poor, backward, suffering from post-Soviet depression and clearly at the opposite end of the spectrum from the well-developed West (see Musiał and Bartnik-Świątek 2016) – several films from that decade question the simplicity of such divisions. In the following, I discuss two films that illustrate this: the romantic comedy *The Birthday Trip* (1990) and the pseudo-documentary *Screwed in Tallinn* (1999), made as one of four one-hour films ('Fyra små filmer'/'Four small films') by the very popular Swedish comedy group 'Killinggänget', with a style influenced by the mockumentary genre (Larsson 2010: 24). The two films produce a boundary discourse that disrupts the narrative on the Baltic's 'eastern' periphery constructed by Nordic protagonists – not by reversing oppositions, but by attributing a similar peripheral status to the Nordic characters and locations. An important question remains regarding whether this gradually established similarity between protagonists and regions is a strategy for 'taming' the other by 'affixing the unfamiliar to something established' (Bhabha 2004: 105) or whether difference is recognised, preventing appropriation of the unknown by means of familiar cognitive frames.

As mentioned earlier, borders are delineated by those situated at the centre and who claim power (Casey 2011: 386).[2] The same applies to the distinction between the centre and the periphery. As A. V. Seaton emphasises, the idea of the margin or periphery rests on the imbalance of power existing between people living in different countries or regions. Most frequently, such power relations are shaped by those who perceive themselves as belonging to the centre (Seaton 2000: 322–3). Seaton conceptualises centre/periphery in relation to three domains: physical, psycho-cultural and politico-economic. Within the physical domain, distance, language and the 'exotic' appearance of the local people function as important markers of the periphery. Within the politico-economic domain, the centre is associated with economic vitality, metropolitan sophistication, innovation and a modern and fulfilling lifestyle. Within the psycho-cultural domain, Seaton identifies the following binaries: mundane comfort/extraordinary hardship or ease; familiar/dangerous; classic/romantic; ordered cultivation/disordered wilderness; ego controlled and 'civilised'/id or superego driven and 'natural' (336–8).

These contrasting domains are inherent in numerous, often overlapping discourses about the periphery. Two are of significance here – the romanticising and the imperial. According to these two discourses, the periphery can serve as a discursive site for the 'spiritual raptures' of 'romanticism' and as the site of an 'imperial mission' and 'adventure' (Seaton 2000: 324).

Romantic depictions of peripheries typically offer a critique of, and compensation for, the shortcomings of one's own society (Ibid. 334). In the imperial discourse, peripheries are seen as colourful sites of exploration and adventure. Within this discourse, the inhabitants are usually imagined as 'barbarians' and often cast in gendered and sexualised terms. Most often, 'European civilization is endowed with a stereotypically male sexuality. Its superiority gives civilization the right to penetrate, decipher, and give meaning to the female Asian mystery' (Boletsi 2013: 97). Both discourses, the romanticising and the imperial, are invoked in *The Birthday Trip* and *Screwed in Tallinn*. However, the assumed imbalance in power is challenged within all three spheres distinguished by Seaton – physical, psycho-cultural and politico-economic.

In *The Birthday Trip* and *Screwed in Tallinn*, imperial discourse is evoked by the very fact that the plots revolve around the travels of male Scandinavian protagonists to the 'other' shore – Poland (*The Birthday Trip*) and Estonia (*Screwed in Tallinn*) – in order to meet local women. In both films, the relations between the two sexes metaphorically stand for the imagined relations between the two countries and regions. An implicit factor underscoring the imperial nature of the practices of Swedes and Danes is the historical circumstance that both countries were active colonisers of these areas in the Middle Ages and later.[3] Likewise, the fact that in both films Russians are figured as either soldiers (*The Birthday Trip*) or as 'pimps' (*Screwed in Tallinn*) reinforces the position of the local inhabitants (Poles and Estonians) as peoples colonised by a foreign power.

The relation to Russia requires further explanation. In *The Birthday Trip*, Russians are represented by numerous soldiers, who in 1990 were indeed still stationed in Poland. In the film, they seem a natural part of the local landscape. In *Screwed in Tallinn*, one of the central characters is Lembit, a Russian local businessman. His aggressive macho-like behaviour epitomises the antipathy felt towards Russians by citizens of the oppressed societies within the former Soviet Bloc. In both Scherfig's and Alfredson's films, Russians represent the established order on the 'other' shore, even in a post-Iron Curtain Europe. But unlike in stereotypical crime narratives that conflate Russians and East Europeans, Russians are clearly distinguished from Poles and Estonians.

Early on in both films, it seems that the Scandinavian characters, as successors to the Russian colonisers, are going to assume the superior position of those possessing, literally, 'the right to penetrate' (Boletsi 2013: 97). In *The Birthday Trip*, however, it quickly turns out that the Russian soldiers incite fear in the Danish visitors, and the Danes are hardly up to the role of 'new colonisers'. Unlike the Poles, Russians are seen as distant others by the Danes, a contrast made explicit through their uniforms. Compared to Russians, Poles appear more familiar. In *Screwed in Tallinn*, the Swedish organiser of the trip cooperates with the bossy Lembit (who treats both his wife and his staff badly), who arranges meetings between Estonian women and Swedish men. The two middlemen, a Swede and a Russian, collaboratively broker transactions in which Estonian women are the prime commodity. This evokes not only Sweden's distant colonial past in the region, but also the more contemporary frame of Sweden's implicit support for (and thus complicity in) the Soviet colonial order, expressed by Sweden's 'neutral' ideological behaviour that supported Moscow's interests during the Cold War (see Malmborg 2001: 169).

Unlike the Russians' position in the two films – that of distant other (*The Birthday Trip*) or business partner (*Screwed in Tallinn*) – the Poles and Estonians are initially orientalised in the imaginations of the Scandinavian travellers, only to ultimately transform from 'others' (although much closer than Russians) to 'distant neighbours'. The figure of a distant neighbour combines distance (here signified by the sea) with a sense of proximity, commonality and sharing. While a 'close neighbour' (based on direct territorial adjacency or cultural communality) can pose the threat of absorption, which may prompt impulses towards the solidification of borders, in a distant neighbourhood, like that between Denmark and Poland or Sweden and Estonia, the threat of such destructive drives seems less tangible (see Mazierska et al. 2014: 24).

This neighbourliness, although distant, translates to the fact that the Scandinavian protagonists prove to be less 'central' in Seaton's terms than they initially assume. In the beginning, the distance across the Baltic is imagined as being huge, suggested by the difficulties in reaching the 'other' shore (although both Poland and Estonia are easily accessible by ferry). Distance is also created through language barriers. Poles and Estonians are represented as lacking skill in English, but able to speak Russian fluently, which associates them with a different sphere of influence. At the same time, the English spoken by the Scandinavians is also far from perfect.

While the travel arouses anxiety in the protagonists, which undermines their self-assurance, the (unfamiliar, almost dangerous) Baltic is also imagined as offering liberation and hope for fulfilment. Whereas Denmark is narrated as the site of a bored attitude to sex (romantic raptures destroyed by legalised pornography) and Sweden as a site of loneliness, the Scandinavians expect to find genuine connection and intense emotions on the other shore. In *Screwed in Tallinn*, the liberating potential of the sea is rather grotesquely signalled by travellers being locked in their bus and not allowed to enter the ferry deck, as if to restrain their latent wildness; meanwhile, the Swedish middleman and his bus driver indulge in the 'wild' pleasures of spending the night on the ferry, including attending a discotheque, drinking excessively and sleeping comfortably in a cabin.

Within the politico-economic sphere, the protagonists initially imagine themselves as dominant agents, travelling to fulfil their needs and desires, which (as they assume) they can achieve due to their superior economic position in the impoverished ex-communist countries. However, this 'imperial' mission goes unfulfilled. Rather than being identified with positive features (economic vitality, a metropolitan, modern lifestyle), the Scandinavians are defined by a lack of such advantages: for instance, in *The Birthday Trip*, the wealthy Danish Toyota dealer Jan, with whom the Polish Magdalena is supposed to meet, never arrives in Poland. In his place, the protagonist, Kaj, a hot-dog stand owner, meets Magdalena. Neither Kaj and his friends, nor the Poles belong to the innovative, metropolitan core. When Kaj passes through the Danish capital, he feels both excited and out of place in the political and economic centre. In *Screwed in Tallinn*, the Swedish organiser advertises his trip as luxurious, which contrasts sharply – in an exaggerated manner characterising the strategy of Alfredson's film – with what viewers see (the men travel in a dilapidated bus and stay in a shabby post-Soviet hotel in Estonia). The male protagonists of *Screwed in Tallinn* hearken from provincial villages in the northern, sparsely populated region of Sweden called Norrland – an area marked with depreciating connotations and stereotypes, their inhabitants perceived as uncommunicative, poor, uncultivated and lower-class (see Öhman 2007: 60). The occupations of some of the Swedish characters (such as a sewage treatment plant cleaner) classify them as belonging to the lower rungs of Swedish society.

It is only in relation to the Eastern European 'periphery' that the Scandinavian protagonists are able to construct their self-image as dominating, 'better' subjects. Thus, the real potential – the capability to empower – rests on the other shore of the sea, even if not fully manifested in these films from the 1990s. It gradually becomes clear that encounters between Scandinavians and East Europeans are staged as encounters between two, albeit very different, peripheries. The characters are all equally marginal within their respective societies. They differ mainly in their orientation towards different centres: whereas Poles and Estonians are still marked as belonging to the Russian zone of influence, the Danes and Swedes fall outside the 'centre' of their own societies and its norms, represented in Scherfig's film by the metropolitan core (Copenhagen), and in *Screwed in Tallinn* by the trip organiser Percy, who embodies a hybrid of neoliberal, unbridled capitalist rule and the Swedish welfare state (Mrozewicz 2013a: 133–4).

Moreover, in both films, the Scandinavian protagonists demonstrate unconstrained, wild behaviours and/or are exploited as victims – tropes that usually serve to describe oppressive colonisers and/or the colonised. Scherfig's film, moreover, invites viewers to reconsider the stereotype of Russians as dangerous and wild. After a round of poker with some Russian soldiers, Kaj orders vodka for everyone. At the bar, some Danish tourists offend him and incite a fight, in which he is wounded. It is thus the Danes who start a fight in the style of a western saloon brawl, forcing both Russians and Poles to intervene. The 'bad guys' are depicted as neither the Russians nor Poles, but the 'barbaric' Scandinavian visitors. Although Scherfig depicts neither a unified Danish nor monolithic Eastern European subject, Poles and Russians seem more 'civilised' than the 'id/superego-driven' Danes.

In *Screwed in Tallinn*, the Swedes likewise become 'barbaric'. Magnus, for instance, uses both verbal and physical violence, unable to control his physical reactions; the wild behaviour of Banan (suggested by his racist nickname, meaning 'banana') elicits a racist reprimand from Percy: 'Mr. Banana, behave a little more like a Christian. You are a guest in Estonia, not a baboon in Africa'. Meanwhile, the Estonian women appear cultured. Despite these contrasts, similarities are emphasised through the Swedish and Estonian characters' respective peripheral and subdued positions within their own societies.

The genre adopted in *Screwed in Tallinn* is, as previously noted, a comedic pseudo-documentary that incorporates characteristics of the mockumentary genre – that is, a fiction film that employs various documentary strategies, exposing itself as a 'joke' for purposes of parody, critique or deconstruction (Roscoe and Hight 2001). The plot can, indeed, be seen as a mockery of the so-called 'Swedish theory of love', inherent in the welfare state ideals of (gender) equality and independence, which according to some was threatened after the opening of the borders of the previous Soviet countries (see Larsson 2010). According to this theory, 'only after both parties have achieved economic and legal social parity and independence is a healthy love, freed from unequal power relations and potentially damaging dependencies, possible' (Trägårdh 1997: 271). This theory is, indeed, gravely threatened in the film: most of the participants seem to be seeking emotional dependency, which is why they have chosen to travel to Estonia. Some of them imagine that precisely because they come from a richer country, it will be easier for them to find a partner in Estonia than in Sweden. At the same time, through the film's foregrounding of similarities between the two sides at the physical (both the Swedes and the Estonian women look old-fashioned and provincial), socio-economic (both are poor), psycho-cultural (both expect adventure and liberation from the other part) and even politico-ideological (both are exploited by their respective systems embodied by Percy and Lembit) levels, the Swedish theory of love is fulfilled in a subversive manner: the two sides are indeed equal, but this equality exposes the normativity of the Swedish model as based on the exclusion of those who do not fit in the 'centre'.

Thus, what *Screwed in Tallinn* expresses is not a fear of foreign 'elements' contaminating Sweden in an increasingly globalised world (Larsson 2010: 37), but a desire for contamination, for openings in the Swedish normativity – for porous boundaries, rather than solid borders. In fact, it is Percy and Lembit, representing specific economic and political forces and interests, who need the border, or the centre and the periphery, so that their business can prosper. As soon as the border transforms into a boundary (which is most forcefully expressed through Svetlana, Lembit's wife, and Banan establishing a relationship), their whole enterprise seems to be threatened.

Both *The Birthday Trip* and *Screwed in Tallinn* question the fixed positions of the two Baltic shores – Scandinavian and Eastern European – within the centre/periphery binary, while maintaining it as an overarching cognitive structure. The Swedish, Estonian, Danish and Polish protagonists represent different peripheries in relation to different centres. In both films, their relation is ultimately depicted as non-hierarchical and the self-image of Scandinavians as 'better' and 'central' is repudiated – notably, in *Screwed in Tallinn*, this is communicated in a highly sarcastic manner. Although Russia still functions as the centre for both the Estonian and Polish characters, the Russians seem much less frightening than those depicted in the films discussed in Chapter 1.

Spatio-temporal Boundary and the Finnish Periphery

Another Nordic film from the 1990s that expresses self-criticism by drawing on the cognitive frame of centre/periphery is Aki Kaurismäki's *Take Care of Your Scarf, Tatjana* (1994), which implicitly thematises Finnish national identity as represented through an encounter with the Russian Other and an Estonian other. However, whereas the films analysed thus far have approached the issue of border/boundary primarily in spatial terms, in *Tatjana* the boundary is of a different kind: it is above all spatio-temporal, with stress on the temporal. The past and present comprise a fluid continuum that is horizontal rather than vertical, uninterrupted rather than disjointed, with one layer not fully distinguishable from the other, commingling in the filmic 'now', which has crucial implications for the 'Finnishness' represented in the film.

Tatjana is a black-and-white road movie that tells the story of two middle-aged, working-class and conspicuously non-talkative Finns, Valto and Reino, who go on a road trip through Finland without any precise destination. They are soon joined by two tourists, the calm Estonian Tatjana and the bossy Russian Klavdia, who ask for a lift to the harbour to catch the ferry to Tallinn, Estonia's capital city. The four characters travel together and all end up in Estonia. During the trip, Reino falls in love with Tatjana and decides to remain in Tallinn. Valto returns home to his previous life, while Klavdia continues on to Russia.

In his book devoted to the cinema of Kaurismäki, Andrew Nestingen notes that the director often uses 'multinational' discourse to challenge the Finns' self-conceptions about their national identity. The multinational denotes 'the contested multiplicity of any national arena, its heterogeneity' (Nestingen 2013: 117). Indeed, in *Tatjana*, Finland emerges as a site of many cultures – most importantly, Finnish, Russian, Soviet and Estonian, but also Western/American – all intermingling and crossing one another in various constellations and power relations. As I will show below, in its employment of multinational discourse, *Tatjana* offers an ironic reflection on Finland's anticipated globalisation through a strategy we can refer to as the compression of time and space (Katzenstein 2005: 13): the various spatio-temporal layers are condensed into one fluent entity without clear borders between one 'time zone' and the other (such as the Soviet or post-Soviet). Because of the fluidity and porousness connecting the different temporal as well as national layers, this strategy may be called a spatio-temporal boundary.

Temporal ambiguity and the blending of different historical layers are characteristic of Kaurismäki's *oeuvre* (see Nestingen 2013: 92). In the case of *Tatjana*, released in 1994, the temporal layers boil down to two main periods: the 1960s, coded in the *mise-en-scène*, and the early 1990s, shortly after the dissolution of the USSR. The distinction between these two periods is represented in the film as blurred and almost unnoticeable.

This spatio-temporal fluidity is illustrated in a scene during which the two women peel potatoes together in a dilapidated barn (during a temporary rest stop). As usual, Klavdia talks in Russian and uses familiar Soviet rhetoric: 'Our *kolkhoz* set a five-year potato crop record. Over 30,000 kilos in a single week'. She continues speaking with a mix of pride and sentiment: 'There was a dance that Saturday. I had on this red, tight-fitting dress. They kept me dancing all night long'. After a short silence, Tatjana replies in Finnish (functioning here implicitly as Estonian): 'Estonia also grows a lot of potatoes in the summer'. Whereas Klavdia speaks of the USSR using Soviet rhetoric but in the past tense (grammatically speaking), Tatjana mentions Estonia as an independent country using the present tense. The two women represent two different places of belonging within two different periods: the Soviet and the post-Soviet. They speak past each other, in their own languages, and yet they agree. Moreover, from this dialogue it can be inferred that the action is set after the dissolution of the Soviet Union and not – as the *mise-en-scène* indicates – in the 1960s. But it is not only the Soviet/post-Soviet distinction that becomes blurred in the potato-peeling scene: the potato is a familiar, nationally coded symbol in Finland, which refers to national iconography and the agrarian character of the country (Nestingen 2013: 119). Thus, the film seamlessly combines different historical and national layers: Russian/Soviet, Estonian and Finnish. The fact that all of the film's protagonists are played by Finnish actors only enhances the idea of Finnish nationality as heterogeneous.[4]

Hence, the film elicits not only the spatial closeness, but also the temporal/historical relations tightly connecting these countries – Finland, Estonia and Russia. The two distinct historical periods, Soviet and post-Soviet, interweave without a clear distinction, with Russia remaining present in Finnish reality, no matter whether the plot is set in the 1960s or the 1990s. Indeed, Russians seem to be almost everywhere during Valto

Figure 3.1 In the potato-peeling scene the Russian/Soviet, Estonian and Finnish layers interweave seamlessly. *Take Care of Your Scarf, Tatjana*. Photograph by Malla Hukkanen. Courtesy of © Sputnik Oy.

and Reino's road trip. Importantly, the protagonists travel in a Soviet-built Volga, thus even at the level of transportation, they carry Russia with them. In turn, references to Western/American culture coded in the road movie genre (ridiculed in its Finnish 'version'), in popular culture (music), commodities (such as a Coca-Cola sign) and the English language (heard in rockabilly songs and in conversations between passengers on the ferry to Tallinn) connote the unattainable and suppressed dreams of the Finnish protagonists.

The mingling of the national layers reflects the power relations between them, with both Finland and Estonia being portrayed as spaces where the Russian language is often heard in the background. This, together with the use of Finnish as Estonian, creates the impression that Finland and Estonia are similar (to each other). This similarity is also reflected at the level of plot: Tatjana and Reino, an Estonian and a Finn, embark on a (successful) relationship, whereas romantic relations between the domineering and talkative Klavdia and the unsociable Valto prove to be unworkable. Klavdia and Valto can be defined as distant others, divided by an impassable border, while Reino and Tatjana are distant neighbours, who, although both are shy, turn out to be open to connections and new possibilities.

At the same time, Russia (represented through Klavdia) functions as the great Other, on which the others depend. Indeed, Tatjana and Reino's relationship is possible only through Klavdia's agency, as it is her idea to join the Finns, and thus she is the character who pushes the plot forward. She is the link through which connections between Finland and Estonia are facilitated, but with whom no equal relationship is possible. Also significant is that the protagonists travel to Tallinn (and not, for instance, to St Petersburg); although Finland and Russia share a long border, only Estonia is represented as a neighbour. Moreover, although Klavdia eventually leaves, she still shapes the future destiny of Reino and Tatjana by being responsible for their connection.

In contrast to *The Birthday Trip* and *Screwed in Tallinn*, where the crossing of the Baltic is permeated with the ambivalence of anxiety and attraction, in *Tatjana* the sea clearly connects. When the four protagonists drive towards the harbour, the atmosphere changes considerably. Once on the ferry, the Finns enter its huge comfortable interior, leaving behind the confined space of Valto's Volga. The first long shots and panoramas in the film, depicting the sea from the vantage point of the ferry deck, convey the liberating potential of the Baltic. These frames are dominated by bright tones and are filled with light and white elements. The journey across the sea embodies a state of freedom, with Finland now appearing far behind them and Estonia still lying ahead. The moment of arrival into the Estonian harbour is full of elated spirits. Picturesque wide-angle shots, showing Tallinn in much brighter tones than the non-spectacular, agrarian Finnish landscapes, suggest that Estonia – despite the similarities mentioned above – is more metropolitan and less peripheral than Finland. Estonia, 'a frequent haven in Kaurismäki films' (Romney 2003: 45), is an escape and an alternative to Finnish entrapment, earlier signified by the enclosed space of the car.

Thus, *Tatjana* both focuses on Finland's (and Estonia's) subordinate position towards Russia and stresses Finland's Baltic affiliation, within which Estonia seems brighter and more promising, although both countries are peripheries in relation to Russia. The national self-image of Finland as being influenced by Russia and appearing much closer to a Baltic country than to any Western country mentioned or represented in the film is rather unusual. After WWII, Finland's position as part of the Baltic region, associated with the USSR, was kept low-key in official discourse, and instead its regional affinity with *Norden* was stressed – not only rhetorically, but also due to the fact that Finland joined the Nordic Council in 1955. Kirby mentions that in the post-war period, the misconception of Finland as lying behind the Iron Curtain was not uncommon, and errors occurred even in 'maps printed in German newspapers'. Such misconceptions 'continued to occur in spite of vigorous and sustained efforts to promote an image of Finland as a neutral Nordic democracy which was acting as a bridge-builder between east and west' (Kirby 1995: 424).[5] Official Finnish discourse shifted in the early 1990s to focus on Finland's place as part of the European Union (1995), to which an affirmative voice regarding joining was given by Finnish citizens in 1994. As Kirby explains, in the 1990s, '[a] new vision of the North is being propounded, not as a periphery of Europe, but as a region with highly developed national economies, a valuable cultural and natural heritage, and an internationally social and intellectual infrastructure' (380–1). At the same time, as the Estonian historian Pärtel Piirimäe points out: '[T]he Baltikum as we know it today is first of all a Soviet creation and therefore not a heritage people wish to belong to' (2011: 112).

Official Finnish self-conceptions, both post-war and post-1989, are implicitly challenged in *Tatjana*. The film can be seen as a mockery of globalist and capitalist pro-EU discourses, according to which Finland should be situated in the Western European zone, rather than that of the Baltic or Eastern European. If globalisation is understood as transcending spaces and compressing time, in *Tatjana* these processes only relate to Finland's closest neighbours: the Western/American zone remains vague and distant, while Russia acts as the 'globalising' power, which evokes the slogan of 'global communism', rather than the pro-EU discourses of the 1990s. *Tatjana* thus represents a sarcastic take on Finland's aspirations to a neoliberal conception of globalisation, epitomised by the official preparations to join the EU.

The hardly self-promoting depiction of Finland as a peripheral, rural country represented by two working-class men – who speak only Finnish, if they speak at all – and as a country whose journey is determined by its former enemy, overseer and partner (by necessity) on security issues, rather than by any Nordic or EU country, remains in startling opposition to official representations of Finland and is itself peripheral within Finnish national discourses. Moreover, in its nuanced and non-stereotypical rendering of the relation between the four characters, the film is vastly different to those of the Eastern noir narratives and to the dominant Finnish cultural imagination from the 1990s, within which Russia and/or the Soviet Union is represented in an extremely negative light, in part due to the long suppressed Russophobia during the Cold War (Arvas 2011: 115–16; Kirby 1995: 426–7). Kaurismäki's film avoids such polarisations. Even though Klavdia is in many ways opposed to Reino, Valto and Tatjana, she is neither a positive nor negative character.

Thus, rather than separation, a synthesis is promulgated between Finland and its eastern neighbours. Although Estonia is the only literal (though distant) neighbour in the film, the neighbourliness shared by Finland and Estonia is facilitated by their common relation to Russia. This confirms Russia's centrality in the film, even after Klavdia (the centre, the great Other) has left. At the same time, this common centre brings the northern and Eastern European countries closer to each other than in any of the films discussed so far, and calls into questions both Finland's northernness and Estonia's easternness, mixing them together in an endemic spatio-temporal palimpsest.

A Route to Freedom

As Kazimierz Musiał and Dominika Bartnik-Światek observe in their recent study of the Danish press and their output covering Poland, the perception of Poland in Denmark has shifted in recent years, from narratives of periphery to narratives of freedom and modernity (2016).[6] Indeed, the cognitive frame of the centre/periphery – persisting in the films discussed above – is either challenged or completely abandoned in more recent films that engage with discourses of freedom and modernity. This shift also reflects the declining relevance of the Russian frame of reference.

Narratives of freedom, utilised primarily in relation to Poland and the

GDR, depict the Baltic as offering an escape from their oppressive systems. This discourse was anticipated in *300 Miles to Heaven* (*300 mil do nieba*, Maciej Dejczer 1989), a Polish-Danish-French co-production depicting the Solidarity (*Solidarność*) migration, released shortly after the end of communist rule in Poland (see Mazierska 2009: 114). The film is about two underaged brothers who escape from Poland hidden under a lorry that ends up travelling by ferry to Denmark.[7] The escape and crossing of the border is depicted as extremely dangerous and strenuous, representing a tragic choice rather than the fulfilment of a dream. Although in the film Denmark is depicted as close to 'heaven' when compared with Poland, and the boys receive assistance in the form of support and money while staying at the refugee camp in Sandholm and are finally granted asylum, the atmosphere in the film's final moments is poignant. A boutique signboard reading 'Made in heaven', which is seen in the background as the boys walk aimlessly down the dark streets of Copenhagen, festively and lavishly decorated for Christmas, is an ironic comment on the boys' bitter reality. The boys are uncertain about their future, sad and alone in a foreign country. The taste of freedom is bittersweet.

A similar discourse about the Baltic Sea as a route to freedom, this time seen from the 'other' side, is found in the Danish documentary *The Escape* (2014), which tells the story of the tragic escape of a German family from the GDR in 1977.[8] The film was made as a follow-up to journalist Jesper Clemmensen's book about stories of escape from the GDR to Denmark via the Baltic Sea during the Cold War (Clemmensen 2012). Various images of the Baltic – from idyllic beaches to stormy waves – and other references to water underpin the film as a leitmotif. Rather than offering a straight route to the free world, the Baltic here represents an 'invisible wall', as dangerous as the one in Berlin. Sometimes described as a 'blue border', the sea in Clemmensen's documentary is dark, stormy and life-threatening – this 'Baltic noir' is contrasted with the horizon, promising a 'better' life ahead. *The Escape* combines the Eastern noir trope of border crossings, which are associated with pain, fear and danger (and recalling the stories of escape over the Berlin Wall), with that represented by *The Birthday Trip* or *Screwed in Tallinn*, in which the act of crossing to the other side offers hope. Yet in *The Escape* this hope is lost at sea, under a dark, cloudy sky, when it becomes clear the refugees are going to die. Of the five family members, Christoph's two sisters and his father drown, while Christoph and his mother watch helplessly, soon to be rescued by a Danish ferry.

The film is structured as a detective story. The 'investigation' starts with the film's protagonist, Christoph Sender, visiting Stasi archives and seeing old friends in an effort to find answers to questions about his past:

Figure 3.2 The ambiguity of the Baltic Sea as 'Baltic noir' and a horizon of hope. *The Escape*. Courtesy of Jesper Clemmensen.

why his parents moved from West Germany to the GDR in early 1961 and why they were so desperate to flee sixteen years later. However, the pain, danger and sudden changes that enter the lives of the young Christoph and his family during their crossing of the Baltic, as well as the investigation he is conducting, involve significantly different contexts than those in the Eastern noir narratives. In spite of a similar narrative frame, viewers witness the film's protagonist coping with a traumatic event and coming to terms with the past. Christoph returns to significant places of his childhood and to the beach from which his family began their ill-fated escape. 'We were going to die', he says. 'That was something which very quickly became absolutely clear. I think we encouraged them . . . to die'. The last sentence, referring to his drowning sisters, is uttered twice in the film – in the beginning and at the end. Between these lines, it becomes clear that Christoph does not discuss (and, indeed, is not capable of discussing) everything that he is struggling with. Questions such as whether he could have swapped places with one of his sisters remain unanswered – and probably unspeakable.

In her study of representations of the Berlin Wall in German cinema, Marta Brzezińska suggests approaching such films as a 'cinema of trauma' (2014: 143ff.), in which a traumatic event occurs suddenly and unexpectedly, disrupting the former order – an event such as erecting a wall or escaping 'to freedom'. Clemmensen's documentary adheres to the examples analysed by Brzezińska: a good family life and a happy, almost idyllic childhood are abruptly interrupted by the tragic event on the sea. Old photographs of Christoph's father and smiling sisters are contrasted with the prison-like oppressive system his parents experienced, in the film symbolically visualised by the barbed wire of the Berlin Wall – a recurring trope in imagining the Wall as that of a prison (Brzezińska 2014: 159). The sea in Clemmensen's documentary is an extension of the Wall. Like the Wall, which divided families through its erection, their attempt at escape also results in the breaking up of Christoph's family. But rather than simply expressing trauma – which is, as such, unspeakable (Ibid. 147) – the film, structured like Christoph's journey both in space and time, is a process of reworking the past. The last person to visit is Christoph's mother, with whom he never speaks about these events. The tragic events are not named directly in their conversation. Facial expressions and clasped hands shown in close-ups and silence communicate more than words.

In its depiction of an individual story against the background of a wider political reality, using archival materials from the GDR period, propaganda films, as well as images of the Wall's construction, Clemmensen's film narrates both a personal and a cultural trauma. Brzezińska emphasises that cultural trauma needs to be mediatised in order to be noticed (2014: 146). Although there are numerous films about individuals and families escaping from the GDR in German cinema (though not about crossing the border via the Baltic), in Danish cultural memory this subject is almost non-existent. Therefore, if measured against German films that focus on escape from the GDR, Clemmensen's documentary is one of many; if seen from the Danish perspective, it is an important reminder to both Danish and German audiences about their common history, which the sea embodies. Thus, *The Escape* combines the East German perspective on the experience of fleeing via the East–West border with a Danish perspective. The fact that the Danish context is non-explicit in the documentary can be seen as reflecting the Danish silence around these events (see Clemmensen 2012: 248). Clemmensen's book and his documentary make viewers aware that between 1961, when the Berlin Wall was erected, and 1989, more than 6,000 GDR citizens tried to escape through the Baltic. Only 1,000 escaped safely, whereas at least 164 died.[9] Raising the topic as late as 2012/14 testifies to the fact that transnational memory across the Baltic still needs to be worked through. Whereas the instances of escape across the Berlin Wall were internationally mediatised, the route via the Baltic Sea remained largely unnoticed.

If there are white spots on the cultural memory of the Cold War, other topics can be called 'hot spots'. As Musiał and Bartnik-Światek observe, the main impulse behind the cognitive 'frame of freedom' in narrating Poland in the Danish media is provided by living memories of Polish history, especially those related to the resistance to communism and figures such as Lech Wałęsa and Pope John Paul II. In this discourse, Poland is narrated as a synonym for freedom and the epicentre of positive changes, relating both to 1989 and to Poland's role in Europe since joining the EU in 2004. A frequently used metaphor describes Poland as the country that generated the 'wave of freedom' in Europe (Musiał and Bartnik-Światek 2016: 259). The metaphor of the wave (Danish *bølge*) points to the Baltic Sea as a symbol of freedom. The Polish city most closely related to this symbol is Gdańsk, the birthplace of the independent trade union Solidarity and home of Lech Wałęsa, its leading figure. However, these connotations with freedom have roots much earlier in the history of Gdańsk, which has long enjoyed significant independence; as a 'free city' for most of its recorded history, Gdańsk developed a unique, cosmopolitan character. As the Free City of Danzig, the city was granted the status of an independent quasi-state during the interwar period, under the auspices of the League of Nations.

Depictions of Gdańsk and the Baltic Sea as symbols of freedom are directly evoked in the Swedish short feature film *Coffee in Gdańsk* (2008), directed by Per-Anders Ring, who studied at the National Film School in Łódź. Set in 1968, the film tells the story of a seventeen-year-old Swedish sailor, Nocke, who during a stop in Gdańsk on the way to England has a one-night stand with an older Polish woman, Izabela. Early next morning, Izabela asks her brother, Lech (Wałęsa), to help Nocke find the way to the harbour so that he can catch his boat. As soon as they walk out in the street, obstacles arise. Lech is accosted by a friend, who appeals to his sense of solidarity, to help him steal a motorbike, which causes them to take a detour. Nocke's anxiety grows as he agrees to drive on the stolen motorbike with Lech. When it breaks down, Nocke chooses to leave Lech behind and try to find the harbour himself. Lost in the city's labyrinthine streets, he finally finds himself back where he started when he left Izabela. There, in a long queue in front of a shop, Izabela is waiting to buy coffee. Upon discovering that coffee is no longer available, a riot breaks out. The angry and disappointed crowd are confronted by the police (then Civic Militia). Meanwhile, Lech returns to his neighbourhood. He takes command of the crowd and leads them to the harbour, which he tells the people contains all the commodities they need. The final shots depict the sea and the Swedish sailor finally onboard his ship. At the end of the film, Wałęsa's accomplishments are listed on the screen against the background of the sea.

The film maintains a humorous tone, resulting mainly from the employment of two strategies: first, the young Nocke does not quite understand what is going on around him, not the least due to a language barrier; second, Wałęsa is depicted as an ordinary, friendly, but at the same time cunning, working-class man. The first strategy creates a contrast between the two men that serves to emphasise Nocke's lack of experience, immaturity and innocence. The contrast also signifies a difference in approach: whereas Nocke wants to walk straight to the harbour and becomes irritated by any impediment, the paths of the Poles are convoluted and obstacles need to be tackled. The path to the harbour – a 'liminal zone, connecting Poland with the West' (Näripea et al. 2016: 57) – is not easy and requires effort and consolidation of common forces (solidarity).

The result of the second strategy employed in the film is that Wałęsa is depicted as one of many Poles involved in the solidarity effort. While leading the rioting crowd to the harbour, he does not stand out as an individual. This communicates the specifically Nordic idea of freedom as a value that can (only) be achieved collectively and by joining forces (Musiał and Bartnik-Światek 2016: 260). At the same time, the 'common people' fighting for freedom are romanticised, which evokes the Nordic and particularly Swedish ideals of social democracy, according to which 'the workers' movement as the main agent of history [. . .] leads the country from the ineffective and unjust rule of the upper classes to a *folkhem* (or "home for the people")' (Jørgensen 2008: 239). A shot of people running in slow-motion fades to black and cuts to the white-crested waves of the Baltic Sea. As this elliptical cut suggests, the 'wave' of people standing up for their rights results in a wave of freedom. In the final frames, the Swedish flag in the foreground and the path left on the water's surface, leading from the ship to the Polish horizon, imply a connection between Sweden and Poland. The grey labyrinthine streets and confined frames – a common trope in imagining Eastern Europe – are now replaced by an open wide shot of the sea and a straight path. The connection between Sweden and Poland, as viewers can infer, is not only physical, but also denotes shared values. The Swedish flag and information about the Nobel Peace Prize received by Wałęsa in 1983 can be seen as a reminder of Nordic appreciation for Poland's contribution to triggering the 'wave of freedom' in Eastern Europe, but also as a Nordic/Swedish perspective on these events. This perspective is underscored by a similar importance attached to the Swedish flag on the poster advertising the film.

Coffee in Gdańsk, released in 2008, adheres to typical narratives on 1989 in the present-day Nordic media, which tend to romanticise the heroic acts of the people and the common effort, the Polish spirit of freedom that stimulated the chain of transformations.[10] Inner complexities or negative aspects, often debated in the Polish media, remain absent (Musiał and Bartnik-Światek 2016: 260). Ring's film can be seen, moreover, as being more typical of the historical moment when it was made than of the time to which it refers. The Swedish and Danish authorities reacted with ambivalence rather than enthusiasm to the changes in Eastern Europe related to

Figure 3.3 The Swedish flag implies the Swedish/Nordic recognition of the Polish 'route to freedom'. *Coffee in Gdańsk*. Courtesy of GötaFilm.

Solidarity (1980–1) and 1989 (see Lundén and Nilsson 2010; Lauridsen et al. 2011: 510). The fact that the action is set in 1968 – a year that is symbolic in Western and, not least, Nordic history for its association with the domination of the political left, as well as with leftist radicalism and student revolts – seems to remind Swedish audiences that Poland in 1968 was marked by power struggles which included protests against communist rule, and as such did not have much in common with its Western or Nordic counterparts. Nevertheless, this is a very simplified depiction of Poland in 1968 (see Garsztecki 2008), resulting from the fact that 1968 is here subordinated to ideas surrounding 1989 some two decades later.

Two Danish documentaries, Jacob Dammas' *Dresser* (*Kredens*, Poland, Denmark 2007) and Jacob Kofler's *Stateless* (*Statsløs*, Denmark 2004), engage more deeply with the events of 1968 in Poland, primarily with respect to the exodus of Poles of Jewish heritage from Poland (forced on them by an anti-Semitic campaign instigated by the authorities), many of whom arrived in Denmark. Both directors, though born in Denmark, are children of Polish-Jewish migrants, and their documentaries have a strongly personal, autobiographical dimension (see Mrozewicz 2014). In these documentaries, Denmark is seen as a country offering freedom and escape from an oppressive reality. Another film tackling the Polish-Jewish migration to Denmark after 1968 is Marian Marzyński's *The Ship* (*Skibet*, US 1970–2010), an extended version of a personal reportage made for Danish television by Marzyński in 1969–70, entitled *A Letter from St. Lawrence to Poland* (*Et brev fra Skt. Lawrence til Polen*) (Jazdon 2011). This documentary combines interviews and observational scenes of daily life onboard the *St. Lawrence*, a ship anchored in Copenhagen harbour and transformed into a hotel, where the refugees from Poland lived 'suspended between two coasts divided by water', with Denmark still 'far away', as the director says in a voice-over.

Female Faces of Polish Modernity

Whereas the freedom narratives above thematise historical contexts, two Danish short feature films narrate Poland as modern and independent, freed from old narratives and the shackles of politics and history, a venturesome country looking forward into the future rather than back into the past. Poland here is embodied by young, modern and mobile female protagonists. They are remarkably different from the passive and non-mobile 'local' women, embedded in history and tradition, represented in Scherfig's and Alfredson's films, which do not fully recognise their female agency (see Mrozewicz 2013a: 136).

The main character in *You Can't Eat Fishing* (1999) by Kathrine Windfeld (who studied at the National Film School in Łódź) is a young Polish woman named Renata.[11] She is active and enterprising – a startling contrast to the passive Scandinavian men whom she encounters. Renata decides to travel alone to Denmark to visit Jens, a Danish man she met earlier in Poland. Not only the gender and nationality of the traveller, but also the direction of the travel is here reversed when compared to Scherfig's and Alfredson's films. The untroubled crossing of national borders and mobility 'in spite of' gender is largely the result of Renata's generational and educational background. Even if she does not represent the Western idea of leisure travel, she is well educated and speaks English. In addition, Renata appears unbound by any national issues. Notably, it is a Dane, Tim, who (sarcastically) mentions Solidarity when he learns that Renata is from Poland – which evokes history as one of the clichés associated with Poland.

Nevertheless, the discourse of the periphery, although challenged, is still present in this late 1990s film. Renata is framed within a conventional representation of Eastern Europe: the establishing shot shows rows of grey blocks of flats. Jens is depicted as living deliberately far from the centre in a squat-like, chaotic area by the waterfront, opposite from, and contrasted with, the most majestic church in Copenhagen, the Marble Church. Renata, a Polish capitalist (she holds a degree in business management), encourages Jens, a Danish design school graduate, now unemployed and living a carefree life financed by the state (which Renata is initially unaware of), to return to a previously abandoned lamp design and signs a contract on his behalf with a lighting company who wishes to produce it. For a time, Jens works diligently. Although Jens and his friend Tim consider Renata's actions embarrassing, such as her effort to negotiate prices ('you don't do things of this kind in Denmark', 'you Polish gold-digger'), it is the pioneering, enterprising Polish woman (strikingly different from the entrepreneur Lembit in *Screwed in Tallinn*) who, according to Seaton's model, would be defined here as the 'centre'. Tim and Jens choose to place themselves at the 'periphery', but their attitudes reveal them as being slavishly dependent on the system – the centre.

When Renata travels to Denmark by ferry, the distance between the two countries is depicted as almost non-existent. From a block of flats in Poland, the film cuts to the unsightly vicinities of the Danish waterfront. The sea is not visible – only the upper parts of the ferry moving behind an embankment signal that the two countries are connected by water. At

Figure 3.4 The 'northbound' Polish woman. *You Can't Eat Fishing*. Photograph by Søren Kuhn. Courtesy of Angel Films.

the end of the film, when Renata leaves Jens after he disappoints her by not fulfilling the agreement, the sea fills the frame as the ferry sails back to Poland. The distance now seems much greater than in the beginning. While earlier Renata was framed within confined spaces, after she leaves Jens she is shown walking towards the Marble Church – the implicit centre within the depicted universe (devoid of religious connotations).

On the ferry, the open sea lies ahead for Renata – not least because she feels independent and triumphant, travelling back with the instalment she earned on the lamp project. And whereas in the beginning the direction towards which the ferry moved was from the 'eastern' to the 'western' edge of the frame, the boat is now moving smoothly north-west (although diegetically this is south-east) – which echoes Renata's movement towards the Marble Church and the 'northern' edge of the frame. Associated with the 'east' early in the film, such a framing of Renata is no longer valid: she turns out to be closer to the 'north' or 'west' than to the 'east'. This detaches Poland not just from its eastern heritage, but also from the master narrative of East *versus* West. The clearly successful Renata is much closer to the financial and metropolitan core, embodied by Copenhagen's representative buildings, than Jens, who stays 'behind' and stands 'still', dependent on state benefits.

While Windfeld's film depicts the female protagonist as an enterprising individual primarily in terms of economics and cross-border mobility, Lisa Aschan's graduation film *In Transit* (2005) focuses on the cosmopolitan Polish woman Zofia, whose job is directly related to crossing borders – she is a flight attendant at the Polish company LOT. The space of the Baltic Sea is no longer crossed by ferry, but by plane, and is now seen from above the clouds, which considerably diminishes the distance. And while Windfeld's film portrays a Polish-Danish encounter resulting in a clash between two systems of values, Aschan's short feature thematises Poland in the context of globalisation (it is worth noticing that the film was made shortly after the enlargement of the EU in 2004). Zofia's life incarnates globalisation understood as 'a new cultural and sociological situation', in which '[t]he movements or "flows" of different symbolic forms, objects, and subjects simply transcend national borders with an unprecedented intensity' (Stavning Thomsen and Ørjasæter 2011: 14–15). Constant movement is ingrained in Zofia's existence. Rather than being associated with Poland, she is connected to non-places – that is, 'spaces of circulation, consumption and communication' symptomatic of the era of globalisation (Augé 2008: viii). These places include the airport, subway and a hotel, their impersonal sterility emphasised by grey and blue tones. Zofia represents the modern face of Poland. In this respect, she is more modern than the Danish Kasper, whom she meets in the hotel during a stop in Copenhagen: when Kasper confesses that he is afraid of flying, Zofia assures him that there is no reason to be.

Although it thematises human relations in a globalised world, the film does not assume a universalising and celebratory optics. Zofia speaks perfect English; however, in a cosy bar outside the hotel, Kasper and Zofia engage in a conversation in which each speaks their own language, but still understands the other perfectly. This symbolic scene illustrates the mutual understanding and attraction between them, but it also shows the easy transnational communication flow across borders, while at the same time recognising and respecting these borders (see Augé 2008: xv). The ability to speak English connotes the homogenising globalisation and impersonal relations (Zofia uses it in non-places), whereas the Danish–Polish conversation signifies the possibility of creating communities not based on sameness. It is important that Zofia is depicted as lonely and unhappy because of her rootlessness. Although she resists establishing a relationship with Kasper, at the end of the film she leaves her telephone number and thus enables a future connection. As in *You Can't Eat Fishing*, the Polish female protagonist is ascribed the agency to decide about the future of the cross-Baltic relationship. In one of the final shots, the plane on which Zofia is flying back to Poland is filmed from below against the background of a blue and white sky – and, as in Windfeld's film, it is on a straight course towards the 'northern' edge of the frame. In the discourse of modernity embodied by Polish women, the sky eventually replaces the sea.

Conclusion: From Sea to Sky

The Baltic Sea does not instigate 'infiltrated' or hybrid (trans)national identities such as those tackled by the films discussed in Chapter 2. Nor does it produce extensive divisions, like the 'hard' borders in Eastern noir (Chapter 1). Instead, Baltic imagery triggers various degrees of a distant connection. I have called this connection, accompanied by emotions ranging from anxiety to attraction, a 'distant neighbourhood'. Distance, as the films demonstrate, is a fluctuating category which is difficult to measure and dependent on more than spatial parameters. The shifting distance is expressed by changes in the forms of transnational communication, symbolised by means of transport. From ferry to plane, from sea to sky, from difficult journeys making up a significant portion of the narrative to a cinematically enhanced transcendence of space and the compression of time, the Baltic imagery encodes the changing grades of distance between the Nordic region and the eastern neighbours across the past three decades. This distance is never replaced by proximity and the Nordic identity is not replaced by a transnational, regional Baltic identity – contrary to what many hoped for in the early 1990s (see Wæver 1992). However, the Nordic films discussed here demonstrate that communality and connection do not need to be based on fluent supra-national and universal communication. Rather, similarity respecting differences is the new common 'ground'. Detachment of the neighbours across the Baltic from the Russian frame of reference becomes an important element in creating this common ground. Whereas Russia remains *Norden*'s Other, the Baltic countries (here represented by Estonia) and Poland become less removed, which is expressed by the discourse of the periphery giving way to narratives of freedom and modernity. The East–West axis is finally eclipsed.

The emergence of the depiction of mobility across the Baltic boundary in Nordic cinemas is related to the re-emergence of historical facts, narratives and feelings, which, when the waters were 'icebound', remained latent and inactive. But whereas the overarching frame 'from sea to sky' offers a positive narrative on the transforming imaginery of the 'other' shore, this narrative does not encompass the whole story. In the next chapter, I explore Nordic films addressing the murky encounters with the Baltic Sea and porous boundaries.

Notes

1. A similar 'threat of the thaw' was conveyed in the Cold War imaginary of the Arctic Sea in American films (see Stenport 2015: 164).
2. Following parts of this section of the chapter have previously appeared in an article published in the *Journal of Scandinavian Cinema* (see Mrozewicz 2013a). I am grateful to the editors of the journal for granting me permission to republish parts of this article.
3. The Danish road documentary *The Wild Hearts* (*De vilde hjerter*, Michael Noer 2008) about a group of Danish men travelling by motorbikes to northern Poland evokes similar colonial tropes.
4. Later in the same scene, another spatio-temporal layer – English/Western – is added through the music score (a song from the rockabilly 1960s band The Renegades).
5. It is interesting in this context that Helsinki often acted as Russia's 'body double' in Western films during the Cold War (see Paasonen 2015).
6. However, positive narratives on Poland in the Danish press have recently been replaced by expressions of disappointment over the nationalist right-wing government (in power in Poland since November 2015).
7. A similar trope of the Baltic as Poland's gate to the West is found in *The Last Ferry* (*Ostatni prom*, Waldemar Krzystek, Poland 1989).
8. I am grateful to Jesper Clemmensen for providing me with access to the film.

9. A total of 138 people died while attempting to cross the Berlin Wall between 1961 and 1989 (Brzezińska 2014: 155).
10. The romanticising view on 1989 is challenged in the docudrama *1989* (Østergaard and Rácz, Denmark 2014), discussed in the Introduction to this book. The fateful decision to open the border between Hungary and Austria was sanctioned by the Hungarian Prime Minister Miklós Németh, and thus came 'from the top'.
11. I analyse this film in an article previously published in *Journal of Scandinavian Cinema* (see Mrozewicz 2013a). I am grateful to the editors of the journal for granting me permission to republish parts of this article.

CHAPTER 4

Guilt and Shame in
(Trans)national Spaces

In the previous three chapters, the primary focus has been on the spatial adjacency of *Norden* and Russia/Eastern Europe, and the multifaceted imagery of both division and connection triggered by borders in Nordic films. One aspect of these spatial dialectics is economic inequality across borders. The current chapter explores films made on the eve of the 2004 enlargement of the European Union, with a focus on the extreme economic disparities among the nations bordering the Baltic Sea. This inequality is portrayed in two films that adopt the issue of sexual exploitation as a lens: Lukas Moodysson's fiction film *Lilya 4-ever* (*Lilja 4-ever*, Sweden, Denmark 2002) and Pål Hollender's documentary *Buy Bye Beauty* (Sweden 2001). Both films stage the Baltic as a physical, economic and moral division/connection. This chapter focuses on how these films approach this economic inequality on an emotional level – particularly through the guilt felt by the Nordic subjects. These films may be seen as counter-narratives to the freedom narratives generated across the Baltic (and analysed in Chapter 3), where the Baltic is imagined as a gateway to the northern world of freedom.

Whereas Moodysson's and Hollender's films both epitomise guilt, the last section of this chapter is devoted to shame – a feeling often conflated with guilt. Shame is as equally relevant as guilt in the context of transnational inequalities. Here, I will discuss a film which may not seem an obvious choice to draw a comparison with – Pirjo Honkasalo's documentary, *The 3 Rooms of Melancholia* (*Melancholian 3 huonetta*, Finland, Denmark, Germany, Sweden 2004). Whereas Moodysson's and Hollender's films tackle the sex trade in the Baltic Sea region, Honkasalo's documentary deals with the Russian–Chechen war. Aesthetically, these films differ substantially: *Lilya 4-ever* is a feature film shot in a para-documentary style with non-realistic inserts, while *Buy Bye Beauty* uses a shabby aesthetics mocking television documentary, and *The 3 Rooms of Melancholia* combines observational, reflexive and poetic documentary modes (see Nichols

2010). Nevertheless, these films share similarities insofar as they all posit the primacy of feeling in their approach to Nordic/Eastern European/Russian encounters. Such a comparison helps to illustrate how Nordic encounters involving guilt and shame with Russian and Eastern European neighbours involve two very different ways of negotiating the Nordic self in the increasingly globalised world.

Cinematic evocations of guilt and shame carry fundamentally different consequences for our understanding of the borders between self and other. Whereas guilt narratives foster division and the exclusion of unfamiliar bodies, shame has the potential to trigger critical self-evaluation. In view of the differentiation between border and boundary, according to which border produces and reinforces binary divisions, while boundary dissolves binaries by promulgating engagement and connection, guilt adheres to the patterns of the border, whereas shame is capable of opening the self up to the inclusiveness of the boundary. In this chapter, the discussion of shame in relation to Honkasalo's documentary is preceded by examples of shame in a number of films analysed in previous chapters. In these films, cinematic evocations of shame are related to Nordic submissiveness to, and/or fear of, Russia, while guilt narratives are found among films dealing with the neglected Eastern European (Baltic) neighbours.

Guilt and shame can be difficult to distinguish from one another (Ferguson et al. 2007: 345) because both are emotions of self-assessment – that is, directed towards the self and its status. However, they differ significantly in their structure and approach to the self. As philosopher of ethics Gabriele Taylor emphasises, shame concentrates on the (flawed) self, whereas with guilt 'the guilty concentrates on herself as the doer of the deed' (1985: 97). In other words, guilt does not relate to what the person 'really' is, but to actions (or omissions) that are forbidden according to some authority (a law, a taboo, moral standards). Authority plays a crucial role in guilt: '[I]n accepting what he has done as something forbidden the person feeling guilty thinks of himself as being under some authoritative command' (Ibid. 86). Guilt, moreover, is not only an emotion, but also a legal concept: in view of the law, the guilty is liable to punishment – or may be forgiven. The punishment is for 'what he has done and not for what he is' (Ibid. 89). Thus, guilty acts, in contrast to shame, can be compensated for and 'erased'. Furthermore, because guilt is related to punishment and repayment, it is also connected to responsibility. This is another important feature that distinguishes guilt from shame. This difference is illustrated by the fact that in contrast to shame, guilt 'cannot be vicarious, and feelings of guilt similarly cannot arise from the deeds or omissions of others' (Ibid. 91). In other words, one can feel shame (but not guilt) for the acts committed by others, but one can only feel guilty and thus responsible for personal misdeeds or omissions.

Just as authority plays a crucial role in guilt, with shame the crucial element is the conjuring up of an audience (Taylor 1985: 86). Even if alone and not observed by anyone, the person feeling shame 'thinks of himself as being seen through the eyes of another' (Ibid. 57). It is useful to quote an observation on precisely this aspect of shame by Sara Ahmed, who noted that: '[S]hame feels like an exposure – another sees what I have done that is bad and hence shameful – but it also involves an attempt to hide, a hiding that requires the subject turn away from the other and towards itself' (2014: 103). In other words, shame forces us to confront ourselves. In psychoanalytic reflection, 'the conflict of shame has been characterized as a conflict between ego and ego ideal, in contrast to guilt, where the conflict is between the superego and the ego' (Ibid. 106). The ego-ideal is the perfect self to which the ego aspires, while the superego denotes the cultural rules internalised by the ego. In the present context, the superego can be defined as the Swedish/Nordic welfare state (*folkhem*), which includes its values and focus on gender and economic equality, state-provided care and general physical and mental safety for everyone.

In the post-1989 era of open European borders and extensive migration, the Nordic self has been suddenly confronted with much closer non-Nordic others, forcing it to become aware of its own privilege, which awareness is often accompanied by a guilty conscience. As Elisabeth Oxfeldt observes:

> [. . .] [F]eelings of guilt function as a symptom of the discomfort we, Scandinavians and Norwegians, feel facing global injustice and the fact that our privileges are anchored in structural economic and political (dis)parities that allow our privilege to be generated by the others' lack of privilege. (2016: 10)

Oxfeldt emphasises that the Nordic countries see themselves as distinguished by happiness, affluence, trust and equality. The Nordic self-image is characterised by the perception of the region's nations as innocent and inclusive, non-aggressive and non-complicit in colonialism, imperialism or the slave trade – a perspective typical of the 'Nordic exceptionalism'.

Numerous Nordic films problematising guilt in transnational contexts challenge this self-complacency. However, such narratives of guilt are often caught in dilemmas aptly illustrated by a brief example from Sara Johnsen's film *Upperdog* (Norway 2009), discussed more thoroughly in Chapter 6. This film is one of many in Nordic cinemas tackling the guilt felt towards distant and much less privileged global others. In a central scene, a young Norwegian man, Per, a former soldier who served in Afghanistan, has a nightmare reliving a fateful event from the war. In Per's nightmare, the incident begins much as it did in real life – when he was patrolling a road at night. Seeing a car approaching, he panics and kills the driver, who turns out to be a local inhabitant travelling with his two kids. The terrified children are commanded to leave the car, and the panicked soldier points his gun at them. A Norwegian photographer captures this scene, and the image, published on the cover of a magazine, shocks Norwegian society. In the nightmare, Per is sitting in the back seat together with the children, observing the drama play out from inside the car. Suddenly, a shot shatters the windshield, and Per's perspective shifts to view himself from the outside, decked out in uniform, pointing the gun at him(self). He falls out of the car. The following close-up reveals he has been shot in the forehead. He dies. When he wakes up, visibly shaken, his girlfriend, Yanna, asks him about his dream. After explaining, Per yells 'You know nothing about guilt' and storms out of the apartment. Yanna later explains to her brother: 'He is pitying himself'.

This short scene neatly illustrates the main pitfall of Western guilt narratives: their narcissism or – the true 'face' of their concern, which is not concern for the other, that is, the victim of the wrongdoing, but for the perpetrators themselves and their own conscience – their egoistical self-concern. Indeed, 'self-pity' seems a much more appropriate term than 'guilt' to describe the feelings of the young soldier. Throughout the film, Per never expresses concern for how the children of the man that he killed might have felt and what happened to them afterwards, but rather focuses almost single-mindedly on his own 'trauma', lamenting his experience as a 'victim' of the photographer. Thus, narcissistically, he chooses to only consider himself; his so-called guilt prevents him from considering his victims. The image of Per shot in the forehead by himself captures his double position of both perpetrator and victim, whereas his account of the dream to Yanna reveals his inability either to confront his own misdeed (and thus to feel guilt and take responsibility) or to confront himself (and thus to feel shame).

Moreover, the nightmare scene creates a transnational space that comments on privilege: the Norwegian man can sleep calmly in his bed, at worst, haunted by nightmares, whereas the children in Afghanistan live with the real threat of death (in this scene embodied by Per). The film also reflects on the invisibility of privilege that frequently accompanies self-pity disguised as guilt. If we compare privilege to the wind at your back – wind you never feel or see, but which provides you with the ability to walk effortlessly – and the lack of privilege to walking against a strong headwind (Kimmel 2003: 1), then Per is privileged in comparison to Yanna, who was adopted as a child and is depicted in the film as coming from a less privileged social background. Privilege is often invisible to those who have it – thus it can be named and made visible more easily by those who do not enjoy it. This is illustrated through the character of Yanna, who has the necessary insight to describe the Norwegian boyfriend's behaviour as self-pity.

The films discussed in this chapter, situating guilt in a transnational – or 'transBaltic' – context, in a similar manner epitomise the privilege of the Nordic subjects as preventing them from seeing and taking into account the 'other'. The question remains whether the Nordic guilt unfolding in relation to the Baltic neighbours differs from the bad conscience felt towards far-removed global others. Without providing a definitive answer, I would suggest that a distinguishing element is the Nordic countries' past relations with the 'other side' of the Baltic Sea.[1] Therefore, understanding guilt in Moodysson's and Hollender's films requires a brief historical con-textualisation. Apart from addressing the complicity of Swedish men in sexual and economic exploitation across the Baltic in the post-Iron Curtain era, both films – by invoking colonial relations between the (powerful, male) self and the (powerless, female) other – implicitly point to Sweden's colonial past in this region. Because *Lilya* was shot in the Estonian town of Paldiski, which was the Swedish town of *Rågervik* in the seventeenth and eighteenth centuries, Sweden's previous position as a coloniser constitutes a 'subtext' in Moodysson's film (see Larsson 2010: 33). Regarding more recent 'present pasts', to use Andreas Huyssen's term (2003: 12), Swedish half-heartedness in recognising the independence of the Baltic countries at the end of the Cold War should be mentioned among the potentially guilt-inducing contexts (see Lundén and Nilsson 2006: 29–31). Another context is the infamous extradition of Baltic refugee soldiers from Sweden to the Soviet Union in 1946 (known as *baltutlämningen*), for which the Swedish government apologised in 1994. The extradition and the underly-ing guilt related to the event was explored in a 1970 film entitled *A Baltic Tragedy* (*Baltutlämningen*) by Swedish director Johan Bergenstråhle, co-written with Per Olov Enquist and based on Enquist's novel from 1968 (Enquist 1973: viii). The film implies that the decision was influenced by Swedish fear of Russia and the wish to recuperate neutral Sweden's unoffi-cial cooperation with Germany during the war. Its political ambiguity and 'neutrality' towards the subject provoked divergent reactions (see Wright 1998: 208): the film was seen by some Swedish commentators as a critique of the Swedish welfare state, while the Baltic diaspora in Sweden accused the authors of being pro-Soviet.[2]

Although these contexts remain implicit in Moodysson's and Hollender's films, historical circumstances are relevant, not least because *Lilya 4-ever* and *Buy Bye Beauty* deal with the exploitative, rather than the cooperative, side of the north in the post-1989 reality (see Galt 2006: 118). In the end, both films reinforce the binary discourse of the us/them border, even if they also problematise the ongoing mechanisms of bordering.

Both films received significant public attention in Sweden (see Johansson 2001; Hedling 2004; Kristensen 2007), sparking debates concerning the illegal sex trade in the Baltic Sea region and the ethical implications of directors from complicit countries representing its victims. *Lilya 4-ever* was praised for successfully avoiding the victimisation, eroticisation or objectification of the characters (Coxe 2010: 30), while *Buy Bye Beauty* faced accusations of breaking the accepted rules of ethical representation (Johansson 2001; Zaremba 2008: 53–4). As a feature film positively reviewed internationally,[3] *Lilya 4-ever* reached a substantially broader audience than Hollender's documentary and undoubtedly contributed to raising awareness about trafficking for sexual purposes in Europe. *Buy Bye Beauty* 'enjoyed' a largely negative reception, with the Latvian authorities even demanding the film be banned in Sweden.

These two films are interesting to examine alongside each other, precisely because they employ radically different tactics in approaching a similar subject and the related question of guilt. Yet what needs to be examined here is not how the films relate to the real phenomena of prostitution and sex slavery, but how they function as cinematic mediations. It is important to ask how they frame bodily encounters between the oppressors and victims so as to evoke a feeling of guilt in the Nordic viewers – their primary audience[4] – and what consequences follow from this evocation. In Moodysson's, Hollender's and not least Honkasalo's films, feelings of guilt and shame are evoked affectively in the viewer. As I argue below, the strongly affective strategies in *Lilya 4-ever* serve to induce guilt in order to reunite the Swedish self.

Lilya 4-ever: Swedish Self and Invisible Privilege

Moodysson's film tells the story of a teenage girl from an unspecified post-Soviet country, its description limited to 'somewhere in what was once the Soviet Union'. Suddenly abandoned by her mother (who emigrates to the United States), Lilya copes on her own in the harsh reality of a provincial post-Soviet town. Abandoned by everyone apart from her younger friend, the forsaken boy Volodya, she turns to prostitution in order to survive. Lilya is approached in a nightclub by an agreeable young man, Andrej, who seduces her and convinces her to become his girlfriend. Andrej turns out to be a mid-

dleman in the international sex trafficking business. To Volodya's despair, he arranges to send Lilya to Sweden, telling her that he has found her a job and will soon join her. In Malmö, Lilya is met by a Polish pimp, Witek, who confiscates her passport and imprisons her in a flat, only letting her out to visit Swedish clients. Lilya sinks into depression, her only mode of escape being through her dreams, in which she has conversations with Volodya (who commits suicide after Lilya's departure). In the end, Lilya manages to escape, but commits suicide by jumping from a highway overpass.

In an interview featured in the DVD version, Moodysson directly mentions the guilt and responsibility he feels as a Swedish (and Western) director in relation to the (representation of the) post-Soviet countries. His focus on the sex trade and trafficking not only confronts viewers with the very real societal problem of trafficking across borders, but also serves as a metaphor to describe these countries' social position within the transnational arena: 'One of the ironies and tragedies of history is that those societies that were raped by Soviet communism are now being raped by capitalism. So, it's like a double abuse'. One way in which *Lilya 4-ever* evokes the feeling of guilt – primarily in male viewers – is by making them identify with the abusive sex buyers. This is forcefully implemented through a montage sequence showing Lilya engaging in sexual intercourse with Swedish men of various ages, representing diverse social environments and ethnic backgrounds, not simply a homogeneous Swedish 'self'.[5] The copulating men's bodies are positioned and remain extremely close to the hand-held camera and are seen from Lilya's point-of-view, while Lilya remains invisible. Mariah Larsson has pointed to three functions of such an approach: first, Lilya never becomes objectified and eroticised through the camera gaze; second, the extreme close-ups distort the faces and bodies of the men, which enhances Lilya's nightmarish experience; finally, the strategy conveys the gradual loss of the self experienced by the girl, which ultimately leads to her suicide (2006: 256).

However, further significant functions of such filming, closely related to the evocation of guilt, are at stake here: when watching the distorted faces and bodies of the copulating men, the male viewers are presented with a reflection of themselves. The viewer may experience a strong bodily reaction, such as repulsion, while at the same time seeing 'himself' in the role of the trick. The evocation of the (distorted) self is crucial: as mentioned earlier, guilt cannot be vicarious, and feelings of guilt cannot arise from the acts committed by others. In effect, the magnifying, 'convex' mirror exposing the abusive male self to itself is capable of inducing the viewer's feeling of guilt. The self is here both individual and collective, constituted by the viewers' recognition of the social reality to which they belong –

Swedish/Nordic and/or Western European.[6] Moreover, although the viewer is made to experience the events from Lilya's position, her invisibility conveys the impossibility of fully uniting with her, her experience remaining beyond the viewer's experience. Lilya's invisibility may further be said to epitomise Europe's involvement in invisible processes of exploitation and the failure to recognise them. At the same time, Lilya's point-of-view allows our perception to become carnal rather than distantly visual and thus to disturb the audience's comfortable (viewing) position.

It is precisely this embodied vision, intensified by the film's documentary aesthetics and its 'reality effect', that generates a strong affect in the viewer. In film scholar Tarja Laine's words, affect denotes 'the pre-reflective bodily mechanism that underlies all emotion and gives pre-semantic meaning to information that originates from our bodily systems, and, more particularly, from our senses' (Laine 2015: 22). While affect cannot be verbalised, emotion 'is the semantic account of the affective appraisal that can be narrated and remembered' (Ibid.). Just as affect is not individual but rather relational (as discussed in Chapter 2), emotions are likewise irreducible to the private 'I' – they are socially and culturally conditioned.

As an emotion, guilt is elicited in *Lilya 4-ever* by the strong affectivity framing the abusive acts of the tricks. Importantly, guilt is regarded as a moral emotion: it results from doing something that is forbidden from the viewpoint of some authority and thus morally wrong (Taylor 1985: 86–9). In the Swedish context, the actions of the men on-screen contradict the national construction of good and morally sound sexuality inherent in the Swedish welfare state's ideals (see Trägårdh 1997: 271; cf. my discussion of *Screwed in Tallinn* in Chapter 3). However, as previously mentioned, guilt is not only an emotion, but also a legal concept (Taylor 1985: 85). In Sweden, the morality of love is secured by legal regulations embodied by two laws. The first is the sex buying law, enacted in 1999, making it illegal to buy – though, crucially, not to sell – sexual services. Its aim was to enhance gender equality and diminish violence against women, but it was also meant to counteract trafficking for sexual purposes (Larsson 2010: 26–7). In 2002, another law was introduced specifically against human trafficking for sexual purposes. As Larsson emphasises, the political and social changes in the former Soviet Union were a part of the justification for introducing the law (see Ibid. 28). Larsson concludes that these laws and Swedish films thematising sex trafficking both reveal the same national anxiety related to the idea of a borderless Europe, but 'whereas the films express that anxiety, the laws attempt to contain it' (Ibid. 37).

However, I would argue that the wrongdoing on screen, eliciting guilt because of its moral iniquity, combined with the affective evocation of guilt

through the embodied vision, does more than express national anxiety and condemn morally bad acts. It also serves to unite the Swedish self. As Taylor emphasises, being guilty and feeling guilty are two different things. In order to feel guilty, one must accept the underlying authority, due to which guilt 'becomes the voice of conscience' (1985: 85). But for viewers to feel guilty (and thus to accept the authority), they must be involved affectively. Thus, affect serves in Moodysson's film to confirm this authority – the moral standards secured by the law – and to re-establish the welfare state as 'the voice of conscience'. As an act of acceptance of authority, the evocation of guilt can thus be seen as providing grounds for claiming national identity (see Ahmed 2014: 109). Hence, the strategy of admitting the failure of living up to the welfare state ideal serves here to confirm and reinforce this ideal. And because both the laws and the film are a response to a specific transnational situation, the identity of the Swedish self they express is reconciled to itself in relation to the post-Soviet (Baltic) other.

Paradoxically, in *Lilya 4-ever* this reinforcing of borders around the national self is itself reinforced by a blurring of distinctions between Swedish locations and 'the former Soviet Union' (as the general(ising) description provided at the beginning of the film says), depicting Sweden as similar to an Eastern European location. Distinctive to Moodysson's films, space is a semantically marked layer and 'an authentic conveyor of social and affective ambivalence' (Stenport 2012: 9). In *Lilya 4-ever*, this ambivalence is, indeed, striking. On the one hand, the visual erasing of borders provokes reflection on the official non-existence of borders in the 'new Europe', as opposed to existing divisions (Galt 2006: 118). Importantly, however, it is Sweden that resembles a post-Soviet country. This 'direction' of resemblance should not be ignored. As I argue below, this strategy functions as a means of hiding Swedish privilege in the film.

This resemblance is most prominently illustrated in the prologue. It is not clear to the viewer watching the film for the first time that the prologue, located in anonymous, grey industrial areas evoking Nordic/Eastern noir imagery, with concrete blocks of flats in the background, is set in Sweden. The establishing shots following the prologue (with the 'somewhere in what was once the Soviet Union' note), showing blocks of flats in a post-Soviet country, blur the visual differences between the Nordic/Eastern settings, creating the impression that the preceding images were also set in destitute post-Soviet areas.

Suburban locations and provincial aesthetics, which are typical of Moodysson's films, can be interpreted as 'deemphasiz[ing] the spectacular or unique' about Sweden and questioning 'an urban, cosmopolitan, and neoliberal subject position, understood as significant components in the

globalization of Swedish culture at the turn of the twenty-first century'
(Stenport 2012: 96–7). However, if Moodysson wished to address the
urban 'neoliberal' subject position (as some critics have emphasised, see
Hedling 2004: 331), the Swedish agents of such a position are hardly
visible in the film, and thus not a possible point of identification for an
'urban, cosmopolitan, and neoliberal' viewer. The unattractive, Soviet-
esque aesthetics of the anonymised Swedish outskirts conveys the idea
of social determinism, evoked in the film by Lilya's alienation and her
hopeless situation of no escape, but it also causes a significant portion of
the potential Swedish/Nordic (and other metropolitan Western) audience
to feel alienated. The zones of privilege remain almost entirely invisible.[7]
Thus, apart from the sex montage sequence invoking guilt, a large group
of spectators can barely identify with the on-screen reality. Because the
locations and events remain alien to them, they are unable to feel responsible. In consequence, the film misses its point in producing social critique.

Part of this 'erasing-of-Sweden' strategy involves the identification
of the pimp as Polish and the middleman as Russian, which relegates
the entire chain of the sex trade to the previous Eastern Bloc countries.
Additionally, Swedish is spoken only scarcely, which further contributes
to the anonymisation of the areas and tricks. But whereas Sweden is barely
recognisable as Sweden, the manner in which 'the former Soviet Union'
is depicted rests on a perfectly recognisable, stereotypical image. The area
of Estonia where the film is shot – represented by dilapidated concrete
blocks of flats, dirt, garbage and corroding car bodies in the streets, empty
post-industrial buildings with political leaflets featuring USSR General
Secretary Leonid Brezhnev scattered over dirty floors, children sniffing
glue – functions as a synecdoche of the whole 'former Soviet Union', which
reinforces the stereotype of the previous Eastern Bloc as one homogenous
area, and at the level of representation repeats the gesture of the former
Russian coloniser, who strived at denationalising the countries that made
up the Soviet Union. Thus, whereas the gloomy 'Eastern noir' settings
seem natural for the 'former Soviet Union', in the case of Sweden, they
function as a prophecy of an approaching dystopia.[8]

Thus, the invisibility of Swedish privilege implies that this privilege can
be lost if the transnational, borderless Europe becomes a reality – and 'we'
will become like the 'others'. Isolina Ballesteros suggests that '[b]y empha-
sizing similarities, the film minimizes the differences between East and
West and challenges the glorification and mystification of immigration to
America and Europe and the prosperity it promises' (2015: 100). However,
it is exactly this implication, coded in the *mise-en-scène*, which debunks the
guilt-imbued discourse: by depicting Sweden as similar to the post-Soviet

Figure 4.1 Lilya and Volodya with a (stereo)typical 'post-Soviet' concrete block of flats in the background. *Lilya 4-ever*. Photograph by P.-A. Jörgensen. Courtesy of Memfis Film.

areas, the film fails to mobilise responsibility in the Swedish viewers.

As Michael S. Kimmel has observed: '[I]t is hard to generate a politics of inclusion from invisibility' (2003: 5). Indeed, the invisibility of Swedish privilege in *Lilya 4-ever* makes inclusion hardly possible, because Sweden is no less dystopian than 'the former Soviet Union' (apparently also in relation to gender in/equality); for the post-Soviet 'other', the wealthy Swedish society remains invisible – *ergo*, it does not exist.

The failed evocation of guilt in *Lilya 4-ever* is reinforced by the fact that Lilya is the only one punished in the film. This is explicitly thematised in the afterlife epilogue, in which Lilya makes good all the 'sins' committed during her lifetime: she tells Andrej that she is not moving to Sweden, instead she helps her elderly neighbour who has dropped a bag of potatoes on the staircase. Her existential fall is reversed: now she is on her way up to the flat, unlike in the 'original' scene. The 'rising' is reinforced by Lilya throwing a ball upwards, after which she is seen playing with Volodya on a roof in their hometown. The epilogue points indirectly to her guilt and responsibility for Volodya's death; leaving Volodya behind enacted a repetition of Lilya's mother's abandonment. This strengthens the implication that Lilya's greatest sin was to travel to Sweden (see Kristensen 2007), for which she was punished by the fate she suffered.

Hence, although Sweden is almost invisible in Moodysson's film, it does not prevent the film from falling into the main trap of Western guilt narratives – narcissism. *Lilya 4-ever* adheres to Kimmel's observation that when 'you are "in power", you needn't draw attention to yourself as a specific entity; rather, you can pretend to be the generic, the universal, the generalizable' (2003: 5). The film itself exercises a form of homogenising transnationalism (despite its critique of the same), in which 'we' communicate only with those similar to 'us' (see Hjort 2010: 17; Kristensen 2007: 5). While the Swedishness is implicit for the Swedish audience, Lilya is not supposed to see Swedish privilege. At the same time, the national self can be reconciled to its 'welfare-superego': the 'guilt' felt towards Lilya can help recover the sound Swedish sexuality and values associated with the *folkhem*. Thus, the film is not about taking responsibility for Lilya and approaching her exclusion critically, but about recovering oneself. And because the film alienates its primary (Swedish urban middle-class) audience, the depicted abusers come to embody some 'alien doer[s] of the deed' (Taylor 1985: 96–7). Such alienation is questioned in *Buy Bye Beauty*.

Making Privilege Visible: *Buy Bye Beauty* as a Meta-narrative of Guilt and Shamelessness

Moodysson's film, *Lilya 4-ever*, can be said to exploit Lilya rather than protect her, despite the successful avoidance of unethical representation strategies. It could thus be asked whether films that are openly exploitative are not more honest about exploitation than films which, in trying to protect their characters by not victimising them, in fact exclude and exploit them in more obscure ways. How to resolve the problematic fact that the victims of the sex trade are represented by those indirectly complicit in their fates? William Brown urges that 'filmmakers must make films that are unrecognisable, that shake, shudder and tremble audiences out of their silent complicity with the contemporary slave trade' (2010: 48).

If *Lilya 4-ever* makes its viewers shudder, perhaps *Buy Bye Beauty* does so even more. However, in contrast to Moodysson, Hollender radically foregrounds Swedish complicity by focusing on privilege and the privileged. And whereas Moodysson effaces differences through an all-embracing dystopian *mise-en-scène*, Hollender operates through a politics of visibility, exposing difference as key to understanding why and how one group of people abuses another. Hollender's film is a meta-reflection on privilege and exploitation: by openly flaunting the rules of ethical responsibility in documentary, it demonstrates the lack of ethics in the real world. In effect, the film can be seen as a meta-narrative of guilt.

The documentary caused controversy because it depicts Riga as a city populated by prostitutes; indeed, Hollender goes so far as to claim that 'half of all women in Riga between the age 18–30 at least once performed a sexual service in return for money'. The greatest controversy, however, was provoked by its final scenes, in which the filmmaker, using the conventions of hard-core pornography, has sexual intercourse with his 'interview objects' – six Latvian women. As a representative for The National Federation of Social Democratic Women in Sweden (*S-kvinnor*) asked in the programme *Folkhemmet*, during which the film was screened and debated: 'Was it necessary for you to abuse these women?' She also accused Hollender of taking advantage of the fact that the women could not say 'no' to the money he offered them (three minimum wage salaries in Latvia). But as Hollender answered: this is exactly the point of the film.

In order to understand why, according to Hollender, such a transgressive act was indispensable, we need to look at the participatory and performative aspects of the film. Hollender's provocation appears more complex than just an attempt to shock through authentic sex scenes. The participatory dimension relates to the filmmaker's interaction and active engagement with the subjects in front of the camera, involving the (transgression of the) ethics of encounter. Its performativity concerns the effects the documentary exerts outside the film itself. The ultimate goal of the film is affective and not persuasive. As in the case of Moodysson's film, viewers should not simply acquire knowledge, but also engage bodily and emotionally. According to Hollender, he thought of *Buy Bye Beauty* as a catalyst, 'a work the real contents of which is first and foremost found outside the film itself' (Hollender 2005).

In interviews, Hollender has emphasised that the film was made specifically for Swedish audiences and is primarily about Sweden and Swedes. It is thus intentionally narcissistic – created to expose the narcissism which, according to Hollender, is a typical attitude among Swedes visiting Latvia. Within the dynamics of the local and the transnational, the film exposes the privilege that normally remains invisible to those who have it. It claims that Sweden 'owns and controls a minimum of 10% of all business and trade in Latvia', and that Swedish investors intentionally keep Latvian wages on a level below that required for minimum existence, thus creating Latvians' need for extra income and fuelling 'implicitly the supply of the women and girls for sale'.

Hollender's documentary evolved from the idea of shooting a film that would expose the fact that every (documentary) filmmaker exploits his or her subjects, irrespective of intentions (Hollender 2006). Hollender remained faithful to this idea and construed the film so that the only person held responsible for anything that occurs within, or as part of, the film is the filmmaker himself, literally incarnating the 'bad guy', the exploitative abuser, which is strengthened by the fact that no real experts or authorities appear to confirm Hollender's statements. His incarnation of the 'bad guy' is carried out in the most radical and uncompromising manner in the final sex scenes, which prompted – as Hollender counted on – a fierce critique from various sides.[9] Hence, a meta-narrative on the general relation between the filmmaker and his subjects evolved into the specific relations between the male filmmaker, representing the collective Swedish self, and Latvian women, standing for Sweden's Latvian 'other'. Staging sexual abuse[10] and using the camera not only to objectify and victimise the women, but also to evoke hard-core pornography, Hollender brutally exposes his complicity. Unlike Moodysson, who at the level of representation only applies acceptable strategies, the performative gesture in Hollender's film rests upon himself doing 'bad things'. He deliberately violates the ethics of (participatory) documentary: he uses deception, manipulation and distortion and insists that the subjects appear on-camera, no matter how painful the experience may be (see Nichols 2010: 182). In this way, he claims to take full responsibility and any subsequent punishment that results from the production of the film, unlike the 'bad guys' from Sweden, understood both as individuals and a collective entity.

Hard-core pornography can be seen as the 'most masculine of film genres' and 'the most extreme example of what women abhor about male power' (Williams 1999: xvi, 4). Hollender's choice of the hard-core pornography convention not only serves to illustrate Sweden's exploitative attitude towards Latvians, but also enhances the affective impact of the documentary: the viewers are moved, 'whether to anger or arousal' (Ibid. xvii). In this case, however – and this is an important point – it is difficult to imagine 'arousal' or pleasure on the part of any spectator. The sex scenes include not only close-ups of genitals, but also of the women's faces – serious, sad and tense. Hollender himself appears, like the women, naked. But his nakedness differs crucially from the women's: it demonstrates that he has no shame. This open demonstration of shamelessness (his own and of the Swedes who exploit the weaker) results not least from the fact that, by staging himself as the trick, Hollender emphasises the unity rather than the alienation between himself and his deed. By showing the television audience that he is shameless, Hollender 'perversely' comments on the flawed and shameless Swedish self.

Hollender also demonstrates that the Swedish man/Hollender feels no responsibility for acts resulting from his privileged position (he can easily afford six 'prostitutes' and make a documentary film), *ergo* – he feels no guilt. On the other hand, Hollender's nakedness can be read as the director's refusal to cover and protect his own person, and as a radical way of making privilege, here envisaged as his 'male power', visible – literally 'laid bare'. In effect, the responsibility and resulting punishment for his deeds (both the abusive acts and the documentary) rests exclusively upon the director. The attacks from both Swedes (although there were also positive reactions) and Latvian officials, who issued threats that they would file an international criminal case against the director, only confirm his point.

It is important to realise that the documentary implicitly relates to the image of Latvia created in the Swedish media around the time when Hollender was working on his film. The fifty-minute-long documentary originally ran to 124 minutes and contained television excerpts covering Latvia during the ten years after the country regained independence. As Hollender said in *Folkhemmet*, the Swedish media depicted Latvia as a very poor country suffering from depression after the Soviet regime, prostitution being one of its symptoms. At the same time, Swedes boasted about providing aid to its neighbour. What Hollender missed in these official representations was the connection between the Swedish investments and the poverty in Latvia, as well as the fact that the aid provided by Sweden was very modest when compared to Swedish profits. As a way of commenting on these – in his view, false – official media representations, Hollender employs manipulation – for instance, exaggerating the number of prostitutes in Riga mimics the manipulation carried out by official institutions (Hollender 2006).

Thus, Hollender manages to demonstrate what kind of reactions the exploitation should provoke, but which it normally does not provoke. He shows that the radical difference between Sweden and Latvia, which makes exploitative behaviours allowable on the 'other' side, is assumed to be natural. This difference is visualised by the trope of the border: the filmmaker has his passport issued, panoramas of Stockholm are juxtaposed against ones of Riga, and a few shots are taken on the ferry. But if the (spatial, economic and moral) border can be crossed effortlessly by a Swede, this is because he can afford it. By making Swedish privilege visible for the (Swedish) audience and disclosing the ways in which the border is generated, Hollender questions the 'natural' status of both the border and privilege (or its lack). By staging himself as guilty, he prompts and embraces the mechanism of guilt and punishment, reaching beyond the documentary itself. Moreover, by demonstrating his shamelessness, he encourages viewers to recognise their own lack of shame – and thus, through the eyes of the 'audience', which viewers become, potentially makes them reconsider the relation of the Swedish 'self' to the Latvian 'other'.

Shame as Sharing: *The 3 Rooms of Melancholia*

Audience, as stated above, is crucial in the creation of shame; the 'person feeling shame feels exposed: he thinks of himself as being seen through the eyes of another' (Taylor 1985: 57). Through the audience, the subject recognises his/her flawed self. As a result, '[s]hame is felt about injury to, or loss, or lack of self-respect' (Ibid. 131). These two aspects of shame – the question of self-respect and the audience/observer (which may be internalised by the subject, who becomes his own 'critical assessor'; Ibid. 58) – are crucial to what can be defined as the shame of submissiveness to Russia, noticeable in a number of Nordic films discussed earlier in this book. Before delving into the role of shame in *The 3 Rooms of Melancholia* (2004), it is worth reflecting briefly on these films. Although previously analysed in view of the tropes of Russia as a crime scene and the Baltic boundary, they are also important expressions of the Nordic shame reappearing in cinematic depictions of Russia.

In *Orion's Belt*, *Take Care of Your Scarf, Tatjana* and the television series *Occupied*, Russia functions as the great Other – the 'imperial centre' from which the subject is being observed. This observing gaze prevents the Nordic self (whether Norwegian or Finnish) from taking the fully sovereign subject position. The three films express the omnipotent position of the Russian Other and the awareness of the Nordic subject as existing within its gaze. Different solutions to this position of submissiveness are offered, one resting upon establishing a discursive and imaginary border through which to subordinate Russia to the Nordic subject. In *Orion's Belt*, this is only partly successful. Even though Russia is represented as utterly 'other' – the aggressive and faceless enemy embodied by the Russian helicopter – the Norwegian self is doubly humiliated: first, because the Norwegian authorities internalise the controlling Russian gaze; second, because the Norwegian self becomes expelled from itself (see Ahmed 2014: 104),[11] which is most radically emphasised by the authorities' silent acquiescence to the murder of Tom. By evoking submissiveness to Russia, *Orion's Belt* forces the Norwegian self to take the position of its own audience and recognise 'his or her lost status as an "omnipotent" subject' (Laine 2007: 31).

Quite an opposite solution is offered in *Occupied*. The submissiveness to Russia embodied by the Norwegian Prime Minister Jesper Berg, who allows for a soft occupation of his country, is experienced by the society as shameful. The shame is tackled by establishing firm borders around the Norwegian self and regaining control against the hostile 'outside' by establishing a resistance movement, thus restoring self-esteem and making it impossible for the self to be expelled from itself. In the end, the great Other is dislocated from its omnipotent position, with Norwegians winning back the status of the 'master of the situation'. But rather than using the self-critical potential of shame to open up to new subject positions, the series turns to a firm national identity, emphasising borders as a remedy against the national shame of submissiveness.

Finally, shame generated by the Russian gaze is ironically expressed in *Tatjana*. As noted in Chapter 3, the Russian Klavdia functions as the great Other, in whose gaze the other characters are constituted, particularly the silent Valto. Klavdia embodies Valto's unattainable ego-ideal and is the 'audience' through which he can see himself. In Klavdia's eyes, Valto is passive and not masculine enough to be treated like a 'real' man. Klavdia serves as a mirror reflecting and subsequently condemning Valto's masculinity as weak and opposed to Russian masculinity, of which she often speaks. Her presence makes Valto recognise his 'impotence'. It is worth noting that Valto's Volga lacks the phallic function ascribed to vehicles in classic road movies. Both the desired and fearsome femininity Klavdia embodies, which Valto cannot possess, and the 'ideal' masculinity Klavdia longs for, which Valto cannot give her, are thus coded Russian. At the same time, Valto's shame is coded Finnish, which is strengthened by his silence, in Kaurismäki's films often conveying 'Finnish' emotions (see Nestingen 2013: 121–3). Considering the national entanglements thematised in the film, it is hardly an exaggeration to recall here that during the Cold War 'Finns *dutifully listened to* their [Soviet] neighbour[s]. [. . .] The Soviet Union *closely watched* the Finnish media and actively interfered in Finnish affairs [. . .]. Finns themselves engaged in *wide-ranging self-censorship*' (Arvas 2011: 116 [emphasis added]). Valto's inertia and the resulting shame can be read as a (post)colonial anxiety paralysing the Finn's power to act.

Whereas in *Tatjana* and the Norwegian films mentioned above shame is generated within the gaze of the Russian great Other, the 'imperial centre' through which the Nordic subjects recognise their own lack and dependence, Honkasalo's documentary *The 3 Rooms of Melancholia* introduces a different take on shame in the context of Finland's relation to Russia. In the above cases, shame designates an impassable distance between the 'self' and the 'Other'. In Honkasalo's documentary, the role of the audience/observer is not ascribed to the 'imperial centre', but to the 'others', whom 'we' are prone to perceive as 'not-us'. Due to this, unlike the guilt narratives in *Lilya 4-ever* and *Buy Bye Beauty*, the film has the potential to question the subject/object opposition.

This is not to claim that all viewers experience shame while watching *Melancholia*.[12] Despite this, this chapter will dwell on the potential for the evocation of shame, as it is a textual layer of Honkasalo's documentary that can be activated in many viewers. Interestingly, Honkasalo has mentioned shame as a driving force behind the film (Koivunen and Soila 2005: 259–60). This shame could be tentatively defined as the 'shame of Finlandisation' and thus related to Finnish historical reality.[13] Film scholars Anu Koivunen and Tytti Soila point out that Honkasalo reflected on how 'she grew up in Finland with full knowledge of Soviet prison camps and the state's ongoing harassment of dissidents. She accepted all this – along with most of her leftist generation – as an internal Soviet matter' (260). Laine observes that as 'a mode of social engagement [. . .] [shame] has a long history, and perhaps nowhere more so than in Finland' (2007: 68). Honkasalo's documentary does not include any direct references to Finnish history, but as demonstrated later in Chapter 5, the theme of Russia as a war-mongering aggressor may evoke images deeply anchored in Finnish cultural memory, represented by the popular Finnish war film, *The Unknown Soldier* (Edvin Laine 1955).

The documentary contemplates the impact of the Russian–Chechen war on Russian and Chechen children. It consists of three parts – labelled metaphorically as three 'Rooms' – each introduced with an English title and information about the location. Room 1 (entitled Longing) is set in a military school for boys in Kronstadt, a town on a small island in the Gulf of Finland, close to St Petersburg. Room 2 (Breathing) unfolds in the post-apocalyptic landscape of Grozny, Chechnya's capital city. Room 3 (Remembering) is filmed in the Russian Republic of Ingushetia, in an asylum for child war victims, located close to the border with Chechnya. All three 'rooms' are located in one big 'flat' – the Federal Republic of Russia. Lying next to each other, they are neighbours – and yet they are also sharply divided.

The potential evocation of shame in Finnish/Western viewers is, first of all, encouraged through the use of strategies connecting viewers with their own socio-historical reality. A female voice-over in Finnish, briefly narrating the personal stories of the children, marks the cultural situatedness of the speaker. A comparable effect is produced by the English titles for the three Rooms. Additionally, a number of references evoke cultural memories potentially recognisable to Western, but also Russian, audiences. Among these references is black-and-white footage of the ruins of Grozny, recalling images from WWII of the devastation in Europe and Japan

(Bonsdorff 2005: 32). Numerous visual references, such as stylised foggy shots of horses in Room 3, evoke the cinema of Andrei Tarkovsky.[14] Other references eliciting the viewers' socio-cultural belonging through activating their transnational cinematic memory include Sergei Eisenstein's *Battleship Potemkin* (USSR 1925), *We Are from Kronstadt* (Efim Dzigan, USSR 1936) and Finnish war films (see Chapter 5).

These references make the viewers aware of their cultural belonging, but also remind the (educated, cultured and thus resourceful) viewers that they cannot become utterly familiar with the reality they are witnessing. In the film, a feeling of exclusion or of being an outsider might occur, for example, when we watch the religious (Orthodox and Muslim) communities immersed in their rites. Untranslatability is no doubt involved here – and Honkasalo ensures that these moments remain untranslated.

But while the viewers may feel like intruders, they also become emotionally involved, due to the highly affective load of the film. The key element of the affective appeal is the focus on children. Many of the children are orphans who were either abandoned by their parents or whose parents died in the wars in Chechnya; some were found homeless in the street. As the most innocent human victims of war, children are more prone than adults to evoke compassion and protest in the viewer (Mąka-Malatyńska 2012: 45–6). Honkasalo's camera manages to get very close to the young people depicted, following them in close-ups from the time they go to sleep to the moment they wake up, catching moments of sadness, longing, joy and other feelings and moods. Long takes of details of their bodies and faces appeal to the viewer not only visually, but also by means of tactile qualities: their skin, hair and the fabric of their clothes are often filmed in extreme close-ups, evoking the sense of touch, and thereby creating intimacy and proximity. The soundscape, and especially non-musical sounds, such as an insistent female voice waking up the babies or the children's whispers, suggestively create intimate spaces into which the spectators are allowed.

This double strategy – evoking the feeling of sharing one's intimate space with the children and experiencing exclusion as Western 'intruders' – is combined with an emphasis on the viewers' position as passive witnesses, watching from the safety of their comfortable chair. Such a mechanism, common in fiction cinema and known as safe involvement, provokes (blocked) action towards the subjects – like the desire to reach out and help (Laine 2007: 14). However, unlike in fiction films, here we are confronted with real people and a (then) contemporary political issue. In this specific situation of transnational spectatorship, our safe position reminds us of our (Western societies') inertia regarding the real and ongoing conflict in Chechnya. Moreover, through close-ups, extreme close-ups and macro-sound, all of which create proximity, viewers experience the subjects looking back at them, proving that their inertia is witnessed by the children.

By appealing to Western viewers affectively and by making them recognise – through the children's perspective – their inability to act, the documentary confronts the viewers with their own flawed selves. Importantly, Ahmed observes that only certain others can make us feel shame. The prerequisite for invoking this shame is 'that a prior love or desire for the other exists' (2014: 105). In *Tatjana*, Valto feels shame because he desires Klavdia. In Honkasalo's documentary, the love for the other is promulgated by the affective strategies and the invitation to participate in the children's reality. The feeling of shame involves the recognition that the desire to share their reality is impossible to fulfil – we are adults, they are children; they suffer, we remain unharmed. Our reality is one of peace and comfortable armchairs; theirs is one of war. Their nomadism and movement are caused by the need to flee, while their transnationality, if one can call it that, is enforced by imperialist conditions. Our reality is that of the European Union – the ideal of free and unrestricted mobility and transnational film productions. These are all reasons why viewers may feel shame.

However, Honkasalo's documentary shows that shame can open the self up to a sense of community based on social and cultural dissimilarity. If in *Lilya 4-ever* the alienation of the (metropolitan Swedish) viewer reinforces the border, in Honkasalo's documentary the recognition of one's own cultural belonging, combined with the failure of identification with the other, is transformed into a sense of community based precisely on the lack of identification.

The most telling example of this is provided by two scenes utilising television news coverage related to the Russian–Chechen war – more exactly, to the event known as the Dubrovka Theatre attack (or the Moscow theatre hostage crisis), carried out by Chechens in October 2002. The television excerpts are inserted twice in the film, in a way that makes the two scenes almost indistinguishable from one another. In both scenes, we see groups of boys in a living room gathered around a television. Thus, the viewers watch the news twice – first with the boys in the Russian military cadet school in Kronstadt (Room 1) and later with the boys from Chechnya now living in Ingushetia (Room 2). The news segments serve to both represent Russian propagandist rhetoric and remind Western audiences of the images from the Russian–Chechen war that reached them through the mass media. Therefore, the television screen can be seen as embodying

Figure 4.2 Facing the television screen. The viewer and the children are involved in an analogous act of spectatorship. *The 3 Rooms of Melancholia*. Photograph by Pirjo Honkasalo. Courtesy of Pirjo Honkasalo.

the great Other – the 'imperial centre', from which the 'other' is seen and narrated. Honkasalo's documentary, however, confronts this 'centre' by facilitating an encounter between the self (viewer) and the others (children) through the analogous situation of spectatorship and by literally facing the Other. Experiencing recognition (having seen similar accounts of the event in the mass media), the (Western) viewer is reflected in the television news, while at the same time connecting – as a viewer – with the children-viewers. While viewers can recognise themselves in relation to what is depicted on the screen, they may feel shame that they unreflectively accepted the information communicated through the source of television media. As a result of the emotional involvement in the reality behind the screen – the lives of the boys observed by Honkasalo's camera – viewers are given the opportunity to shift to the others' viewpoint.

Hence, the film prompts viewers to consciously reconsider their own position towards the conflict taking place on the other side of the safe European borders. Shame plays a crucial role in this self-evaluating confrontation. It forces the viewer to reflect on how (s)he, in the eyes of others, fails to meet his/her ego-ideal understood in terms of the Western sense of human rights (shown as irrelevant in the realities of wartime), but also in terms of Christian ethics, evoked by numerous religious references embedded in the film (the icon of the Holy mother, religious rituals, music evoking Catholic traditions). In this context, it is worth mentioning that the original concept behind the film was to make a cinematographic commentary on the Eighth Commandment: 'Thou shalt not bear false witness against thy neighbour'.[15] Indeed, 'neighbour' is here a central idea, with the term referring to someone living close by (on the other side of the border), but also to the biblical sense of the word – that is, our fellow human beings for whom we are responsible. The film remains faithful to the commandment in that it strives to bear true and responsible 'witness' to our neighbours.

Conclusion: Exclusion, Sharing and Fear in a Globalised Space

The juxtaposition of the films in this chapter shows that Nordic narratives of guilt and shame, which are two related but not identical feelings of self-assessment, represent two different strategies for approaching the Russian and/or Eastern European neighbours in a broader transnational context. Both cinematic modalities – of guilt and shame – attempt to problematise the murky parts of neoliberal globalisation, with its tendency to 'reinforce pre-existing patterns of exploitation and domination, be they political, economic, or cultural' (Hjort 2005: 26). Whereas guilt narratives are typically activated towards the 'weaker' Baltic others, they may easily reinforce the border between the self and the other, and reproduce exclusion rather than provoke responsibility. Shame, in turn, often articulates the Nordic countries' subordinated position towards larger imperialist powers, particularly Russia/USSR.[16] Shame has the potential to make viewers recognise their flawed self, rather than focusing on the deeds committed by the (uncontested, alienated) self. Honkasalo's affective shame narrative proves this point most radically, destabilising borders around the self at the level of both emotion and reflection, helping to reconsider viewers' relation to the (unfamiliar) other.

What underpins these cinematic expressions of guilt and shame is anxiety or even fear aroused by the underbelly of an increasingly globalised reality. In *Lilya 4-ever*, which represents a form of reactionary resistance to globalisation, and *Buy Bye Beauty*, addressing the economic hegemony reinforcing borders in neoliberal globalisation processes, this anxiety is visualised by the 'demoralisation' of the Swedish self, provoked by the 'newly' emerged Baltic boundary. This deterioration of standards inherent in the welfare state ideals (equality and security for all, sound sexuality) may be seen as reflecting the assumed crisis of the Nordic identity, induced by the political changes in Europe (see Wæver 1992). *The 3 Rooms of Melancholia* is concerned with the victims of contemporary Russia's 'globalising' politics. The threat to Finnish sovereignty posed by Russia earlier in history resonates in Honkasalo's thematisation of the threat Russia currently poses towards other communities – and provokes the urge to take transnational responsibility.

In recent years, the fear of Russia has gained new actuality. Whereas guilt and shame can be seen as two distinct ways of tackling this fear, the next chapter interrogates the fear of Russia in Nordic films as imagined through the – again, historically relevant – militarised social body, drawing on the stereotype of the Russian soldier.

Notes

1. Another question concerns 'Nordic guilt' as compared to 'Western guilt'. In contrast to the Nordic countries, 'American feelings of guilt are directed towards the national and not global Other' (Oxfeldt 2016: 13). When compared to Germany or England, the main difference lies in these countries' colonial and military history. However, it should be remembered that the Nordic countries – especially Denmark – have colonial histories of their own, although their societies are generally less aware of these historical facts than those of England or France.

2. Enquist was criticised by a Swedish journalist for not even mentioning the Stalinist purges of the 1930s when considering the Swedish government's decision in his novel (Holm 1975: 120). Latvian Gunars Pavuls (featuring in the film) criticised the film in *Svenska Dagbladet* (10 February 1970). I am grateful to Lars Kristensen for providing me with access to his (and Christo Burman's) unpublished research on the film.

3. The reception was less positive among Scandinavian film scholars (see Hedling 2004; Hansell 2004; Kristensen 2007).

4. The Swedish/Nordic frame of reference is not a necessary context in the case of *Lilya 4-ever*. It is nevertheless striking that Swedish references are recognisable to Scandinavian scholars (Hedling 2004; Hansell 2004; Larsson 2010; Kristensen 2007).

5. As Oxfeldt emphasises, not all Nordic people are privileged, and the idea of the homogeneous privileged Nordic subject is a construction (2016: 10). Nonetheless, even the least privileged Swedes in *Lilya 4-ever* seem more privileged than 'post-Soviet society' (which should be seen as another construction).

6. The appeal to Western European audiences includes social realism evoking British kitchen-sink cinema; the hand-held camera aesthetics and tragic female fate recall Dogme 95; the opening song, Rammstein's *Mein Herz Brennt*, elicits German affinities; Antonio Vivaldi's Symphony in B Minor for 4, *Al Santo Sepolcro*, establishes an Italian connection.

7. The house of a well-off trick and an H&M store are exceptions. However, as a producer of cheap clothing, although a Swedish company, H&M hardly illustrates Swedish urban middle-class privilege.

8. Dystopia is encoded in Malmö's *mise-en-scène* by references to cinematic dystopian cities, such as the trope of the rooftop (Nestingen 2008: 128–9).

9. See http://www.wikiwand.com/en/Buy_Bye_Beauty#/overview and http://www.ce-review.org/01/8/latvianews8.html (accessed 5 February 2016).

10. The women agreed to such a role, signing a contract in which Hollender explained (in Latvian) that they would participate in a roughly ten-second-long sexual intercourse scene with the filmmaker in a partly 'fake' and partly 'authentic' way (Hollender 2005).

11. As Ahmed notes: '[P]rolonged experiences of shame [. . .] can bring subjects perilously close to suicide' (2014: 104).

12. Parts of the following section have previously appeared in an article published in the *Journal of Scandinavian Cinema* (see Mrozewicz 2016). I am grateful to the editors of the journal for granting me permission to republish parts of this article.

13. Finlandisation was strongest in the 1970s (Salokangas 2015: 77) – that is, when Honkasalo started making films in her twenties.

14. '[T]he theme of lost childhood evokes *Ivan's Childhood* (1962); the juxtaposition of colour and black-and-white film stock evokes *Andrei Rublev* (1966); and the film title focusing on Melancholia obviously suggests Tarkovsky's late study of homesickness – *Nostalgia* (1983)' (Koivunen and Soila 2005: 258).

15. See http://www.millenniumfilm.fi/2004_melancholia.html (accessed 18 May 2016).

16. Also towards the political and cultural domination of the US, signalled in *Orion's Belt*, *Occupied* and *Take Care of Your Scarf, Tatjana*.

CHAPTER 5

Embodying the Fear of Russia:
The Militarised Body

As seen in several films discussed thus far, the soldier is a recurring figure in representations of Russia in Nordic cinemas. Most commonly imagined as an aggressive invader, with a green uniform, red star and military equipment as his main attributes, he encapsulates the stereotype of Russia as a brutal, despotic and expansive nation-state. At the same time, the Russian soldier can also be seen as a construction that embodies the Nordic fear of (Soviet) Russia, of which there are plentiful cinematic examples, most prominently featured in Chapter 1 of this book. This construction is often invoked in opposition to what we might call 'homo Nordicus' – the self-perception of the Nordic body as non- or anti-military – incorporating Nordic peacefulness as integral to its (self-)image during the Cold War (see Wæver 1992: 84–5).

Focusing on the figure of the Russian soldier for the duration of this chapter could itself appear to reinforce this negative stereotype. The aim of this chapter, however, is to investigate Nordic films that challenge this well-established narrative incarnating the 'formula of terror and oppression exploited in countless espionage thrillers and films' (Naarden and Leerssen 2007: 229). As we shall see, a number of films – without denying the vital role of the military in the Russian society – examine and reimagine the trope of the soldier, either by recontextualising it through the historically specific militarised body or by assuming distanced and playful approaches to the Nordic fear of Russia. Although most of these films cannot be said to possess the potential to establish a new dominant discourse – since to achieve this, they would have to enter the big-budget feature film circuit, and many of them are documentary or art-house productions, including one animation film – they are noteworthy as critical reflections on the fear of Russia, encapsulated in the figure of the soldier.

As Andrew Nestingen has put it: 'When the nation is represented by the image of the self-sacrificing soldier, we must ask in what ways men, women, children, and groups distinct from the militarised representation of the nation are encoded in such an image' (2013: 118). Indeed, Nordic films examine specific socio-political power structures encoded in the figure of the Russian soldier, as well as in the figures of women, children and non-militarised male bodies implicitly connected to the soldier. These groups also belong to the militarised body. As Maya Eichler argues in her study of militarisation processes in post-Soviet Russia: '[M]ilitarization relies on both men and women, and on notions of masculinity and femininity. Women have been militarized both inside and *outside of the military*, as soldiers, military wives, prostitutes, nurses, rape victims, mothers and feminist activists' (2012: 87 [emphasis added]).

What connects these cinematic reimaginings of the Russian soldier is implicitly expressed in the words of Michel Foucault: 'Nothing is more material, physical, corporal than the exercise of power. [. . .] One needs to study what kind of body the current society needs' (1980: 57–8). The militarised body, submitted to various forms of training and discipline, expected to fulfil specific societal roles, and pressed into uniform can also be grasped through Foucault's concept of the 'social body'. The social body is

> directly involved in a political field; power relations have an immediate hold upon it; they invest it, mark it, train it, torture it, force it to carry out tasks, to perform ceremonies, to emit signs. [. . .] This subjection [. . .] may be subtle, make use neither of weapons nor of terror and yet remain of a physical order. [. . .] What the apparatuses and institutions operate is, in a sense, a micro-physics of power. (Foucault 1995: 25–6)

The militarisation of contemporary Russian society is an important topic in cinematic explorations of Russia's social body. In the definition of militarisation, this chapter follows Eichler:

> The terms 'militarism' and 'militarization' are sometimes used interchangeably. I differentiate between militarism as an ideology (or a set of ideas), and militarization as a process. I define militarization as any process that helps establish and reinforce a central role for the military in state and society [. . .]. Thus militarization (and the adjective 'militarized') will be used to underscore the socially and politically constructed nature of the military's importance. Politicians, society, and individuals become militarized when their beliefs and actions support a central role for the military. Militarization is thus achieved when militarism is not questioned but accepted as normal and necessary. (2012: 4–5)

The theme of militarisation adheres to what film scholar Mirosław Przylipiak has defined, using Jean-François Lyotard's notion, as 'grand narratives' in documentary cinema (Przylipiak 2011; Lyotard 1984). Documentary grand narratives apply expository and 'objective' methods, often with extradiegetic commentary, and a clear rhetoric and editing supporting the main argument (Nichols 2010: 167ff.). Thematically, they are concerned with 'grand' social and political issues rather than micro-events from everyday life, individual cases merely exemplifying broader perspectives. The engagement with 'grand' themes might reflect the preference for socially engaged themes in Nordic (documentary) cinema (see Bondebjerg 2002). However, it certainly also demonstrates that narrating Russia without taking a political stance – for or against the (past and current) political system – poses difficulties (see Gerner 2000: 40). However, Russian society is also critically approached as the very place where grand narratives are produced, kept alive and used by the ruling power to justify authoritarian methods. The militarised body as such encapsulates one of Russia's grand-scale national narratives. As we shall see, its 'grandness' is not taken for granted by Nordic directors.

As argued earlier, the position Russia occupies in the Nordic imagination is different from that of the Eastern European countries neighbouring *Norden*. Despite the admiration for Russia's rich and refined culture (Naarden and Leerssen 2007: 228), the imagery of (not only Soviet) Russia is influenced first and foremost by fear, for which, as mentioned previously in the Introduction, a word exists in Swedish: *rysskräck*. The word derives presumably from the period of wars between Sweden and Russia during the Great Northern War (1700–21) (Ronström 2009: 121–2).[1] According to historian Matthew Kott, the term *rysskräck* 'not only implies what the pro-Kremlin commentators today describe as traditional Swedish "Russophobia", but also an underlying psychological anxiety of invasion of the Swedish heartland from the East that is not easily assuaged' (Kott 2015). During the Cold War, the threat of invasion from the east was incited by numerous episodes of Soviets infiltrating Swedish territories using submarines – most spectacularly in 1981 near Karlskrona. In the 1990s, after the dissolution of the Soviet Empire, the image of Russia as a military threat was fading from public consciousness. But the fear was soon to return: '[F]ollowing the 2008 Georgian crisis, when Swedish [conservative – AEM] foreign minister Carl Bildt took a vocal stance on Russian military intervention, *rysskräck* has been returning to the Swedish regional security discourse' (Ibid.). This fear is currently being instigated by Russia's military expansiveness, not only in neighbouring territories (such as Chechnya, Georgia, Crimea and east Ukraine), but also in distant areas (Syria). These events activate the old 'oriental despotism' modality in the perception of Russia (Naarden and Leerssen 2007). As the British BBC documentary *World War Three: Inside the War Room* (Gabriel Range 2016), about a hypothetical war in Eastern Europe initiated by Russia demonstrates, the fear of Russia as a military threat is escalating in the contemporary Western imagination.

Within *Norden*, the deeply rooted fear of Russia is not only specific to Sweden. In Norway 'the fear of the "red threat" from the east' (Aas and Vestergården 2014: 189) was already strong during the 1905 Russian Revolution. This fear defined the next hundred years of Norwegian security policy, which during the Cold War escalated into a close internal surveillance of society (Ibid. 188ff.). In Denmark, as mentioned in the Introduction, Russian soldiers have been associated with the occupation of the island of Bornholm between May 1945 and April 1946 (see Lauridsen et al. 2011: 140ff.). Ever since a national Finnish identity started taking shape in the nineteenth century, Russia has been depicted according to the dominant Finnish national narrative as its main enemy (see Østergård 1997: 55–6).

Unsurprisingly, among the Nordic countries, the fear of Russia has left its most prominent mark on Finnish cinema. Difficult relations with the Russian and later Soviet neighbour have been formative for Finnish national identity. War is among the most important and regularly depicted themes in Finnish cinema, and even today 'provides key source material for many important and successful films' (Csoma 2012: 85). Finnish representations of Russian soldiers reach back to the silent era and continue well into the 1930s – a decade marked by strong anti-Soviet views. In the first war film made after WWII, which became the highest-grossing Finnish film recorded, *The Unknown Soldier* (*Tuntematon sotilas*, Edvin Laine 1955), based on the bestselling novel of the same title by Väinö Linna (1954), Russian soldiers are barely visible, although they represent a destructive hostile force. The novel was readapted by Rauni Mollberg in 1985. In this film as with its predecessor, Russian soldiers appear almost exclusively as an anonymous army, visible from a distance and embodied by planes, tanks, the roar of gunfire and exploding bombs. A similar anonymity in the portrayal of Russian soldiers is strikingly evident in another important Finnish war film, *The Winter War* (*Talvisota*, Pekke Parikka 1989). What distinguishes Finnish representations of Russian militarised bodies from those of other Nordic cinemas is that the Russian soldier is inherent to the construction of the Finnish soldier. Finnish soldiers are contrasted with Russians through features such as honour and virtue, and are depicted through personalised portraits. In recent war films, such representations are challenged. An example is the Civil War drama *The Border* (*Raja 1918*), discussed in Chapter 2 of this book, depicting a friendship between the Finnish (White Guard) protagonist and a Russian major. The common recurrence of war as a theme in Finnish cinema testifies to its significance.

Depictions of war and the militarised national 'self' in relation to the Russian soldier are less common in Swedish, Norwegian and Danish cinemas. In the context of WWII, for example, the militarised Scandinavian body is most frequently imagined as saboteur, partisan and provider of humanitarian aid, rather than as a regular soldier (regarding Sweden, see Kahn 2012). In neutral Sweden military service was obligatory until 2010, and recently plans to reintroduce compulsory conscription were announced by Swedish politicians as a response to ongoing escalating tensions with Russia.[2] The genre of military farce flourished in Sweden before WWII, as it did in the other Nordic countries (see Laine 2012). During the war, a number of Swedish 'state of alert' films were produced, expressing 'a spirit of community, watchfulness, silence' in the country, which was in a state of partial mobilisation (Soila et al. 1998: 182). In these films, the image of the enemy is obscure, and the actions are set either in the distant historical past or in unnamed countries.[3] However, WWII never truly became part of the official Swedish national memory (Östling 2013: 180).[4] In the case of Norwegian and Danish militarised bodies, the main enemy is German rather than Russian. In Norway, where the war experience plays an important role in the discourse on national identity, the genre of the occupation (docu)drama emerged in the 1940s and continues today (Iversen 1998: 123; 2012). The militarised body of the enemy is predominantly German, similar to Danish representations of war (not only WWII, but also the traumatic Second Schleswig War fought between Germany and Denmark in 1864). In relation to WWII, Denmark is not imagined as a nation at war (Bondebjerg 2012: 242), and during the Cold War the Danish public was in general 'latently anti-militarist' (Wæver 1992: 82). Nevertheless, the Cold War and the fear of Russia were acutely real for those who knew what was going on 'behind the scenes'. A recent documentary television programme entitled *Zealand* [the largest Danish island – AEM] *in the Cold War* (*Sjælland i kold krig*, TV Øst, Denmark 2016) began with the following words:

> On 3 March 2014, an SAS plane flying over the Baltic Sea with 132 passengers onboard came within 5 metres of a Russian spy flight. This was just one event out of 66 during that year provoked by the Russians, who themselves accuse NATO of making such flights. In recent years it seems as if the Cold War has returned, though if you go back to that time, the threat from the East was much more violent and tangible.

A number of Nordic films deal with this threat – one which is felt more or less intensely in the various Nordic countries – by interrogating, complicating and/or ridiculing the fear of Russia. Focusing on the Russian militarised body, the films especially foreground two aspects inscribed in it: enemy and gender. The previously analysed documentary *The 3 Rooms of Melancholia* (Pirjo Honkasalo, Finland, Denmark, Germany, Sweden 2004) is invoked here as an example exposing the mechanisms used to construct the militarised body through the figure of the enemy in post-Soviet Russia. Honkasalo's documentary approaches war both from the perspective of the soldier and of the women and children dragged into processes of militarisation. Jerzy Śladkowski's *Virgins* (Finland 2003), focusing on education in one of Russia's elite schools, deconstructs the Russian soldier through a focus on gender. Gender also plays a remarkable role in (self-) ironic takes on the Russian soldier, such as Torill Kove's animated short comedy *Me and My Moulton* (Norway, Canada 2014) and Roy Andersson's *A Pigeon Sat on a Branch Reflecting on Existence* (*En duva satt på en gren och funderade på tillvaron*, Sweden 2014), both assuming an ironic distance to the Russian militarised body in opposition to the disarmed Nordic body. I also evoke the Russian film *The Cuckoo* (Alexandr Rogozkhin, Russia 2002), which 'demilitarises' both the Russian and Finnish soldier in humorous ways, while at the same time showing them as mutually connected. The adherence to heteronormative models of gender and patriarchal societal norms implicit in the construction of the Russian soldier is ultimately disrupted in the comedy *Popular Music* (*Populärmusik från Vittula*, Reza Bagher, Sweden 2004). Finally, Ada Bligaard Søby's short documentary, *The Naked of Saint Petersburg* (*De nøgne fra St. Petersborg*, Denmark 2010), is discussed as an example of a rare non-political approach to Russia in Nordic cinemas – reaching beyond the prevailing grand narratives.

(De)constructing the Enemy

The fear of Russia together with Finland's specifically troublesome relation with its eastern neighbour gained renewed fervour with the two wars in Chechnya (the first led by Russian President Boris Yeltsin, the second by his successor Vladimir Putin), lasting from the mid-1990s until 2009. These two wars were highly controversial, although reportage on them in the media was, to some degree, limited. *The 3 Rooms of Melancholia* was shot in places 'where the international news reporters never dared to go', and has been called 'one of the strongest films ever made about war', its message being both historically specific and existentially universal (Niskanen 2012: 232). For a Finnish viewer, Honkasalo's representation of the Russian–Chechen conflict would likely evoke associations with Finnish war films depicting the Soviet–Finnish conflicts. Indeed, the documentary rethinks the constructions of not only the Russian soldier, but also its Finnish counterpart by appealing to the viewer's cinematic memory.[5]

To understand how the Finnish soldier is inscribed in Honkasalo's depiction of the Russian soldier, we must take a brief look at the seminal Finnish war film: *The Unknown Soldier*, both the 1955 original and its 1985 remake. In Linna's novel, on which Laine's 1955 film was based, the 'frog perspective' of the individual Finnish soldier enabled the author 'to direct harsh critique against the officers and the nationalistic [Finnish – AEM] propaganda' (Sundholm 2013b: 212; see Sundholm 2007). This perspective, as film scholar John Sundholm observes, is missing in Laine's adaptation: '[T]he particularity of the soldiers in the novel was ideologically transformed into the collectivity of the nation. Whereas in the novel, the soldiers [fought] in order to stay alive as autonomous human beings, in the film they fought as and for Finland' (2013a: 36).

Sundholm sees Laine's film as a cinematic 'founding trauma that explained the events in such a way that the nation could move on' (2007: 127). By far the most important Finnish cinematic war narrative, the film produced a general consensus in Finnish society on how to regard war events (Sundholm 2013b: 212). In it, Finland is represented as a self-defending and victimised nation with a '"tragic geography"', sandwiched between two extreme evils' (Ibid. 225) – that is, Germany and the USSR. Interestingly, Rauni Mollberg's adaptation from 1985 shifted the perspective 'from the nation as victim to that of the common soldier' (Ibid. 219). Even though the national discourse of victimisation remains unchallenged, it does not claim that the causes of the Continuation War (during which Finland was allied with Germany) were justifiable (Ibid. 218). This is one of the main reasons why, according to Sundholm, the 'hegemony' of Laine's 1955 adaptation remained intact and strongly rooted in Finnish cultural memory (the film is screened annually on public television on Finnish Independence Day). It is telling that the 1985 version includes a scene absent from the 1955 film, involving a Soviet soldier who is caught by a group of Finns. Lost and scared, he evokes the viewer's empathy. When a shell is found in his pocket, a Finnish soldier jumps to the conclusion that the man intended to use it to blow himself, and the others, up, and thus kills the Soviet soldier by shooting him in the back. In this short episode, the inhumanity and evilness of the stereotypical Russian soldier is, for a brief moment, suspended, and a defenceless human being, whose frightened face is shown in close-ups, is contrasted with the ruthlessness and dishonourable behaviour of the Finnish soldier.

In its depiction of Russian soldiers, Honkasalo's documentary engages the (Finnish) viewers' cinematic memory by, among other references, triggering visual associations with *The Unknown Soldier*(s). Thus, it rethinks not only the stereotype of the Russian/Soviet soldier, but also the myth of the Finnish soldier persisting in the Finnish cultural imagination. At the same time, the documentary engages with an actual war, embedding the Russian soldier in a specific historical moment.

The collectivity of the social body mobilised in the name of the nation (represented by Laine's adaptation), and the particularity of the individual human being (emphasised in Mollberg's version), can be seen as the two poles between which Honkasalo's documentary unfolds. *The 3 Rooms of Melancholia* begins with close-ups and extreme close-ups of sleeping cadets in the military school in Kronstadt, a fortress island near St Petersburg. The images and sounds lead the viewer directly into the intimate sphere of the future Russian soldiers. The opening sequence registers the hands, ears, heads and cheekbones of the sleeping children; viewers witness the boys waking up and making their beds. This is quite an unusual depiction of the Russian soldier when considered in the context of Finnish war films – first, because of the proximity and private situations in which they are shown; second, because they are children.[6] But although the camera employs extreme close-ups of the boys, it never approaches adult soldiers in the same manner. The superiors at the Academy remain anonymous and distant, closer to the typical figures of Russian soldiers, their main role being to issue orders and instil discipline. At the same time, adult soldiers embody the future of the still-innocent boys. The initial waking-up sequence is followed by a morning gathering, during which all the boys are wearing uniforms. Here, the camera scrutinises their shoes, hats, repetitive gestures and concentrated facial expressions. Intimate images of particular bodies are replaced by the collective, social body – the militarised body.

The Russian soldier in Honkasalo's documentary is a multi-layered construction. The numerous scenes showing the boys being trained and submitted to various forms of military discipline evoke scenes from both versions of *The Unknown Soldier* (1955 and 1985).[7] However, Honkasalo's film is much closer to the 1985 polemic take on Finnish national mythology. The opening sequence emphasising the individuality of the soldiers evokes the initial images in Mollberg's adaptation, which begins with a conscription scene showing naked young men being measured and weighed. The camera lingers on their bodies and boyish faces, framed in medium shots and close-ups, and their nakedness is set in sharp contrast to their uniformed superiors. By prompting these intertextual references, the documentary implies that the Russian soldier is not much different from the Finnish soldier: he is also made of blood and flesh; he suffers, longs and doubts; he is (at least initially) innocent; and he has equally been submitted to processes of indoctrination, both through the practices of militarisation and through the specific (national/ist) discourses by which he is framed. Thus, the image of Russian soldiers as highly negative characters and barely visible distant figures – sometimes not even perceived as humans (as the Finnish soldier Rokka says in Mollberg's version) – is here challenged by their resemblance to cinematic representations of Finnish soldiers, as well as by an emphasis on the cadets' humanity.

Linking Russian and Finnish soldiers is a double-edged strategy, as it also evokes meanings only latent in *The Unknown Soldier*. The novel and its adaptations deal with the Continuation War (1941–4), which is controversial in light of the national discourse of the innocent Finnish soldier defending his motherland. This is due to the fact that Finland was at that time allied with Nazi Germany, and Finnish troops crossed the border and advanced into Soviet territory. Thus, Honkasalo's documentary not only implies that the Russian soldier is as innocent as the Finnish soldier, but also that Finnish soldiers were not as innocent as these films, and especially *The Unknown Soldier* of 1955, suggest. Through the intertextual juxtaposition of Russian cadets in Kronstadt and Finnish soldiers, the documentary implies that although they are both victims of war, they are at the same time not only victims but also (future) oppressors. A similar refusal to accept black-and-white divisions concerns the Chechens. Even though they are unambiguous victims of the Russian–Chechen war, and their situation is much more critical than that of Russian children, Honkasalo's documentary does not hide the structures of violence present on the Chechen side by showing, for example, violent Muslim religious rituals or the Dubrovka Theatre attack conducted by Chechen militants in October 2002.

The working of ideology is illustrated not only through evocation of the dominant Finnish national discourse, but also by means of evoking the most iconic Soviet pro-revolutionary propaganda film, Sergei Eisenstein's *Battleship Potemkin* (1925). The opening sequence in Honkasalo's documentary strongly recalls the early-morning sequence in Eisenstein's film, focusing on close-ups of the faces and bodies of sleeping marines just before their literal and ideological awakening. This evocation reminds us that ideology lies at the base of all militarised bodies – whether Finnish, Soviet, Russian or Chechen. It also emphasises the propagandist dimension of war narratives, not just cinematic ones, but also those upon which existing processes of militarisation feed, embodied by the cadet school in Kronstadt. Another relevant image is the well-known Soviet propaganda film *We Are from Kronstadt* (1936, Efim Dzigan), about Red marines from

Kronstadt defending Petrograd in 1919 from White counter-revolution-
aries. Notable in view of the theme of forsaken children subordinated
to ideology in Honkasalo's film is a scene in *We Are from Kronstadt* in
which children from an orphanage observe Red soldiers preparing for
battle. Thus, through a network of intertextual references, Honkasalo
shows the Russian soldier as a highly complex and artificially constructed
figure. Importantly, whereas these films foreground a collective hero,
Honkasalo's documentary focuses on individual fates and faces, surpass-
ing the anonymising strategy of the propaganda films.

It is worth emphasising that although *The 3 Rooms of Melancholia*
evokes a number of fiction films related to war, it is itself a documentary.
'Fictitious' grand narratives – relating both to Russia and Finland – are
challenged by means of its verisimilitude and indexical logic, intensified
by its strongly affective appeal to viewers. Moreover, because the documentary focuses on the human dimension of the war experience and the
everyday lives of children, it can be said to effectively challenge the grand
narrative of war from the position of minor narratives. From this 'frog perspective', the film deconstructs the Russian soldier's assumed (and thus
taken-for-granted) opposition to the Finnish soldier. Above all, however,
the documentary challenges the very idea of the enemy – a concept necessary to justify any war. This is due to the fact that children on 'both
sides' (Russian and Chechen) are represented, and emotional involvement
towards both of these groups is fostered among viewers. As a consequence,
viewers are unable to perceive them as mutual enemies. An important role
in questioning a clear-cut notion of the enemy is played by the recurring
figure of the absent or dead mother and mother-warrior – of which the
boys and the narrator in the voice-over often speak. Among the televised
images from the Dubrovka Theatre attack, two dead women (Chechen
suicide bombers, so-called 'black widows') are visible in medium close-
ups, wearing black robes and black scarves around their faces. As Eichler
explains: 'Later in the second war, the female suicide bomber appeared
as a feminized version of the terrorist enemy' (2012: 48). Having become
acquainted with the stories of both the Russian and Chechen boys, when
viewers see the dead women, they are already aware of the socio-historical
factors that have led them to their desperate terrorist acts. Thus, the
televised depiction of the Chechen women as unambiguous terrorists
becomes complicated and exposed as official mass-media rhetoric rather
than an ultimate truth.

Honkasalo's documentary removes the soldier from strictly national
frames by placing the militarised body (including that of children and
women) in a transnational perspective. As the Finnish and Russian cin-

ematic references discussed above imply, the Russian soldier is remark-ably similar to the Finnish soldier. He is not simply a threatening enemy, but, primarily, a sad child longing for home and a stable identity. The spatialisation of memory through transnational intertextual framing has the potential to challenge 'the narrative structure of national/ist history' (Sundholm 2013a: 33). This potential is present in Honkasalo's documentary – both because the film confronts the Russian soldier in Kronstadt with his entrenched image in Finnish cinema, and because it shows the Russian soldier outside of official Russian national/ist dis-course, embodied by Russian television news coverage and state institu-tions. Moving closer to the 'enemy' from both sides of the conflict, and upsetting the clear distinction between 'friend and foe', the documentary dismantles the binary construction of the soldier.

(De)constructing the Gender Order

Another binarism upon which the figure of the (Russian) soldier is con-structed involves a specific gender order. This dimension is closely exam-ined in Jerzy Śladkowski's documentary *Virgins*, produced by a Finnish company, Magic Path Entertainment Oy, and broadcasted by Swedish national public television SVT under the title *Kadetter och oskulder* (*Cadets and Virgins*). The film demonstrates what Eichler emphasises in her study of the militarisation of men in post-Soviet Russia: 'To study men [. . .] is necessarily to study them in relation to women, and vice versa' (2012: 5). Śladkowski, who comes from Poland – a country with a historically tense relationship with Russia – but has lived in Sweden since 1982, has devoted the majority of his critically acclaimed (and prize-winning) documentaries to focusing on post-Soviet Russia.

The documentary focuses on a boarding school for girls (between the ages of ten and seventeen years old) neighbouring a cadet school in the Siberian city of Krasnoyarsk. *Virgins* investigates the intersections of mili-tarism (understood as a set of ideas and an ideology) and gender through an examination of the processes of militarisation in the state institution educating girls. As Eichler emphasises, modern states not only play a role in shaping their respective society's gender, but also rely on

> the gender order for its own functioning and ideological legitimization, as is evident in the politics of militarization. The basic claims states make – to sovereignty, protec-tion and security [. . .] have historically entailed dividing society into those who bear arms and defend state and nation (men) and those who are relegated to the private sphere and defined as in need of protection (women as well as children). [. . .] In militarized societies, state and military leaders define woman's patriotism in terms of

her willingness to sacrifice her son, and man's military service as intrinsic to his citizenship and identity. Militarization is gendered in that women's and men's identities can become informed by militarism. (2012: 6–7)

A scene in Śladkowski's documentary neatly illustrates Eichler's words: in an airborne shot, a group of girls is shown standing in the school courtyard. Young cadets, all in dark uniforms, approach the girls, encircling them with a thick 'protecting wall'. As this image shows, in the centre of the militarised masculinity, a specific type of femininity is found. In another metaphorical scene, young cadets marching in regular columns are cross-cut with girls dressed like ballet dancers, training to do splits and preparing for a ballet class. Two iconic images of Russian bodies, the soldier and the ballerina, are here combined.[8] Even though these two images are worn-out clichés in depictions of Russia, Śladkowski situates them in a specific social and political context, and shows their ideological interconnections, thus avoiding the ahistoricity of stereotype by which history is transformed into 'one solid block' (Rosello 1998: 23).

Virgins employs methods typical of television documentary. The film's own grand narrative, which could be formulated as the 'body and nation in post-Soviet Russia' investigated through the lens of the educational institution, emerges by means of talking heads and evidentiary editing. But the film also focuses on 'small' narratives told by the girls and on non-verbal details, transforming them into metaphorical images that ironically comment on the grand narrative disseminated at the school. The

Figure 5.1 Militarised masculinity with a specific type of femininity at its centre. *Virgins*, screen capture. Courtesy of Jerzy Śladkowski.

film's critical edge rests upon uncovering silent symptoms and uncritically accepted ways of thinking.

The documentary opens with one of many scenes focusing on disciplining female bodies: a class is taking place during which the girls are being instructed on proper ways of sitting during various social occasions. The voice of a female teacher explains how to hold your knees together, cross your legs, put one leg on the other, in front of the other and so on. The girls, all around thirteen years old, are dressed identically. The camera focuses on their legs, all in identical positions. We are witnessing the collective disciplining of bodies – the production of the social body. As the director of the school, a high ranking military officer, divulges: 'People ask me what I deal here with. I answer that what I deal with is production – the production of human souls'. Symptomatically for the dominant discourse at both schools, he does not mention the production of bodies.

The role of the militarist ideology in education is made clear by the information written across the screen following the credits, thus opening the film:

> In tsarist times, Russian girls born to good families received an education in Mariinsky boarding schools. There, they were prepared for the roles of spouses, mothers and housewives. After 1918, Bolsheviks closed all of these schools. In 1998, General Alexandr Lebed established the first Mariinsky boarding school for girls in the post-communist Russia, in the Siberian city of Krasnoyarsk. The Russian Army and the Orthodox Church jointly support the idea.[9]

Indeed, with the support of not just the state and military leaders (Eichler 2012: 7), but also the Russian Orthodox Church, the two schools in Krasnoyarsk define very precisely the gender roles of their pupils. The girls are trained to be dedicated housewives and mothers, whereas the boys prepare to become soldiers faithful to their motherland. This is also how the girls perceive the cadets. One of the youngest girls repeats lines she has learned by heart: a real man is 'an officer, characterised by strong will, bravery, generosity and nobility'. This ideal – and its hegemonic masculinity – is represented by the soldier. The soldier, in turn, relies on a specific construction of femininity, defined by domesticity and patriotic motherhood. But the national ideology promoted at the two schools is not only limited to the surface of the pre-adolescent bodies (outfit, behaviour, manners), it also penetrates the bodies of the girls and legitimises the school's control of their sexuality; indeed, in order to be admitted to the boarding school, one must be a virgin. The girls are submitted to regular checks to confirm that they have continued to abide by the school's condition; losing one's virginity results in immediate expulsion.

In commenting on the education policies at both schools, the authorities do not hide its direct connection with national ideology and its reliance on militarisation processes:

> These people receive an education and upbringing on an appropriate level. They owe it to the uniform and discipline, [. . .] necessary for every young man. [. . .] Young people should be isolated from what is called the democratic variant, that is, a way of upbringing and shaping youth that exposes them to drugs, prostitution and the like.

It is useful to evoke here the notion of banal nationalism coined by the American sociologist Michael Billig to describe the routine practices and symbols (flags, coins, banknotes) filling everyday life, which 'flag' the nation by 'providing banal reminders of nationhood: they are "flagging" it unflaggingly' (1995: 41). According to Billig and anti-essentialist approaches to the concept of nation in general, people's sense of belonging to a particular nationality is constantly being constructed through numerous, repetitive, 'banal' everyday activities and verbal expressions. As he emphasises: '[B]anality is not synonymous with harmlessness. In the case of Western nation-states, banal nationalism can hardly be innocent: it is reproducing institutions which possess vast armaments' (Ibid. 7). At the Krasnoyarsk boarding school, the nation is, indeed, present in the form of small narratives: banal activities and micro-events, such as collective prayers or ballet lessons, are caught by Sladkowski's camera. However, the film also shows that the nation is just as strongly present in the schools' discourse as in 'grand narratives' or, rather, in any given grand narrative or particular national/ist ideology. Sladkowski's documentary manages to depict not only what Foucault defined as the 'micro-physics' of power (the numerous scenes of training and disciplining of bodies), but also the strictly hierarchical structure of power, on which a particular conception of the Russian nation rests. In his discussion of the concept of the nation-state, Billig observes, in the spirit of Lyotard, that '[g]rand "meta-narratives", which aim to establish clear boundaries between truth and falsity belong to the modernist past' (1995: 131). As Sladkowski's documentary implies, in Russia such an understanding of the nation-state does not belong to a bygone era. Quite the contrary, the interviewed authorities emphasise the need to return to and preserve pre-Bolshevik Tsarist traditions. The nation (and the ideas underpinning it, militarism included) constitutes the main frame of reference for everyday life at the schools. Hence, the grand narrative operates in the documentary as a meta-subject: in Sladkowski's depiction, Russia is a place for constructing and cultivating grand narratives.

Most importantly, Śladkowski's documentary – as a result of observations and interviews rather than presuppositions – exposes a hidden side to the 'truths' preached at the schools. Even if the documentary can be said to belong to the genre of films thematising the return of pre-Soviet traditions in contemporary Russia (Jazdon 2016: 140), *Virgins* also reveals the undercurrents of this officially proclaimed rebirth: the strengthening of state power and the implementation of militarist ideas in the new Russian society. Behind the promoted ideal of masculinity lies a very particular purpose: attracting soldiers and, ultimately, carrying out specific military tasks (see Eichler 2012: 3). Thus, even though there are no direct references to the military conflict in Chechnya, certain scenes resonate powerfully within the depicted context of militarisation – for example, when the camera focuses on the youngest girls speculating about the meaning of the Russian–Chechen war.

Śladkowski's camera captures the generational gap concerning traditional ideas, which are revealed (sometimes unconsciously) by some of the girls. During a religion class, the camera lingers on yawning faces and catches ironic smiles. Not all the girls uncritically accept the 'truths' told by the bearded Orthodox priest, such as that the primary role of a woman is motherhood. As a teenage girl admits, she has difficulties accepting this idea and supports the 'emancipation of women'. A critique of what is hidden behind the façade of the 'real' Russian man and the promoted family model is conveyed when the girls talk about alcohol abuse in their families. Similarly, the youngest girls make fun of their fathers, who, according to them, do nothing but snore on the couch. Their rather unconscious critique of the official family model is mediated by a fully conscious camera.

Śladkowski's documentary shows that according to the ideology of the two schools, the relation between a man and a woman is mediated through their relation to the nation. Such rhetoric and practices concerning gender seem not unlike those of the Soviet era, with the main difference being that it is now the nation, not the state, which is the overall dominating frame (see Tartakovskaya 2000: 134). Śladkowski's study of the militarised body stages the Russian soldier and the ballet dancer as both metaphorical and real, historically specific figures, closely related to one another – two sides of one coin, to evoke a metaphor mentioned earlier. It is a meaningful choice made on the part of the director that the central figures representing the militarised body – the cadets – remain 'silent'; they are never interviewed or approached directly by the film crew. We learn nothing about the boys' social backgrounds or their experience at the school. The cadet is a powerful but distanced figure – and thus remains a two-dimensional figure. Symbolically, this static, impersonal figure constitutes the central point of reference for both the interviewed girls and the authorities.

Whereas *Virgins* relates an ideal masculinity to an ideal femininity in the national/ist discourse of the new Russia, the films analysed next examine the figure of the Russian soldier through the optics of how Nordic bodies are implicated in this construction. But in contrast to the optics in Honkasalo's documentary, these films undermine the Nordic fear of Russia by means of humour, (self-)irony and other distancing strategies.

Beyond the Fear of Russia

As illustrated by the previously discussed television series *Occupied*, the fear of Russia as a direct military threat thrives in the contemporary Norwegian cultural imagination. However, it is not necessarily considered an existing and serious threat, but rather a heritage to which contemporary directors maintain a safe distance. A scene in the autobiographical short animated movie by Norwegian Oscar-winning director Torill Kove, *Me and My Moulton* (2014), is a noteworthy example that both evokes and mocks the Nordic fear of Russia embodied by the Russian soldier.[10] The film is a humorous, fictionalised first-person narrative recounting the memories of a little girl, Torill, growing up in a small Norwegian town in the 1960s. The narrative focuses on her desire to fit into the community, which sets her apart from her parents – both modernist architects – and their highly unconventional lifestyle. In a particularly telling scene, the father is visually juxtaposed with a group of other dads marching in file during military training. Unlike them, he is not wearing a uniform. As we learn, he 'is almost blind in his left eye and was excused from military service. He says that's ok because he is a pacifist – but the kind who could kill Russian soldiers if they threatened his family'. Meanwhile, an imagined scene – drawn using the graphic convention of a speech balloon – depicts three Russian soldiers arriving in a tank flagged with the red star and violently entering little Torill's family home. In an attempt to protect his family, the father reaches for his revolver and, looking away and with shaking hands, 'aims' it towards the three Kalashnikovs pointed at him. 'That's reassuring', the female narrator says with mild irony, 'but we think Mom should handle the Russians' – following which the mother takes the gun and confidently shoots into the air. As a result, the soldiers flee through the open door, leaving their Kalashnikovs behind.

The scene lasts only thirty-five seconds. Nevertheless, it is thought-provoking that Russian soldiers, imagined as invaders of the Norwegian family's house, are included in this thirteen-minute-long animation

Figure 5.2 Faceless Russian soldiers invading the Norwegian family home. *Me and My Moulton.* © Mikrofilm AS and National Film Board of Canada. Courtesy of National Library of Norway.

inspired by memories of Kove's childhood. The fear of Russians invading Norway is imagined humorously as part of everyday reality in Norway at that time. The three soldiers are literally depicted as faceless, which playfully alludes to the stereotype of Russians as the 'faceless enemy'. Importantly, the Russian militarised body is depicted in opposition to the non-militarised, 'pacifist' Norwegian father. At the same time, it is implied that the necessity to militarise Norwegian men – and to discipline the Norwegian 'social body' – is related to the threat of invasion from the east. However, Kove's story includes a comical gender twist: whereas the father clearly fears the Russian soldiers, the mother 'handles' them without hesitation. The Russian soldiers flee because they fear the modern, self-assured Norwegian woman, who, in contrast, is depicted as fearless. The scene comments ironically on what some would call the crisis of (Nordic) masculinity, represented by Torill's father, who belongs to the 'creative class' (to use a contemporary term), while at the same time demonstrating a rare ironic distance in relation to the fear of Russians. Likewise, in *Occupied* – which is devoid of the ironic coolness characterising Kove's animation – a female character, the PST leader, also frightens Russians, in this case by taking the leadership of the resistance movement. Norwegian women in both cases assume traditional 'manly' roles, while the men are exposed as weak and passive (like Jesper Berg in *Occupied*). But while the Russian soldier tends to embody a strong, patriarchal masculinity, against which the Scandinavian men seem feeble and soft, in *Me and My Moulton*,

Russian masculinity is also ridiculed by the depiction of a strong femininity, embodied by Torill's mother.

An even more ironic – we might even say, sarcastic – approach to
modern Nordic (specifically Swedish) masculinity, and in general, society
as inert and impotent when confronted with the figure of the Russian
soldier, is adopted in Roy Andersson's film *A Pigeon Sat on a Branch
Reflecting on Existence* (2014). This film evokes the Great Northern War,
with the Swedish Army's crushing defeat at the Battle of Poltava in 1709,
which ultimately saw the termination of Swedish dominion over the Baltic
Sea and triggered the beginning of a period marked by 'Russia's dramatic
impact on Europe' (Malia 1999: 9).

The ignominious defeat of the Swedish Army is imagined in two lavish
scenes in Andersson's otherwise ascetic film. The plot is set in contemporary Sweden. However, employing his characteristic strategy of condens-
ing time and space into a single long shot against a stylised static tableau
(see Brunow 2010), Andersson interweaves several historical layers into
one scene. Trabant guards of Charles XII enter a modern-day lunch bar.
Shortly afterwards, the young Swedish king himself – recalling (a much
older) Gösta Ekman, who played this role in the epic historical drama *Karl
XII* (John W. Brunius, Sweden 1925) – rides into the bar on horseback.
In the background, his troops head vigorously towards the 'eastern' edge
of the frame. The king explains that the soldiers are on their way to 'spank
the Muscovites'. A few scenes later, the same soldiers are seen walking
back limping, exhausted and unarmed. They are retreating from Poltava,
where they were defeated because the 'sly Russians' 'had armed themselves in secret'. The defeat at Poltava is here played out as the beginning
of Sweden's downfall, leading to the loss of its strength and virile potency,
symbolised initially by the king's horse and his proud 'vertical' posture.
The fact that the king is depicted as a homosexual (he invites a young
bartender to his tent) emphasises the monarch's association with masculine power (preceding the king's arrival, women are thrown out of the
bar). After the defeat at Poltava, the king, who was wounded in the battle,
returns to the bar lying inertly on his horse's back. A striking contrast is
created between the gallant and courageous Swedish soldiers from the
beginning of the eighteenth century – and, implicitly, the even more potent
and 'sly' (though invisible) Russians – and the passive, weak, apathetic and
pigeon-hearted contemporary Swedes. 'You became widows at Poltava',
an old bartender says to two women from the present, who have been
sitting at the bar, at which they both start crying. The scene is followed by
a young contemporary couple shown on the beach engaging in apathetic
foreplay, during which they remain almost completely motionless, with no

Figure 5.3 King Charles XII after the defeat at Poltava (1709) in a modern Swedish bar. *A Pigeon Sat on a Branch Reflecting on Existence.* Photograph by István Borbás. Courtesy of Roy Andersson Filmproduktion.

signs of sexual excitement. Thus, in Andersson's film, Swedish virility is lost, together with 'half of the kingdom', in a fateful confrontation with the Russians. Here, the fear of Russia is not embodied in a threat of invasion from the east; rather, Poltava serves as a symbol marking the downfall of Sweden's greatness, leading to a spiritually and emotionally dwarfed, apathetic and asexual modern Swedish society.

Another interesting example of a distanced approach towards the Russian soldier is offered by the Russian film *The Cuckoo*. The film is a playful take on the construction of the Finnish soldier in opposition to the Russian soldier. Although it is not a Nordic film, the figure of the Finnish soldier is central, and the Finnish language, as well as Sami, is spoken on an equal basis with Russian. The film features both Finnish and Russian actors and a Sami actress. Most importantly, it provides an uncommon perspective on the mutual entanglement of the Russian and Finnish militarised bodies, which 'disarms' soldiers on both sides.

The plot is set in 1944, a few months before the end of the Continuation War. It tells the story of a Finnish soldier named Veikko. Because of his pacifist views, Veikko is put in shackles and chained to a rock in Lapland by his Finnish and German comrades. Using force, they dress him in the uniform of the Waffen-SS – the formation most hated by the Soviets – to compel Veikko to engage and retaliate when confronted by the enemy. However, instead of shooting at the enemy, Veikko uses all his ammunition to blow up the rock to which he is chained, freeing himself. As he searches for tools to remove his shackles, he comes across a reindeer farm run by a lonely Sami woman, the shamaness Anni. Some days before Veikko's arrival, Anni stumbles across a wounded Soviet soldier in the forest, whom she is nursing back to health in her hut. In this way, the Soviet and Finnish soldiers meet under one roof, where they stay for several months. The three characters all speak different languages and represent three different cultures: Finnish, Russian and Sami. The plot is driven by humorous, as well as tragic, misunderstandings that arise between them. Most importantly, however, the protagonists communicate despite language barriers.

Initially, differences between the two soldiers are emphasised. Whereas Veikko repeats that for him 'the war is over' and the only thing he dreams about is returning home, the Soviet Ivan expresses hostility towards Veikko, calling him a fascist because of his Waffen-SS uniform. Veikko emphasises that he is a democrat and only fought for Finland's independence. Ivan attacks Veikko several times – first with a knife, later with an axe and finally with a revolver, this time almost killing him. Nevertheless, Veikko is depicted as the more masculine of the two, while the threat posed by the Russian soldier is ridiculed. For instance, Ivan is shown wearing Anni's skirt when his clothes are hung up to dry, which makes both Anni and Veikko laugh. This scene exposes the performativity of the functions attached to the uniform and to clothing in general. Later, Ivan is shown picking mushrooms, which again associates him with a stereotypically feminine activity and undermines the roles associated with military uniforms. When the young Veikko is chosen by Anni for her lover, the middle-aged Ivan feels jealous and rejected. The Russian film thus reverses the typical Nordic perspective on the Russian soldier. The Finnish soldier is both the more virile and the friendlier of the two. However, when Ivan finally almost kills the Finnish soldier, not understanding that the war is over, the Russian threat regains its tangibility. Veikko's near-death experience at Soviet hands just after the end of the Continuation War can be seen as referring to Finland's highly precarious position after the war as a neighbour to the victorious Soviet Union.

In the film, the militarised male body, inextricably linked with an enemy, is gradually invalidated. Both soldiers become 'disarmed' over time, with the Sami Anni (whose ethnicity surpasses national belonging) acting as the 'disarming' force. While from the perspective of the soldiers their uniforms seem natural, to Anni they are not. 'Why are you two so fond of hiding yourselves in your clothes?', she asks. For Anni, the symbols on the uniforms (the red star and the SS insignia) have no meaning – she does not seem to recognise them, just as she seems completely oblivious to the concept of nationality. The first time both soldiers are shown without uniforms is when they sit and talk in the sauna built by Veikko. Although the sauna is an emblem of Finnish national imagery, here it creates a realm beyond the national domain: Veikko's and Ivan's nakedness 'discloses' their similarity as human beings. Anni, whose real name – Cuckoo – is revealed much later in the film, is strongly associated with nature; she lives in accordance with the natural rhythms of Lapland, and she draws super-natural strength from animals. The fact that both men ultimately become Anni's lovers emphasises her role as a disarming and unifying 'natural' force. The film thus suggests that what really links them is human nature – their belonging to one human race. In the film's penultimate scene, the two men are seen leaving Anni's farm, now as friends, both wearing identi-cal clothes made by Anni from reindeer leather, which again emphasises nature as an equalising force in contrast to the nationally coded uniforms' power to divide. They part in friendly fashion at the crest of a hill, 'one went this way, the other the other way, each to his home', as Anni tells her twin sons, of whom one is Ivan's and the other Veikko's. Quite tellingly, she does not mention any directions, such as west or east – terms inherently laden with cultural and political connotations. Through the donning of the reindeer leather clothes and Anni's narrative, the two soldiers become ultimately disarmed. No longer soldiers, they can now part – they no longer need an 'enemy'.

Thus, whereas Kove's and Andersson's films satirise the fear of Russia by ridiculing their own societies – either with mild irony or bitter sarcasm – the Russian film conveys a pacifist message, disarming the soldier by emphasising his belonging to a world beyond national borders. Through her association with nature, Cuckoo is ascribed a typical female role and represents boundary – an attitude that denies the abstract national divi-sions represented by uniforms. The dissolution of the border between the Finnish and Russian bodies is almost literal: Anni conceives twins by two different fathers. Interestingly, the depiction of the Finnish soldier by the Russian director in many ways overlaps with Finnish national self-representations of fighting for Finland's independence (rather than together with Germany) and in self-defence rather than as an aggressor. This may be seen as an attempt by Rogozkhin to repeal the border that has historically divided the two nations.

The ultimately transgressive take on the Russian soldier in Nordic cinemas is represented by a supporting character, called Ryssi-Jussi, in the Swedish comedy *Popular Music* (2004). The film (based on the novel by Mikael Niemi of the same title) is set in Pajala, a small village in northern Sweden close to the border with Finland. Combining the perspective of a child with the memories of an adult, the protagonist Matti describes his childhood spent living in this far-removed place during the 1960s and 1970s. Ryssi-Jussi is introduced in the voice-over as 'the last real pedlar in these parts. One of the countryside's most feared personalities. One to be avoided. If you could'. Ryssi-Jussi's daily outfit consists of an old, worn-out Soviet uniform jacket, decorated with a row of medals, and a red knee-length skirt. Under the jacket, a ladies lace T-shirt is visible. The middle-aged Ryssi is a former revolutionary, signified by the red star on his jacket and his fondness for the colour red in general. In the village, Ryssi-Jussi functions as a local oddball, believed to have supernatural powers. His status as an outsider is primarily related to his non-normative sexuality – his behaviour marks him as a homosexual, an exhibitionist and, significantly, a transvestite. Just as his sexual identity is fluid, so is his national belonging, expressed by his name, which indicates three nationalities: Swedish, Russian (*ryss* in Swedish) and Finnish (Jussi is a Finnish name).

Ryssi-Jussi thus embodies the boundary, most typically ascribed to women – a rather stereotypical pattern into which most of the films discussed in this book fall. His Soviet uniform is detached from a normative nationality or gender; moreover, the combination of nationalities that together make-up Ryssi have historically been considered enemies (in all their various combinations: Russian/Finnish, Swedish/Finnish and Swedish/Russian); thus, the idea of the enemy inscribed in the military uniform is also overturned by Ryssi-Jussi. The uniform of the Russian soldier is just one more piece of attire he wears in a constant performance of identity. Against the strongly conservative and patriarchal community of Pajala, the Soviet uniform appears de-masculinised, and the fear of Russia – the 'fear' of Ryssi-Jussi – is exposed as a fear of something different, unknown, fluid and non-conforming.

Beyond Grand Narratives

Kove's, Andersson's, Rogozhkin's and Bagher's films all adopt a safe distance towards grand narratives about Russia. Nevertheless, grand narratives – such as war, nationality or gender – remain a point of reference in these films. *The Naked of Saint Petersburg* (2010), a Danish documentary by Ada Søby, adopts a different strategy: the film focuses exclusively on 'small narratives', with the 'grand narratives' of today's Russia relegated to the background, as if accidentally caught by the camera. The film belongs to those few Nordic documentaries about Russia made after 1989 that avoid depicting the country directly in political terms. This approach, more typical of the younger generations of filmmakers (Søby was born in

1975, which makes her younger than the directors mentioned above), can be seen as a product of their generational distance from the Cold War with its unavoidable politicisation of West–East discourse.[11]

The bypassing of grand narratives grows out of Søby's documentary method. The camera approaches St Petersburg from a position of '(not) knowing' – which should not be confused with ignorance. In Maria Boletsi's definition, the 'parenthetical "not" foregrounds [. . .] a negative concept pregnant with positivity. [. . .] (Not) knowing thus refers to a kind of knowledge that does not yet exist' (2013: 30–1). The 'knowledge that does not yet exist' is something the director gradually acquires through the process of filmmaking and through cautious contact with the city and its inhabitants. Her 'knowledge' is gathered *en route* and results from interactions, rather than from a self-appointed omniscient (presup)position. The film is therefore a series of subjective impressions from a passerby's perspective, guided by the voice of an insider – a male inhabitant of St Petersburg. The camera's focus shifts from the splendid architecture of the Winter Palace to concrete blocks of flats or the barbed wire atop a prison wall. Street hip-hop dancers are contrasted with small girls training in ballet, guided by the authoritative voice of their instructor.

The documentary is not free from the well-established (Western) iconography of Russian bodies, such as – like in Śladkowski's film – the ballet dancer and the soldier. However, it goes beyond the usual associations these figures evoke (militarism and discipline). In a number of scenes, soldiers are shown as permeating the city space – both just walking in the street and during a spectacular ceremony in front of the Winter Palace. But they also appear in somewhat humorous, non-official situations, bursting out with laughter while smoking cigarettes during a break. Similarly, when the young ballet dancers are shown training, and the camera catches moments of clumsiness or a loss of concentration, the girls' facial expressions are contrasted with the teacher's rigorous reprimands. Nevertheless, the presence of the military seems a natural part of the city, just as ballet classes seem to belong to every Russian girl's education.

Most importantly, unlike the films analysed so far, Søby's main focus is not the disciplined social body, but rather the opposite – the 'undisciplined' individual body. The central figures are naked sunbathers, middle-aged or elderly inhabitants of the city, who come to the bank of the Neva River, covered with running ice floes, and sunbathe collectively in their underwear, observed in long takes. The winter sunbathers function as an image of contrasts and divisions within contemporary Russian society. Their 'social nakedness' exposed on the non-representative bank of the river transgresses the limits of the disciplined body, represented by the uniformed soldiers associated with the official buildings or the ballet dancers being reproached by their teacher. At the same time, the sunbathers can be seen as the powerless and nameless, those whose bodies have no protective cover (the 'naked'), strongly contrasted with the splendour of the architecture on the other bank of the river. These sunbathers, observed from a distance, do not get the chance to speak to the camera.

However, by resisting conclusions, Søby's documentary avoids assigning the camera the role of a superior, intruding subject. It also implies, by means of various strategies, that the encounter with St Petersburg is not 'direct', but mediated through cultural filters, like the colour red tinting a wall behind the sunbathers, added in post-production, hinting at pre-existing grand narratives about Russia (Bolshevism). Most importantly, although not political in its subject matter and not a 'victim documentary' (see Winston 1988), the film manages to raise critical questions about the condition of contemporary Russian society, such as the stark societal contrasts – the river providing a symbolic embodiment of inner divisions.

As a small narrative in its method, form and subject, Søby's documentary offers an alternative perspective on Russia compared to the other films discussed above, which are inextricably linked with grand-scale issues, encoded in the figure of the Russian soldier. However, this cinematic take on Russia freed from politicised and polarised frames seems even more marginal in view of the current political developments. The escalating fear of Russia makes this approach difficult to sustain among Nordic directors.

Conclusion: Declining the Russian Soldier

The Russian soldier interrogated in contemporary Nordic films is neither reinforced as a negative stereotype nor simply denied. Rather than repeating the stereotype (denying a stereotype is also a repetition),[12] the films discussed in this chapter perform a strategy which Mireille Rosello calls 'declining' the stereotype, a concept meant to evoke two meanings of the word 'declining': first, the grammatical term of declension (which reflects what is 'mechanical in our language'); and second, a polite refusal to accept or do something, close in meaning to the term 'dismiss'. To decline a stereotype means to make a 'double movement of inhabiting while displacing' the repetitive thinking (Rosello 1998: 10) and to deprive the stereotype 'of its harmful potential by highlighting its very nature' (Ibid. 11). Exposing the Russian soldier as a construction defining the Nordic body as its positive opposition, the films discussed above demonstrate that this figure has long been 'inhabited' by Nordic projections. By blurring divisions between 'homo Nordicus' and the Russian body, they 'decline' both the Russian and Nordic social bodies by showing them in new, and yet recognisable, manifestations, which underscore similarities between them rather than divisions. The 'declining' rests upon exposing (with the use of various strategies, such as irony, humour and intertextual references to well-known films and images) taken-for-granted structural elements of the soldier figure – most prominently, the enemy and masculinity. Moreover, by shifting the focus beyond the figure of the Russian soldier to something new, the films also displace the fear of Russia, exposing it as a Nordic (self-paralysing, self-ridiculing, self-emasculating) projection.

But the fear of Russia is not simply disavowed. Śladkowski and Honkasalo, drawing on specific political and historical contexts, and perhaps on their own experiences, warn us subtly but confidently against neglecting or dismissing Russian militarism as a mere 'stereotype' that can be uncritically repeated and behind which there is no reality. Rather, it needs to be closely examined.

Notes

1. According to historian Kristian Gerner, an outburst of *rysskräck* (fear of Russia) can be observed at the turn of the nineteenth and twentieth centuries (2000: 34ff.).
2. See, for example: https://news.vice.com/story/sweden-reintroduces-compulsory-military-service-as-tensions-with-russia-increase (accessed 25 June 2017).
3. An exception is *A Day Will Dawn* (*En dag skall gry*, Hasse Ekman 1944), dealing with the Finnish Winter War. Here, a Swedish soldier fighting on the Finnish side dies while trying to help a Russian soldier.
4. Recently, however, several war films were produced in Sweden, reimagining the war experience of a neutral country, such as *Beyond the Border* (*Gränsen*, Richard Holm 2011) and *An Enemy to Die For* (*En fiende att dö för*, Peter Dalle, 2012).
5. It should be mentioned that one of the first Nordic documentaries discarding a stereotypical representation of the Russian/Soviet soldier after the Cold War was Sonja Vesterholt's *Lithuania, Spring 1990* (*Litauen foråret 1990*, Denmark 1990). The documentary depicts the strong urge for independence among Lithuanians shortly before the country regained sovereignty. However, it also gives voice to several Russian soldiers, who are now supposed to leave Lithuania, where they have lived for decades, and depicts their difficult existential situation in personalised and nuanced portraits, beyond the oppressor/oppressed dichotomy.
6. The focus on children in wartime was previously explored in Finnish cinema in *The Boys* (*Pojat*, Mikko Niskanen, Finland 1962). Recent films with a focus on the experiences of Finnish children during WWII include

       the documentary *War Children* (*Sotalapset*, Erja Dammert, Ulla Simonen, Finland 2003) and the feature film *Mother of Mine* (*Äideistä parhain*, Klaus Härö, Finland, Sweden 2005).

7. In 2017, a third adaptation of Linna's novel premiered in Finland on the 100th anniversary of Finnish independence. This new version of *The Unknown Soldier* (*Tuntematon sotilas*, Aku Louhimies, Finland 2017) was released too late to be considered in the current book.

8. The ballet became associated with Russia's refined cultural life in the nineteenth century and recurs in representations of Russians (Beller and Leerssen 2007: 228; Boym 1994: 218). As Pomerantsev put it: 'Oh nation of ballet dancers!' (2014a: 12).

9. The tradition reaches back to the eighteenth century, see: https:// en.wikipedia.org/wiki/Institute_for_Noble_Maidens (accessed 13 February 2017).

10. I am grateful to Adam Trwoga for bringing this film to my attention.

11. Other examples are Maximilien Van Aertryck's (b 1989) *Icebreakers* (2012), Iris Olsson's (b 1981) *Between Dreams* (2011), Kimmo Yläkäs' (born early 1980s) *The Queue* (2005) and Lise Birk Pedersen's (b 1974) *Nastja's Heart* (*Nastyas hjerte*, Denmark 2010). Other 'small narratives' include the documentaries *Hotel Russia* (Kristoffer Nyholm, Denmark 1993), *The Photographer from Riga* (*Fotografen från Riga*, Maud Nycander, Sweden, Finland, Latvia 2009) and *The End of the Road* (*Vägens ände*, Maud Nycander, Sweden 2013).

12. As Mireille Rosello warns us, saying 'All Arabs are x' or 'It is not true that all Arabs are x' can have an equally damaging effect as repeating the stereotype, as it only reiterates and thus 'activates the stereotyped idea' (1998: 38).

CHAPTER 6

Polish Spectres in our House: Revisiting the Nordic Metaphor of the Home

As a number of films discussed in previous chapters demonstrate, the fear of Russia is an enduring topic in Nordic cinemas, articulated either through the modality of Eastern noir, as a subject (self-)critically and/ or humorously approached, or as an emotion expressed at the subliminal level. In this final chapter, I would like to focus on another fear – that of the 'spectre' of workers migrating to the Nordic countries from the so-called 'new members' of the European Union, the largest of these being Poland. As Rosalind Galt has observed, post-Wall European cinemas redraw 'both the discursive and the referential spaces of nations' and are character- ised by co-articulations of 'cinematic space and geopolitical space' (2006: 4–5). Indeed, in a number of Nordic films, Polish labour migrants not only signal the changing structures of societies and emergence of new transnational identities, but also prompt a revisiting and reconstructing of the central political metaphor defining the Nordic welfare states – that of the home. The films discussed in this chapter challenge both the political metaphor and social reality shaped by the concept of 'home'.

Although 'notions of family, home and local community have generally been central metaphoric resources from the very beginning of modern nationalism' (Gullestad 2006: 94), and the 'European house' metaphor (first used by Mikhail Gorbachev in 1985) has figured prominently in European public discourse after 1989 (Stålhammar 1997: 101–3; Van Heuckelom 2014: 73), in the Nordic context, the notion of home carries its own relevance as the most ubiquitous and powerful concept for imagin- ing the Nordic welfare state. Its centrality and prevalence is reflected in Scandinavian languages. Danes and Norwegians often use words denoting home, such as *hjem, hjemme, herhjemme* interchangeably with 'Denmark' and 'Norway' (as opposed to the world outside). The widely used Swedish term *folkhemmet* ('the people's home', 'the folk home') was adopted by Swedish social democrats in the 1930s 'to suggest that familial solidar- ity should be extended to everybody within the modern and progressive welfare state' (Gullestad 2006: 94). Although this term does not translate directly into the other Nordic languages, the links between the welfare state and national identity are equally as strong as those in Sweden (Hilson 2008: loc. 1790). The foundations of the welfare state – like those of a good home – are values such as community and solidarity, helpfulness and cooperation. 'The good home knows no privilege or neglect, no favourites and no step-children', were the famous words of Per Albin Hansson, the Swedish social democratic leader and later prime minister, who in 1928 introduced the term *folkhemmet* (Stålhammar 1997: 97; Hilson 2008: loc. 1781; Hansson 1982: 227). The power of the *folkhem* metaphor lies in its combination of two positively laden notions: folk community in a modern nation-state and family bonds in a secure home (Żmuda-Trzebiatowska 2012: 160).

It is striking that in public discourses on migrants, which involve notions such as 'guests', 'strangers' or 'intruders', home functions as an implicit metaphor (Gullestad 2006: 120). Today, Poles make up one of the largest migrant groups in Scandinavia. In 2016, they constituted the most numerous ethnic minority in Norway, the second largest in Denmark and the fourth largest in Sweden.[1] The main sector of employment for so-called 'foreign workers' – that is, the low-wage labour force from poorer countries – is construction (Bartram 2007: 774). A huge wave of 'foreign workers' from Poland reached Scandinavia in the period following 2004 – after Poland's accession to the EU. Soon afterward, Polish construction and domestic workers began appearing in Scandinavian films, if not abundantly, then certainly more numerously than ever before in Nordic cinemas (which, in general, have historically failed to portray the percentage of immigrants in film in relation to the actual number of immigrants in Nordic societies after WWII), often as lead characters.[2] The films frequently utilise domestic spaces as central metaphors, dissecting the privileged Nordic societies from the perspective of Polish labour migrants (or those assumed to be labour migrants), who, as this chapter argues, due to their precarious social position and outsider perspective possess the insight necessary to question the Nordic home metaphor.

First, however, it is necessary to ask why Polish 'foreign workers' are perceived as a threat to the 'Nordic home' – a discourse frequently raised in the Nordic media. One possible answer is that their presence evokes the inner spectres, both past and contemporary, haunting the Nordic home. As Jacques Derrida put it in his seminal reflections on spectrality: 'The specter is also, among other things, what one imagines, what one thinks one sees and which one projects – on an imaginary screen where there is nothing to see' (1994: 100–1). One way in which the Polish characters evoke inner spectres is their embodiment of the working class in the

Nordic societies, of which they now make up a large part. The figure of the contemporary Eastern European worker has been defined as spectral by Maciej Zaremba, a Polish journalist living in Sweden. Although not mentioning Derrida directly, but similarly drawing on Karl Marx and Friedrich Engels' notion of the communist spectre, Zaremba observed in his essay 'Polish plumber' (first published in the Swedish newspaper *Dagens Nyheter* in 2005):

> We live in peculiar times. One and a half century after *The Communist Manifesto* ("A spectre is haunting Europe – the spectre of communism") the worker again incites fear. But this time he does not wave a banner, he does not try to overthrow the regime [. . .]. All he wants is to work. He really does not demand much. And this is frightening, the fact that he demands so little. [. . .] Just look how he [the Polish plumber] has already transformed Denmark into a stronghold, and provoked Swedish trade unionists to yell to Latvians: "*Go home!*" (Zaremba 2008: 7 [original emphasis]).

Here, Zaremba addresses the divide emerging at that time between Eastern and Western workers within the newly enlarged EU. The conclusion is that solidarity and the sharing of common interests united across the globe (or even across Europe) is a fallacy; instead of urging '[w]orking men of all countries, unite!' (Marx and Engels [1848] 2012: 102), the Swedish workers attack their Latvian 'fellow workers' in what might be called both a location-based conflict (Gajewska 2013: 67–70) and a class conflict. As Gullestad observed, in contemporary (Norwegian) society, 'social class has been replaced by national ethnic difference as the basic categories with which to understand and to defend [oneself] in the face of current changes and the presence of new categories of people' (Gullestad 2006: 100–1). 'National ethnic class', as we might call it, is the new mobile border in the ostensibly borderless Europe of today.

However, Zaremba's observations can be taken one step further: what he touches upon here is the problem of how the spectre of the 'Polish plumber' is produced by the spectralising forces at society's apex, related to contemporary globalisation processes and economic models (post-industrial labour and neoliberal capitalism), or by the 'ruthless economic war among the countries of the European Community themselves, between them and the Eastern European countries' (Derrida 1994: 81), the 'old' EU countries embodied by the Swedish trade unionists protecting their rights and salaries. It is worth recalling that Scandinavian societies are often referred to as those who, on a global scale, represent the northern 'top of the world', and are seen as being among the most privileged regions (see Chapter 4), although it should be remembered that not everyone is (equally) privileged within the Nordic societies.

Polish migrants, and especially Polish labour migrants, have their own history of representation in European cinema. Kris Van Heuckelom has observed a shift between pre- and post-1989 cinematic depictions of Polish workers abroad, one which intensified after the turn of the millennium (2013: 219). Previously, Polish characters suffered harsh and sometimes tragic fates in the host country. An important example in the Scandinavian context is *300 Miles to Heaven* (Maciej Dejczer 1989), mentioned earlier in Chapter 3. Even though this film depicts two underaged refugees who embrace a better life in Denmark, their new existence could hardly be called 'heavenly'. Nowadays, according to Van Heuckelom, the primary role of migrants from poorer countries is to 'rejuvenate and cure the European continent' (2013: 220). Yet the trope of critical self-examination of Western society against positively valorised non-Western newcomers is hardly new; it is, in fact, one of the most clichéd conventions in representing migrants, often resulting in stereotypical discourses like those defined by Mehmet Ü. Necef as 'ethnic kitsch' (Necef 2003). Ethnic 'kitschification' rests upon a romanticised, idealised and glorified – and thus simplified – view of others, not considering them in a socio-historical perspective, but instead projecting one's own deficiencies, longings and desires onto them (Ibid. 173–5). According to this discourse, the 'others' – 'noble wilds' – are opposed to the superficial, non-spontaneous, commercialised Western societies. Sociologist Carina Tigervall has observed that since the concern with immigrants became a noticeable tendency in Swedish cinema in the 1970s, representations of 'agreeable others' have become the norm, complying with the official Swedish social democratic 'antiracist' rhetoric (Tigervall 2005; Hedling 2007: 37, 39).[3] As Tigervall argues, in a critique of modernity rooted in the political left, these films often fall into their own trap of colonialist, sexist and patriarchal discourses – or ethnic kitsch-ification. Necef suggests that in order to avoid ethnic kitsch, one needs to present migrants as 'normal', prejudiced against other ethnic groups, and utilise a consciously humorous self-kitschification – that is, a humorous exaggeration of their own foreignness (Necef 2003: 175). Today, humour, sarcasm, self-irony and play with ethnic stereotypes occur frequently in Nordic cinematic depictions of migrants (Jørholt 2007; Larsen 2015). However, although Necef brightly illuminates the pitfalls of ethnic kitsch, his suggestion is problematic: on the one hand, it may be seen as implying that the 'normality' of the host society is something the newcomers strive for; on the other, his call to humorous exaggeration of foreignness can easily lead to anti-immigrant representations.

One frequently used 'kitschifying' strategy rests upon mobilising nos-talgia and a desire for a restoration of the past. In this model, the migrants represent 'pre-modernity' and forgotten past values (on Balkan and Pakistani migrants in Norwegian films, see, for example, Dancus 2011; on Polish migrants in British cinema, see Rydzewska 2012). Indeed, in the films discussed in this chapter the homes are not only spatially but also temporally structured, and ghosts from the past are often invoked. However, Poles are rarely kitschified through nostalgia. Rather than promising a return to the good old days and a restoration of the lost splendour of the Nordic home, they embody change and a need to radically reimagine the home in terms of its future rather than its past.

Bearing the above contexts in mind, this chapter examines Polish migrants from a different perspective, that is, in terms of their agency, or – considering their status as threatening 'spectres' – their 'spectral agency' (Peeren 2014: 16). In order to do this, this chapter applies the metaphor of the 'living ghost' conceptualised by cultural theorist Esther Peeren, who draws on theories of the so-called spectral turn inspired by Derrida's 1993 *Spectres de Marx* (English translation *Specters of Marx*, 1994), departing from Marx and Engel's *Communist Manifesto* and its 'ghost' following the dissolution of the USSR. Derrida's text 'marked the transformation of the ghost and its capacity to haunt from a genre convention or plot device [. . .] into a theoretical "idiom"' (Peeren 2014: 9).[4] If numerous conceptualisations of spectrality see the ghost as a figure of return (for example, the forgotten, ignored or repressed parts of history), Peeren focuses on present, living ghosts (Ibid. 14). These living ghosts are the dispossessed, the marginalised, and those made socially invisible by ongoing spectralising processes – most prominently, the processes of neoliberal globalisation (including the role of the new media, see Ibid. 16; see Derrida 1994: 79). The living ghosts also include the unemployed, homeless, exiles, migrants, refugees and other figures made obscure 'in their growing segregation from everyday life' (Peeren 2014: 17). Some, like contemporary migrants forced to undertake unskilled jobs in wealthy Western countries, can be called 'globalized servants' (Ibid. 103).

Key to Peeren's conceptualisation of living ghosts is what she calls their 'spectral agency' or 'agency of invisibility'. Agency as such is understood as 'the ability to act on one's own initiative and to have this acting taken seriously by others [. . .]. As such, agency potentially enables one to renegotiate one's social position and identity' (2014: 15). As Peeren insists, ghosts can actively and efficiently disturb the spectralising system through their very ghostliness (Ibid. 16). However, due to the social vulnerability of the ghost, spectral agency does not necessarily translate into 'straightforward, deliberate intervention' (Ibid. 22). The spectral agency of a ghost would rely on being seen, including 'the ability to be seen not to act'. An important aspect when considering spectral agency is that of perspective. Peeren shows that the norm is to look at the ghost from the position of the haunted and not through the ghost's eyes (Ibid. 24–9). Zaremba's example quoted above illuminates this 'norm': what the Swedish trade unionists are doing when they yell 'Go home!' to the Latvians is exorcising a 'ghost' perceived by the haunted 'host' as threatening. This approach takes for granted who embodies the 'self' and who embodies the 'other'. Yet, as Peeren contends, because living ghosts 'are materially present and open to exchange, [. . .] not giving the specter the opportunity to occupy the position of a self robs it of agency and exempts it from the task of taking responsibility for *its* other(s)' (Peeren 2014: 27 [original emphasis]).

Whereas the home metaphor looks at the domestic space from the perspective of those included, the metaphor of the living ghost emphasises the external perspective on the house, problematising invisible power relations and exclusions implicit in the home metaphor. The Polish foreign workers can be called 'ghost workers'; contrary to the guest workers invited to Western countries shortly after WWII, they have not been invited, and rather than 'guests', they function as living ghosts.[5]

This chapter will, however, keep the ambiguity of the guest/ghost worker in focus using the concept of the living ghost to grasp the encounters between Polish migrants and Nordic 'hosts'. The films discussed in the following demonstrate that the guest/ghost/host sequence is a fluid continuum, rather than a set of rigidly established roles, and that its contents and positions are not irrevocably fixed. In contrast to kitschifying representations of Muslim immigrants in Scandinavian cinemas, which often take difference as a pre-established given (see Dancus 2014; Mulari 2013), and in contrast to Necef's approach, which looks at the migrant from the normalising standpoint of the host, the social position and identities of the Polish workers are here depicted as construed rather than natural, imposed by spectralising societal forces, such as economic inequality and stereotypes.

Metaphors, as famously stated by George Lakoff and Mark Johnson, function not simply as 'a matter of words', but something we 'live by' – that is, something that shapes our everyday reality (2003: 3). The home metaphor can be said to function as a concept that the Nordic people 'live by'. Cinematically imagined domestic spaces can thus be analysed as reflecting (upon) the socio-cultural reality and conceptual structures this reality is governed by. At the same time, the living ghost – as Peeren proposes – 'is a metaphor certain people (are made to) live *as*' (2014: 6 [original emphasis]). This chapter's engagement with the ghost metaphor, inspired by Peeren's study, will help show that the Polish newcomers – while made to 'live as' invisible and dispossessed ghosts by those 'living by' the home metaphor – are represented as resisting spectralisation. The Polish characters challenge rigidly assigned positions and, by doing this, function as a means for reimagining the national self-image encapsulated in the Nordic home metaphor. Through the Polish newcomers – who undertake various domestic and manual jobs, such as cleaning and repairing houses – viewers are offered surprising and sometimes shocking insights into the Nordic home.

Using domestic spaces as not merely settings, but as vital and semantically laden spaces, the films under discussion in this chapter epitomise the change within the Nordic societies resulting from the changing relations with the external world, embodied by the Polish 'ghosts'. This is particularly apparent in two feature films: *Four Weeks in June* (*Fyra veckor i juni*, Henry Meyer, Sweden 2005) and *Upperdog* (Sara Johnsen, Norway 2009), as well as the (only briefly mentioned) documentary *I am Kuba* (Åse Svenheim Drivenes, Norway 2014) and the television series *Struggle for Life* (*Kampen for tilværelsen*, NRK, written by Erlend Loe, Per Schreiner and Bjørn Olaf Johannessen, Norway 2014–15), analysed in the final section of this chapter.

Tearing the House Down

In the late 1980s and early 1990s, when disillusion and insecurity among Swedes, incited by a severe domestic economic crisis and sweeping political changes throughout Europe, dominated public debates in Sweden, the term *folkhem* proved a highly emotional metaphor for Swedish society and the way of life incarnated by the Swedish welfare model. Important spatio-temporal dimensions of this metaphor became prominent during these debates, some of which are also crucial to a discussion of Polish ghost workers. Expressions such as the '*folkhem* is being dismantled' (*folkhemmet demonteras*) and the '*folkhem* is being torn down' (*folkhemmet rivs*) prophesied the decline of the safe and secure home and, at the same time, articulated sentiment regarding the golden era of the *folkhem*. This pessimism demonstrated the crisis of Nordic identity that followed after the end of the Cold War and gave rise to 'Nordic nostalgia' (see Wæver 1992). During the 1991 election campaign, a slogan stated: 'Per Albin built the *folkhem*. Ingvar Kamprad furnished it. Ingvar Carlsson turned off the lights' (Stålhammar 1997: 93–4).[6] As Mall Stålhammar observes in her study of the *folkhem* as a metaphor, this political slogan, alongside typical leftist rhetoric, imagines the initial, successful period of the *folkhem* by means of the metaphor of building (rather than simply founding), with an implicit reference to physical labour.

In the Swedish psychological drama *Four Weeks in June* by Henry Meyer, released in 2005, *folkhem* materialises as a multi-unit building that could have been built within the so-called Million Programme (*Miljonprogrammet*) – a large-scale public dwelling project implemented in Sweden in the 1960s and 1970s to reduce the housing shortage. The programme was seen as an embodiment of social-democratic ideas of equality and a good life for everyone. However, the house in Meyer's film denies any idea of success: the building is a flimsy construction that is falling apart and is located in peripheral, unsightly areas evoking the suburban aesthetics of Moodysson's *Lilya 4-ever* – a resemblance that, as we shall see, is more than coincidental. Although the walls of the building are covered by scaffolding, it is uncertain whether it is being renovated or dismantled. Considering that a single elderly lady, Lily, seems to be its only inhabitant, it could be inferred that the house has been abandoned by everyone else. To stay there is a form of punishment – which, indeed, it is for the young depressed protagonist, Sandra, who moves into a derelict apartment in the building. Sandra is sentenced to four weeks' community service in a nearby used clothing centre after she attacks her ex-boyfriend with a knife. A crew of Polish construction workers are staying in a nearby house, and a romantic relationship develops between Marek (played by a Polish actor) and Sandra.

The house is the film's central setting. Within the context of the Swedish debates about the decline of the *folkhem*, this pitiable building could be said to visualise the laments about the 'people's home' being dismantled, the safe and secure home destroyed. Sandra is awoken early one morning

Figure 6.1 The run-down house in Meyer's film questions the social-democratic idea of 'the people's home'. *Four Weeks in June*, screen capture.

due to the noise from the renovation of the building and, leaning out of her window, she uses the expression *riva huset* ('tear the house down') when she exclaims first in Swedish and then in English: 'Are you going to break the house down totally, or what?' Slightly confused, Marek answers: 'Yes, I'm sorry . . .', following which he corrects himself: 'No, just a new wall'. Sandra repeats ironically: 'New wall. . .'. This short scene evokes both visually and verbally the metaphor of the *folkhem* being torn down; more-over, it potentially implies that the threat of the house being torn down is a result of the current political changes in Europe, here represented by the Polish worker. Additionally, the scene both verbalises and visualises 'the wall' – the inside/outside border of the house separating Sandra and Marek. But there is an important ambiguity here: if the Polish worker is said to 'tear the house down', the expression is also an overstatement and a joke; while from Sandra's perspective he 'breaks down' the house, his intention is to repair and renovate the building, the deterioration of which started long before his arrival. The building's walls are not solid: they are thin, the plaster is crumbling and the windows through which either the outside or the interiors are frequently focalised accentuate the appearance of the walls as a highly porous boundary, with the transparent scaffolding only emphasising this porosity. Thus, the wall is important, but rather as an obstruction that – in the post-Wall reality – should be removed.

Indeed, the anxiety present in public laments about the Swedish home collapsing and the nostalgia for the golden days of the *folkhem* are not shared by the film's narrative. The film seems to suggest that the home is about to collapse, but that, as such, it should be demolished without unnecessary sentiment, so as to make way for the creation of a new imaginary space for the community to thrive. The house, in fact, seems unrepairable – over the course of a whole month, the work never appears to make any progress. Marek's role is not to make the house 'very, very beautiful' (as his colleague assures Sandra), rather, it is to compel its lethargic inhabitants to understand that the house must be left behind and thus implicitly, the home metaphor abandoned. It is worth noticing that in the scene mentioned above, Sandra wants to sleep, while Marek wakes her up – both literally and as an apathetic inhabitant of the run-down *folkhem*. It is meaningful that Lily exclaims to Sandra (when she plays loud music): 'We want to sleep in this house!' Both Sandra and Lily seem to be 'asleep', imprisoned in their memories of a (past) home: Sandra comes from a broken family and was raised in a foster home; Lily lives immersed in her memories of a past lover, the father of her daughter. She does not want to move out of the house because she is clinging to her past, symbolised by her apartment overflowing with objects she has collected over the course of her life. Thus, the house functions in Meyer's film as a metaphor for imprisonment, but also as a metaphor for the idealisation of the past, recalling the nostalgic discourses of the *folkhem*.

However, the ideal *folkhem* is represented in the film only by its non-existence. Both Sandra and Lily can be seen as the *folkhem*'s ghostly others.[7] Their ghostliness is marked by their isolation from any larger community: Sandra is an outlaw and a prisoner, and – as if to undermine Hansson's words – a stepchild (Hansson 1982: 227); Lily is a German Jew who escaped to Sweden during WWII, which makes her partly an outsider (epitomised by the 'foreign' accent with which the Danish actress Ghita Nørby speaks Swedish). Both of them are, in their own way, homeless in their home country (Van Heuckelom 2014: 87). Interestingly, Sandra's life resembles that of Lilya in *Lilya 4-ever*: abandoned by her family and severely depressed, she also attempts to commit suicide. Other resemblances to Moodysson's Lilya include Sandra's appearance and a scene in which she is raped. These reminiscences are important because they show that 'Lilyas' can also be found within the *folkhem*. Moreover, the resemblance between Swedish Sandra and Eastern European Lilya invites viewers to consider the women as equals, which corresponds with the film's depiction of Sandra and Marek as socially and economically equal individuals. Sandra's and Lily's ghostliness is, moreover, signified by the run-down multi-unit public dwelling, connoting a lower social status. Rather than being 'a cross section of society, across generational and social divides' (Van Heuckelom 2014: 75), the house visualises the less optimistic, spectralising side of the welfare state, producing ghostly subjects within its own structures. It is worth noticing that the house is in poor condition, not only on the outside, but on the inside as well (Ibid. 77).

Whereas the past, embodied by the house, haunts both Lily and Sandra in ways that distract them from their current reality, the living ghost whom Marek initially embodies helps them, in the end, to leave the house. Marek's ghostly status results, above all, from the fact that he works in dangerous conditions on a construction site without a work permit. Marek's social marginality is emphasised through visual associations with the scaffolding – the literal margin of the house. His vulnerable position is made clear when Swedish trade unionists visit the construction site and claim work permits from the Poles. It is thus primarily the house – and Marek's relation to it – that defines and fixes Marek's identity as a 'construction worker' and a ghostly subject. The house seems to imprison each of the three protagonists by fixing their identities in non-changeable positions.

Moreover, Marek's marginal position is emphasised by the caravan where he lives. The caravan signifies not only Marek's social vulnerability and nomadic existence, but also independence and agency. Most importantly, Marek gains agency by making himself visible to Sandra, who initially overlooks him. Later, Marek's position transforms from that of a haunting (in Sandra's view) and marginalised ghost – a 'Polish worker' – to a host. He invites Sandra to his caravan, thus becoming the first character to assume the role of host, offering dinner, hospitality, love and security, and thereby making his agency evident. The ambiguity of Marek's spectral agency is illustrated in a telling scene when, while waiting for Sandra to bring him a tool he dropped, he walks off the scaffolding and into her room, accidentally getting wrapped up in a curtain. When she returns, Marek pretends to be a ghost. Sandra is scared and becomes unreasonably angry, throwing him out of her room as a result. Her over-reaction both reflects and ridicules the fear of the spectre of the 'Polish worker', exemplified by Swedish trade unionists who expel Marek from Sweden. But this fear – and the apparent need to exorcise the ghost – only confirms the power of the 'Polish worker'. Sandra apologises; Marek is no longer the target of her exorcisms. She finally recognises him as being more than the fixed identity imposed on him by economic and political structures, embodied by the house.

In the end, all three characters leave the run-down building. In the final scene, Lily is seen at a cemetery in conversation with her daughter, telling her the truth about her father, and thereby liberating herself from the imprisoning past symbolised by the house. Sandra chases Marek to the ferry after the Polish construction crew escapes from the police. The two protagonists swap roles at the film's end: now it is Sandra who is situated 'outside' and is forced to cross a forbidden border in order to reach Marek. In the harbour, she climbs a barbed wire fence and jumps onboard without a ticket. The lovers reunite on the ferry, framed by the sea in the background.

Hence, even though Marek initially represents a 'Polish worker', who is supposed to fulfill the Swedes' nostalgic hope for restoration of the old house, the building metaphor, used in relation to the founding of the *folkhem*, does not hold as the plot develops. Marek is not a nostalgic embodiment of an unspoiled other who can help recover lost values. At the end of the film, he sheds his identity as a ghost worker, while the irreparability of the house implies that there is no return to the golden era of the *folkhem* – perhaps this era never really existed.

Meyer's film, as Van Heuckelom rightly notes, expresses an integrationist fantasy (2014: 89). However, it is crucial that Marek's role is not reduced to 'making' his way 'into the house' (Ibid. 76). Rather, his spectral agency results in making the inhabitants of the house change their perspective –

both in relation to themselves and to the newcomers. The new insight the film provides lies not simply in changing the focus from the 'strangers' to the 'dysfunctional locals' (Ibid. 90), which has, after all, become a quite common trope, but in questioning and reimagining the house metaphor with its implicit hierarchical divisions into locals/newcomers, guests/hosts, ghost/host and inside/outside.

The run-down and imprisoning house is, in the end, replaced by the open space of the ferry, providing a sharp contrast to the confined and claustrophobic domestic spaces dominating the film's *mise-en-scène*. The ferry functions as a liberating space within which people can unite across borders – and which is able to move freely on wide transnational waters, unlike the house, which stands still, 'rooted' in the land. Thus, the final scenes of the film function to suggest that it is time to replace the home metaphor with new spatial imagery more in tune with the present moment, connoting connection and mobility rather than stagnation and isolation. This new spatial metaphor promises a transnational opening into the future, instead of a clinging to the national past – and to an old national discourse.

Choosing Thin Walls: An-other Norwegian House

'Polish ghosts' also haunt other parts of Scandinavia – most prominently, Norway, where they are the largest minority group. In relation to Norway, however, we should speak of the house, rather than home, metaphor. In 1996, the Norwegian social democratic Prime Minister Thorbjørn Jagland (in)famously coined the broadly criticised metaphor of 'the Norwegian house', which was supposed to refresh the 'social democratic notion of the integrated Norwegian nation-state' (Gullestad 2006: 95). According to Marianne Gullestad, Jagland's metaphor of the house, rather than the home, is indicative of the contemporary stress on borders (or walls) between the inside and the outside in the Scandinavian home discourse (Ibid. 121). Jagland's metaphor of the Norwegian house stresses stability and walls to a higher degree than the Swedish *folkhem*, which 'points rather to moral and emotional phenomena'. The Norwegian house metaphor emphasises, in turn, 'solid material aspects while assuming the relational aspects of kinship and marriage'; the solid house construction 'promises safety and stability [. . .] in a changing world, [. . .] and the establishment of national unity and firm boundaries against the transnational flows of capital, people, images, ideas and pollution' (Ibid. 96). Indeed, Jagland's metaphor may be seen as stressing an ethnically Norwegian frame of reference.

Unlike in Sweden, a large-scale public housing sector was never established in Norway. An ideal Norwegian house is associated with a privately
owned single-family detached house (Ibid. 104–6). In the psychological
drama *Upperdog* (mentioned briefly in Chapter 4), such a type of dwelling is embodied by a *nouveau riche* house in Oslo, inhabited by a family
consisting of Norwegian parents and their adult adopted son of Asian
origins, Axel. His mother employs a maid, a young Polish woman named
Maria, whose job is to clean the house, help prepare food, serve guests and
walk their well-groomed miniature poodle – an emblem of the Norwegian
woman's upper-class ambitions.

Axel's mother embodies a self-enclosed Norwegianness. This is epitomised in a scene when, during a birthday party, she begins singing the
Norwegian 'Happy Birthday' song. Everyone sings, and the ritual aspect
of this unifying act of 'banal nationalism' (Billig 1995) is emphasised by
the circle formed by the guests. The Polish Maria, who does not speak
Norwegian, remains clearly outside the circle, slightly removed, beyond
the threshold of the living room door. The fact that the family employs a
domestic servant is criticised within the film narrative – most importantly,
by Maria, who utters critical remarks about Axel's mother's treatment
of her, but also because the Norwegian woman is presented as lazy (she
refuses to vacuum the house after Maria finds another job) and phony:
she rents out high-priced apartments in a flimsily constructed multi-unit
building, while she lives in a solid thick-walled detached house with a
garden in a wealthy Oslo neighbourhood. One of her tenants is Maria,
who pays a ridiculously high price for a flat with walls so thin that she can
hear her 'neighbours brush their teeth'. The Norwegian woman's hypoc-
risy is also emphasised by the fact that being a (self-perceived) 'perfect'
housewife, she (over)uses cheap labour, and thus creates a construct of
'perfection' that relies upon the help received from other people in far less
privileged situations.

These interdependencies remain unrecognised by Axel's mother and
can be perceived as a suppressed, unconscious layer of the Norwegian
house, inherited by Axel. Initially, Axel embodies a quasi-upper-class
isolation from 'real life' and from the people around him, his attitudes
and behaviour being an exaggerated extension of his adoptive mother's
negative traits, including rudeness, egoism, self-complacency, materialism
and a contempt for other people, especially those who are less privileged.
These resemblances between Axel and his adoptive Norwegian mother
(unlike and regardless of their lack of physical resemblance) convey the
film's implicit view on culture and nation as communities created discursively and imaginatively, rather than inherited 'by blood'. The 'Norwegian

house' – whether understood as a self-enclosed, thick-walled detached building or a more open structure – can thus be inhabited and shared by people who are not ethnically Norwegian. At the beginning of the film, Axel does not reflect upon his origins, fully identifying with the thick-walled, self-complacent version of Norwegianness embodied in his mother. Axel's attitude is illustrated by his attempts to humiliate Maria, such as calling her 'maid' and constantly telling her to get back to work. Maria does not allow herself to be treated as an inferior. She bites back with sharp retorts, like: 'So you think that sitting at home, at your parents' home, is better than doing manual labour?' But unlike his mother, Axel grows throughout the plot and develops a new perspective, in the end moving out of his parents' house into Maria's thin-walled apartment.

The relationship that forms between these two characters is central to the development of the plot – and indicative of Maria's agency. In a similar fashion to Marek in *Four Weeks in June*, Maria functions as a living ghost who acts as a 'catalyst hero'; according to Christopher Vogler's definition, catalyst heroes 'bring about a change in a system without being changed themselves' (2007: 37). It is crucial that Maria provokes change not only in Axel, but within the overall 'system' – the Norwegian house. Most importantly, Maria discovers that Yanna, who she works alongside in an Asian restaurant, is Axel's older half-sibling. Axel was unaware of his sister's existence, as it had been kept secret by his adoptive parents. Maria arranges the siblings' first meeting, which results in the two adoptive families' reunion in the final scene of the film. Maria's power as a catalyst hero rests upon bringing these two families together, awakening Axel's awareness of his origins, and making the transnational connections of Axel's 'house' visible, which contributes to an overall rearrangement of the Norwegian house. Having learned the truth about his birth mother, who lived in harsh conditions and died as a young woman, Axel gradually changes as a person. Enraged by his adoptive parents' lies, he moves out, throwing the keys to the house on his adoptive mother's well-groomed lawn in a dramatic gesture. The final shot in the film shows a picture of Axel and Yanna's dead mother, looking back at the viewers from an old passport photograph – a ghost whose agency is exerted through her children. The ghosts 'haunting' the Norwegian house, both past and present, embodied by Maria, Yanna and the photograph of Axel's and Yanna's birth mother, are recognised by Axel as independent subjects with agency.

Like *Four Weeks in June*, *Upperdog* suggests that the Norwegian house metaphor should be revisited: the thick-walled detached family house is in the end replaced by a multi-unit building with walls so thin that it is impossible to live in isolation and forget about one's neighbours' existence. Walls are also emphasised in a scene in which the camera, employing a bird's-eye view, crosses smoothly between two spaces without a cut, making visible the internal structure of the wall. Due to its thinness, the wall connects rather than divides. This connection is stressed by familial and friendship relations linking the two transnational couples – Yanna and the Norwegian soldier Per, Maria and Axel – living next to each other. The inhabitants of the multi-unit house are also diverse socially, including both the new 'working class' comprised of immigrants (Maria and Yanna) and the Norwegian 'upper class' (Axel and Per). The structure of this alternative, 'other' Norwegian house challenges the divisions imposed by economic inequalities.

Finally, it should be mentioned that the living ghosts in *Upperdog* (Maria, Yanna, as well as the two Afghan children whose father is killed by Per in Afghanistan) embody various homes – all less safe and less privileged than the Norwegian house. Maria's case incarnates the broader context of the large Polish minority in Norway. She has a son, whom she has left with her parents in Poland. This arrangement evokes the phenomenon of so-called 'Euro-orphans' – that is, children left behind by parents forced to work in Western Europe to earn a living and thus support their families. A Norwegian documentary is worth mentioning here: *I am Kuba* (the title referring ironically to the Soviet film by Mikhail Kalatozov from 1964), about a Polish family who falls apart due to the parents' need to work abroad. The documentary follows the everyday lives and emotional struggles of two brothers, aged twelve and eight, left alone in a provincial Polish town. Although the problem of Euro-orphans is only signalled in *Upperdog*, parentless children (Yanna, Axel and Maria's son left in Poland) are an important concern in the film. However, against the colonial trope of representing Western countries' non-Western 'others' as innocent, infantile and victimised children, *Upperdog* depicts adult Norwegians as immature. Initially, both Axel and Per are childish and refuse to take responsibility – until they transform by way of Maria's (and Yanna's) spectral agency, and become adult enough to leave their parents' 'Norwegian house'.

Opening Doors for Polish 'Workers'

As demonstrated thus far, both *Four Weeks in June* and *Upperdog* are highly critical of the ways the home/house metaphor came to shape the reality of Scandinavian societies, the ideals of equality and solidarity having been forgotten long ago, and the spatial organisation of the house incompatible with the globalised reality of today. Both films revisit and reconstruct this metaphor with the help of Polish 'ghost workers', opening up the potential for a new kind of future transnational connections. The recent Norwegian television drama *Struggle for Life* expresses a more pessimistic view on the capacity of its Norwegian characters to reimagine the house metaphor, to which they seem desperately attached. Nevertheless, the series encourages viewers to revisit the premises of their own 'Norwegian houses'.

The series consists of two seasons, each with eight episodes. The Polish protagonist, Tomasz (played by a Polish-Norwegian actor), is a twenty-eight-year-old passionate linguist and a good-hearted, slightly absent-minded academic. He leaves Warsaw for Norway, encouraged by his money-oriented girlfriend. The woman (pregnant, though not by Tomasz – a fact of which he is initially unaware), knowing that Tomasz has an unknown Norwegian father, believes that he should find his father and demand 'alimony' for all the 'lost' years. She arranges for Tomasz to be driven to Norway with a group of Polish construction workers. Reluctantly, Tomasz agrees. In this way, he is suddenly placed in the midst of a 'typical' (and stereotypical) group of Polish workers going abroad to seek work. Even though he leaves them upon their arrival in Norway, in Oslo he cannot avoid getting stuck with yet another group of Polish workers. Apparently, his nationality makes him destined to be seen as a 'Polish worker' by both Norwegians and Poles.

The series consists of several plotlines. Viewers follow not only Tomasz and his Polish comrades, but also several Norwegian families, who live in detached family houses in Ullevål Hageby, one of the wealthiest residential areas in Oslo. The juxtaposition of the Polish migrants with the Norwegian families situates Norwegian society, represented by the upper-middle class, in a transnational perspective, ridiculing the problems faced – or rather created – by the Norwegian characters. An important stylistic and narrative feature of the series is the combination of a realistic plot with the grotesque, irony, black humour and non-realistic elements (such as a character who has turned into a ghost). As one reviewer admitted, the series is 'not easy to categorise: It is absurd, stylised, cunning, dark and funny. It cultivates stereotypes, but also surprises. And it is mild, but shocking' (Lavik 2015: 74). The series oscillates between 'subtle satire through magic realism to burlesque; at the same time, there is often something indeterminable and understated in the scenes. It seems both usual and supernatural, recognisable and strange' (Ibid. 60). *Struggle for Life* plays extensively with stereotypes about Poles (and other foreigners) and seems unconstrained by any form of political correctness. In contrast to the two films discussed earlier, the Polish characters are not flawless (for example, Bartosz is racist, Serafin homophobic, and Tomasz is clumsy and feels intellectually superior to Norwegians). This strategy de-kitschifies them, while at the same time exposes Norwegians' stereotypical thinking about others.

A recurring trope throughout the series is that of a Pole knocking on the door of a Norwegian house and being denied entry because the Norwegians automatically assume them to be a worker. An illuminating example here is a scene when Tomasz knocks on the door of the house of an older Norwegian couple, suspecting that Mr Kiran might be his father. When Mrs Kiran opens the door, Tomasz starts the conversation in English, but the woman interrupts, immediately assuming that he is a jobseeker: 'I'm sorry, we don't need anything. Are you hungry?' In the background, her husband says in Norwegian: 'A Pole? Give him a banana'. Mrs Kiran gives Tomasz an overripe banana, and when he hesitates (he is not hungry and definitely does not feel like eating the banana), she peels the fruit, inferring that he does not know how to eat it. This scene mocks the Norwegians' presuppositions about Poles: Tomasz is here treated almost like a beggar; a man knocking on the door and not speaking Norwegian must be a Pole, and a Pole is equal to a job-seeking manual worker. These presuppositions automatically make Tomasz voiceless, which is ridiculously visualised by the banana filling his mouth. Tomasz is not allowed to express a single word, let alone the intention behind his visit. At the same time, this scene returns the 'boomerang' of the stereotype to the Norwegians – in the end, it is they who are ridiculed.[8]

The door, opened reluctantly to Poles, functions as a protective and exclusionary barrier, while the walls materialise 'firm boundaries against the transnational flows of capital, people, images, ideas and pollution' (Gullestad 2006: 96). The series suggests that the most important factor determining whether one is excluded or included in the 'house' is class belonging, here shown as strongly dependent on one's ethnicity and nationality. This is depicted through a romance between the Norwegian Mina and the Polish labour migrant Serafin. Even though the ambitious and good-hearted Mina is successful in her career, she is perceived as 'other' in Ullevål Hageby because she is a dwarf. Due to this, Mina has high social aspirations. Although she is happy with Serafin, she breaks up with him. Serafin asks her directly: 'Is it a question of class?', which Mina leaves unanswered. Mina prefers to be unhappy than to unavoid-ably sentence herself to a double exclusion – as a dwarf and because of her relationship with a Polish worker. Ballesteros observes that in films about migrants, the excluded and marginalised frequently join forces against the oppressive processes in the society (2015: 40). But, for Mina, joining forces with a marginalised group would mean admitting to her position as marginalised. Only a relationship with a 'normal' Norwegian man can secure Mina's status in society. Even though she is aware of these social correlations, she cannot help surrendering to them. Whereas the impossible inter-ethnic relationship is a common trope in Nordic films about Muslim migrants, the obstacle is typically that of tradition and religion (Jørholt 2007: 24–5). In representations of Polish migrants, their nationality – which determines that they belong to a lower class – seems the main hindrance in climbing the social ladder.

The capacity of the series to revisit the Norwegian house metaphor does not lie in the 'locals' growing and changing their attitudes, positively influenced by the newcomers, as in *Upperdog* or *Four Weeks in June*. Rather, it results from the ironic distance and, at times, cruel sarcasm towards its characters, by means of which the series encourages its viewers – though not the characters – to reimagine the fixed positions and identities imposed by the solid structure of the house.

An important potential for reimagining the rigidly assigned positions lies in the specificity of television as a medium. The numerous scenes when the 'others' approach or enter the Norwegian houses in friendly and peaceful ways can be seen as a parallel to the viewer watching the series on a television (or computer) screen. Through the screen, the Polish migrants 'enter' the private spaces of the Norwegian houses, thus producing what Craig Hight calls 'televisual space', which results from the encounter between the space of reception and the space of the screen. Hight emphasises 'the cultural implications of linking sites of broadcast transmissions and individual sites of reception' (2010: 74). Television viewers 'are typically addressed as members of an assumed national unity, geographically isolated in households but linked discursively' (Ibid. 88). Within this televisual space, the home space 'becomes permeable to the public world [. . .] in ways which effect a radical change in both' (Corner in Hight 2010: 88).

The Norwegian house metaphor is a crucial concept for addressing the Norwegian audience discursively and imaginatively. This audience is embodied by the Norwegian characters portrayed on the screen. Their strong visual and narrative connection to domestic spaces, which marks their social belonging and works as a social border between the inside and the outside, remains in stark opposition to the Poles, depicted as outsiders and associated with public or half-private spaces, such as doorsteps, streets, an airport, a university canteen, a cellar within which Polish labour migrants have to sleep out of necessity, or a tent in a forest where Tomasz is forced to live temporarily, despite the winter cold. Both spatially and socially, the Poles function as living ghosts. But if the Norwegian charac-

Figure 6.2 The Polish living ghost, Tomasz. *Struggle for Life*. Photograph by Helene Amlie/NRK. Courtesy of NRK.

ters lack openness and exorcise the 'strangers' from their doorsteps, the televisual space forces the viewers to open their 'doors' – or, rather, their screens – to the Polish newcomers. The series becomes a space of encounter between the local and the global, which is particularly important in view of the fact that in the NRK (Norwegian Broadcasting Corporation) 'in-house drama production [. . .] migration and the multicultural society have until recently not been particularly prominent' (Larsen 2015: 188). Ullevål Hageby is depicted as enclosed, as well as ethnically and socially homogeneous; so much so that it seems more like a village than a posh neighbourhood in Oslo (the viewers are, indeed, seldom reminded that the action takes place in Oslo). The film places this tiny local space (Ullevål Hageby/the domestic space of the viewer) within a transnational frame, forcing viewers to position themselves in relation to the changing neighbourhood.

Hence, the ghostly potential of the Polish characters functions here to criticise the local community that imagines itself as 'un-mixed', pure, self-sufficient and autonomous. Indeed, even when kept on doorsteps, Poles challenge the self-sufficiency of the inhabitants of Ullevål Hageby, whose members eagerly employ Poles to do various jobs, some of which are quite ridiculous, such as moving a hedge by 60 cm in order to have a better view from the kitchen.

However, while having the potential to open Norwegian houses to Polish newcomers within the televisual space (because television is physically in one's house), the television can also be seen as a spectralising medium: first, because it turns the Polish newcomers into '"mere silhouettes" [. . .] empty, ghostly shells that can be manipulated like "marionettes"' (Derrida

1994: 80); second, because television can easily be switched off if what one sees becomes threatening or unpleasant, and can thus be exorcised. This is what Norwegian audiences largely seem to have done – they have 'closed' their screens to the Polish guests/ghosts. Although Norwegian critics were highly positive about the series, *Struggle for Life* proved too ambitious in terms of style and genre-hybridity, as well as being too critical of Norwegian society – too dark and dangerous – to attract a broad domestic audience.[9]

Therefore, perhaps it is worth taking a look at the darker layers of that particular society, invoked in the series by the Polish ghosts and exorcised by Norwegian audiences. Whereas culturally specific elements conjured in *Struggle for Life* appeal to an imagined (national) community, black humour, the grotesque and the uncanny open this community up to unexpected, provocative and sometimes shocking perspectives on its own house. Many such satirical effects in the series take their cue from discourses related to the social-democratic house metaphor – among them, the ideal of egalitarianism. Equal treatment is not the prevailing attitude among the Norwegian characters. Although Poles assure their agency within the limits possible, this agency is radically circumscribed by the Norwegians. For instance, Tomasz, who quickly becomes fluent in Norwegian, has numerous unskilled jobs; however, he dreams about gaining a position at a university. The fact that Tomasz learns Norwegian challenges the depreciative depictions of migrants as linguistically incompetent and voiceless (see Ballesteros 2015: 41). Similarly, he also proves his agency in refusing to accept money from his newly found father. But he is not treated as an equal. At one point, he wins a difficult linguistic competition held at the university. Professors and students gather to congratulate him. A professor, earlier challenged by Tomasz in a discussion concerning linguistics, comments: 'Just think that we should have such competent cleaning personnel'. After someone suggests that a university position could be made available for Tomasz, he scathingly retorts that 'the corridor has not been painted for ten years, and the toilets are even worse'. The identity of the 'Polish worker' is again imposed on Tomasz, in this case with calculated cruelty.

Another discursive layer evoked in the series relates to the idea of Norwegian society as non-violent, challenging yet another taken-for-granted aspect of the Norwegian house: 'a kind of home where you can dwell safely and securely' (Gullestad 2006: 95). The series suggests that an invisible violence haunts Norwegian society. Most forcefully, it is illustrated by the killing of the well-integrated, Norwegian-speaking Pakistani immigrant Mustafa. During a hunting trip with a group of his

Norwegian colleagues, the somewhat macho Mustafa gets tipsy and challenges Norwegian masculinity in various ways – for example, by accusing
Norwegian men of being passive and feminine. Later, Mustafa has sex
with one of the Norwegian men, who initiates the encounter. The next day,
he is 'accidentally' shot during the hunt. The murderer is never identified;
thus, through collective force, Mustafa undergoes a symbolic (and literal)
expulsion. Interestingly, the motivation here is revenge, normally ascribed
to ethnic 'others', which contrasts with the widely professed Nordic
ability to control strong emotions and inner daemons (Necef and Bech
2014: 263–4). Even though Mustafa appears over-reactive by nature (for
instance, he physically disciplines his child and offends Norwegians verbally), the violence of the Norwegians is much more brutal and calculated.
Compared to the Norwegian characters, both Mustafa and the Polish men
are non-violent and peaceful. Violence, frequently ethnicised and depicted
as a distant feature of a 'different culture' (Mulari 2013: loc. 4040; see
Necef 2003: 177–9), is here transferred onto the Norwegians themselves.

The strategy of switching the fixed and seemingly evident self/other
positions is taken a step further by depicting Norwegians in positions
similar to those of the Polish ghostly others. A powerful example is
Karianne, who becomes a literal ghost after she freezes to death locked in
her brand-new Porsche Cayenne, thus 'incorporating' the non-corporeal
spectralising force of money (see Derrida 1994: 45ff.). Throughout her
life, Karianne embodied extreme materialism and egoism – a caricatured
version of Nordic privilege, which in her case does not prompt even the
slightest feeling of guilt. After death, she is sent to purgatory, where she
learns that her unforgiveable sin was her selfishness. Quite tellingly, in an
earlier episode, Karianne's daughter reads out an epistle from Paul the
Apostle, in which it says that 'those who only want to enjoy life are dead
alive'. In opposition to Polish living ghosts, Karianne is alienated from 'real
life' due to her wealth and privilege and the resulting lack of empathy – she
is 'dead alive'. Karianne's position is turned upside down after her death.
From an agent of selfishness and sickly consumerism, she transforms into
an unwanted ghost deprived of all possessions and family relations. In the
last episode, she returns from purgatory to the living after having passed
the 'empathy, trust, love' test. She knocks on the door of her house, inside
which her husband-widower Hugo now lives in a peaceful and loving
relationship with Mina and his and Karianne's children. Nobody seems
to miss Karianne. Not wanting to interrupt an idyllic moment, Hugo and
Mina do not open the door. The last shot of Karianne shows her sitting
outside, on the doorstep of her own, and yet no longer her own, house,
alone – unmistakably similar to the Polish living ghosts.

Figure 6.3 The Norwegian Karianne as a ghost. *Struggle for Life*. Photograph by Irene Rossland/NRK. Courtesy of NRK.

The uncanny and/or non-realistic elements in the series, such as Karianne-the-ghost or the killing of Mustafa, encode a ghostliness which – through its deformation of the real and rational – serves to undermine the apparently well-functioning Norwegian house. This ghostliness can be related to the Freudian notion of *unheimlich*, most importantly because it encapsulates 'the hidden desires and dangers associated with possessing or belonging to a house' (Peeren 2014: 89). Paraphrasing the observation that the concept of the uncanny 'finds its roots in "bourgeois anxiety about servants"' (Brian McCuskey in Peeren 2014: 89), we may say that *Struggle for Life* exposes the global Nordic upper-class anxiety about 'globalised servants' and a desire to keep them in their place. But as Peeren emphasises, the uncanny remains a figure defined from the perspective of the master of the house, capturing the master's anxieties and not those of the ghost (Ibid. 90). Indeed, *Struggle for Life* encapsulates the master's perspective by means of a 'reactionary' element, materialised in the nostalgic prologue preceding each episode. These prologues consist of black-and-white early twentieth-century photographs depicting Norwegian peasants at work and drawings of Ullevål Hageby houses, built for the working class in 1915–22. Among the old photographs, one shows a modest kitchen interior – a crucial image in the context of the first scene in the series, depicting a perfectly decorated apartment with a modern 'Scandinavian design' kitchen in white. As a kind of ghostly space, the old kitchen reminds viewers of how the houses – and society, poor and hard-working – looked in the past. Through the spatio-temporal jump cut, the prologue illustrates how the idea of the Norwegian house has been deformed over the years. Unlike *Upperdog* or *Four Weeks in June*, which both suggest that the house has never been perfect or homogeneous, *Struggle for Life* idealises the house of the past. The past home represents forgotten values and ideals, haunting the Ullevål Hageby of today.

The function of the Polish migrants in *Struggle for Life* is thus ambiguous: they serve to remind Norwegians of the forgotten values of their past society, but this nostalgia is combined with humour and ironic play with stereotypes. On the other hand, the resemblance between the Polish newcomers and the ghostly Norwegian ancestors can be seen as something that connects Norwegians and Poles: a shared past. This connection is embodied by the hard-working and ambitious Tomasz, who also has a Norwegian father. Most importantly, however, Tomasz embodies a future dimension of the Norwegian house, as he becomes a father to a Norwegian-Polish child. Nevertheless, his belonging to the present moment and to the future is not fully possible in the depicted social realm.

Indeed, in the end, the series suggests that the master's perspective remains uncontested. The final scene uses black humour to once again ridicule the stereotype of the Polish worker, while reminding viewers about the spectralising force of this stereotype. When repairing a window frame in the modest loft apartment where he lives with his Norwegian girl-friend, Tomasz – an excellent linguist, but not a very skilled construction worker – falls. This tragicomic moment is surprising, but also borders on the uncanny. The camera stands still in the empty apartment, remaining unsettlingly indifferent. It then begins tracking slowly from the inside towards a bird's-eye view of Ullevål Hageby. The movement of the camera and the controlling gaze over the area together evoke an invisible spectral power: it feels as if Tomasz did not just lose his balance in a moment of distraction, but was pushed out of the house by this invisible surveying force. In this final scene, the globalised servant/ghost/guest is exorcised by the master's/host's gaze. The perspective of the ghost is displaced by the gaze of the haunted host. Apparently, being neither a proper Polish worker nor a full-blooded Norwegian, Tomasz is not welcome inside the Norwegian house.

Conclusion: The Nordic Home Reimagined?

Enthusiastic cinematic expressions encouraging viewers to reimagine the Nordic metaphor of the home and the social reality it denotes, which followed the growing integration of Europe, seem in retreat today, as *Struggle for Life* demonstrates. The films and the television series analysed in this chapter scrutinise the spectralising forces present in the privileged strata of Nordic societies through transnational encounters with newcomers from less privileged regions of the world – primarily Poles – and by incorporating their perspective. The Nordic self can thus see itself through the eyes of the other – though we should not forget that in the case of Nordic productions, the 'others" perspective is still a Nordic projection. Whereas the films diagnose the change in the Nordic societies' ethnic, cultural and social structures, and the inability of old political metaphors to reflect this change, they also indicate the unwillingness to 'leave' the home – and especially the house – behind, and the reluctance to look at oneself with the other's eyes. Thus, the home/house becomes reimagined in the films, shifting from the metaphor of equality to the metaphor of exclusion and division. If some alternative spatial units are suggested (a ferry, a multi-unit dwelling), *Struggle for Life* drastically suppresses this optimism. This sounds, indeed, like a discouraging conclusion for the last chapter of this book. However, it should be emphasised that these limitations are located not in the other, but in the self. The Polish characters, although functioning as 'ghost workers', are able, at least to a certain degree, to surpass the function imposed on them by the spectralising economic and societal forces and to assume powerful and independent roles as full subjects beyond that of 'globalised servants'. In this way, their 'spectral agency' helps reimagine the 'Polish worker', even if he is eventually pushed out of the house.

Notes

1. Norway: http://www.ssb.no/befolkning/statistikker/innvbef (accessed 5 June 2016); Denmark: http://www.statistikbanken.dk/statbank5a/SelectOut/ PxSort.asp?file=20161124113258181336363FOLK1C&PLanguage=0&Ma inTable=FOLK1C&MainTablePrestext=Folketal%20den%201.%20i%20 kvartalet&potsize=238 (accessed 24 November 2016); Sweden: https:// en.wikipedia.org/wiki/Immigration_to_Sweden#Country_of_origin_for_ persons_born_abroad (accessed 14 January 2017). In Finland, the biggest migration groups are Estonians and Russians (see Bartram 2007).
2. One of the most recent examples is *Strawberry Days* (*Jordgubbslandet*, Wiktor Ericsson, Sweden, Poland 2017), which tells the story of Wojtek, a young Polish 'guest worker', who gets a job picking strawberries in Sweden and falls in love with a Swedish girl – the daughter of the farmer who employs the Poles.
3. Hedling observes that this discourse gained prominence after 1963, when Swedish cinema became dependent on official funding. According to Rochelle Wright, before the 1960s, Swedish representations of ethnic otherness were dominated by negative stereotypes (Hedling 2007: 40–1; Wright 1998).
4. The term 'spectral turn' was first used in 2002 by Roger Luckhurst (see Peeren 2014: 10).
5. 'Guest worker' is a historical term, defining migrant labourers invited by

Western governments between the 1950s and 1970s (see Bakøy 2011: 171; Ballesteros 2015: 33).

6. Per Albin Hansson was the social democratic prime minister (1932–6, 1936–46) associated with the beginnings of the Swedish welfare state. Ingvar Kamprad founded IKEA (1946), which encapsulated the ideals of equality in the Swedish 'home'. Ingvar Carlsson was the social democratic prime minister (1986–90, 1994–5) associated with the economic crisis in the early 1990s. He is known for leading Sweden into the EU in 1995.

7. Importantly, neither Lily's nor Sandra's apartment is furnished with IKEA products, associated with the successful period of the *folkhem*. Lily's interior originates from the pre-IKEA period, while Sandra's resembles an abandoned squat.

8. The trope of Poles knocking on the doors of Scandinavian houses brings to mind *300 Miles to Heaven*, in which the two Polish boys walk around in Copenhagen and knock on doors, asking for work.

9. On the day of the premiere, the audience totalled 509,000 viewers, which fell to 364,000 for episode two and to 255,000 for episode three (Lavik 2015: 74, 80).

AFTERWORD

Beyond Eastern Noir:
Toward a New (Cinematic) Space

In Antti-Jussi Annila's historical horror film, *Sauna* (Finland 2008), set at
the end of the sixteenth century on the border between Russia and Finland
(then Sweden), a professional Finnish soldier named Eerik and his younger
brother Knut participate in a border commission. This commission's task
is to establish a new border between the Russian and Swedish empires following the conclusion of a peace treaty after the Russo-Swedish War. Early
on in the film, Eerik brutally kills a man (who offered him hospitality) for
hiding Russian icons, after which the brothers lock the man's daughter in
a dark cellar, leaving her to die. This gruesome act haunts Knut for the
rest of their journey. The Russian–Swedish border commission arrives at
a marshy area in the woods, inhabited by mysterious people who fear a rec-
tangular concrete hut – resembling a hut in the style of modern construction, rather than being historically accurate – standing in the middle of a
swamp, which they call 'the sauna'. After a number of strange occurrences,
neither the Russians nor the Finns/Swedes want to include the marshy
area within their borders. Meanwhile, Knut becomes obsessed with the
sauna, and when he finally enters its pitch-black interior, the ghost of
the girl who was left in the cellar appears before him. After this, Knut
transforms into the 'agent' of the sauna, due to whom all the members of
the border commission eventually lose their lives, including Eerik, who in
his last moments confronts his darkest sins and fears inside the sauna. As a
result, the border agreement is never brought to fruition.

In the film, the sauna is a multi-layered symbolic space that performs
several plot-related functions. First, it refers, at least by name, to the traditional Finnish bathhouse and can thus be seen as an incarnation of Finnish
national space. At the same time, it is a space where the protagonists'
darkest feelings surface, especially guilt, while also serving as an imaginary
screen that reflects society, primarily by exposing 'the lives lost in the
construction of national community and the imposition of human-made
structures on the natural world' (Kääpä 2014: loc. 1656). The sauna also

impedes the final establishment of the border, thwarting human actions and plans. As a kind of vortex of the marshlands, it absorbs the humans and induces their dehumanisation. As such, the sauna incarnates nature as a force more powerful than humans and a boundary that effectively resists appropriative and inherently human bordering processes. In effect, the border cannot be delineated or solidified. Whereas in the first part of the film, the border (and the desire to establish it) is a catalyst for events, later the sauna assumes the function of propelling the plot forward.

Although the film is permeated by the gloomy atmosphere of Eastern noir, it resists enacting its dichotomous structure: it reimagines the Finnish national discourse encapsulated in the sauna and dismisses national, as well as other (natural/human), oppositions. Moreover, the film endows the boundary incarnated by the sauna – an uncertain, indefinable and transformative space – with agency, demonstrating its power and impact on the human realm (which here is equated with the 'hard' border). As such, *Sauna* is positioned at the opposite end of the spectrum in relation to the docudrama *1989*, discussed in the Introduction to this book, in which the agency lies with the man-made border (as opposed to a natural boundary). Finally, *Sauna* draws abundantly on the aesthetics of Andrei Tarkovsky's cinema, especially his existential science fiction films, such as *Solaris* (USSR 1972) and *Stalker* (USSR 1979). In this way, the film blurs distinctions between the Finnish and Russian domains, not only on the level of the narrative, but also on the level of representation, while combining genre cinema (horror) with art cinema. It thus refers to the realm of cultural discourses and cinematic imagination, rather than to the social reality proper.

The poignancy of *Sauna* lies in its questioning of the border utilising a boundary discourse that reimagines and ultimately deconstructs the border on several levels. A similar qualification applies to the films analysed throughout this book, offering a valuable testing ground for what has been defined as boundary discourses, implemented through a variety of strategies situated on a continuum between the binary border discourse of Eastern noir and the opposite end of the spectrum, where the neighbours are imagined beyond preconceptions structured by national, economic and social divisions. By focusing on the ways in which the geographical, political, economic, cultural and mental borders between the Nordic countries and their eastern neighbours have been reimagined as boundaries in the Nordic cinematic and televisual imagination during the last approximately thirty years, I have sought to expose the specificity and plurality of the discourses on Russia and Eastern Europe in Nordic cinemas. This plurality testifies against the pervading perceptions and narratives, which essentialise Russians and East Europeans as villains, victims and 'others'. However, as the analyses have shown, imagining and reimagining the neighbours beyond the dominant Eastern noir modality does not mean that the East/West, us/them dichotomy is easily or fully renounced – rather, it is closely scrutinised, modified and nuanced by Nordic directors, the stereotypes are 'declined' (to reinvoke Mireille Rosello's term) through a number of imaginative tactics rather than simply denied, which would unavoidably result in their repetition.

Disturbing easy dichotomies and exposing the difficulties involved in such projects is important, because it challenges the authority of the stereotype encapsulated in the Eastern noir narrative and recognises the Nordic/Eastern neighbourliness as a situation open to multiple forms of exchange. Over the past three decades, the Eastern noir narrative has been gradually complemented by other perspectives. Yet, rather than being abandoned, Eastern noir has been displaced from its hegemonic position, and now coexists with a multiplicity of other discourses. These discourses, challenging the dominant negative perceptions of Russia and Eastern Europe and, above all, emphasising Nordic/Eastern connections rather than divisions are typically, although not exclusively, implemented in films that do not fit within popular genres, such as documentaries, short and animation films, art cinema and, occasionally, high-end television series.

The boundary discourses entail a number of strategies that allow us to see *Norden*'s eastern neighbours, both in the present and in the past, otherwise. Some of these strategies have been carefully examined in the preceding chapters. They entail engaging individual perspectives and 'small narratives' on Russia and Eastern Europe, as well as attempts to come closer to the 'other' side, leaving presuppositions behind, while frequently expressing an awareness that abandoning one's own cultural screens is impossible. A noticeable strategy is the effort made to distinguish between Eastern European neighbours and Russians – groups typically conflated in popular crime genres. This detachment lies in depicting Eastern Europeans beyond the East/West cognitive frame as self-conscious, modern and independent countries, as opposed to Russia, which tends to be represented within the 'oriental despotism' and 'crime scene' modes. The image of Russians today differs from pre-WWII and late Cold War depictions of them as primitive, backward and faceless enemies, with Russia now represented as an ultra-modern, self-conscious nation-state (as in *Occupied*), though this hypermodernity is also shown as being employed for authoritarian purposes. Tropes originating from the Cold War, such as surveillance, Nordic submissiveness to Russia, and Russia as the great Other, continue to reverberate in recent depictions. At the same time, tropes that became

widespread after 1989, such as Russian gangsters, villains and mafia, continue to thrive. Nevertheless, in the less popular representations analysed
in this book, especially in the documentary films, Russia is approached in
a nuanced and individualised manner. The Eastern European countries,
in turn, are framed by discourses of modernity and progress, triggering
various degrees of connection to *Norden*. However, this concerns primarily Poland. Just a dozen or so years ago, before the accession of the
Baltic countries to the EU, these countries, unlike Poland, were depicted
as heavily victimised others – by both Russian and Nordic self-interested
subjects, and not only within the Eastern noir modality.

At the same time, a less clear line is being drawn between the Nordic
and Russian self, and especially between the Nordic and Eastern European
neighbours. The diminishing gap between 'us' and 'them' entails evoking
common historical pasts and connections, suppressed during the Cold
War and erased from both official and unofficial discourses, which also
entails imagining present and future connections. As this book has strived
to show, mutual connections are problematised not just thematically, but
frequently also on the level of representation, whether by activating cinematic references to Russian/Soviet cinema (as in Pirjo Honkasalo's, Knut
Erik Jensen's, Tómas Gislason's and Antti-Jussi Annila's films), by blurring distinctions at the aesthetic level (Lukas Moodysson, Ville Suhonen)
or cinematically reimagining the metaphor of the *folkhem*.

Many of the narratives representing strategies of boundary relate to the
historical past, taking their cues from the growing temporal distance to the
defining conflicts of the twentieth century, which once generally defined
Nordic/Eastern relationships. Again, their strategy can be neatly illustrated by *Sauna*. Although this film is set several centuries ago, by reimagining the border as preceded by a transnational realm (or in the context of
the Middle Ages, we should perhaps say trans-communal), the film invokes
present conceptualisations of borders and transnationalism. The fact that
the film is a historical fantasy – or imagined history (Hendrykowski 2000:
45) – is emphasised by its vague historical specificity. Both thematically
and aesthetically, *Sauna* makes us rethink the means available for engaging
one's own national, regional and transnational (hi)stories – whether recent
or past – rather than simply striving to depict the past. The same applies to
the films examined throughout this book; while they offer alternative perspectives and enter into polemical dialogues with the past, as well as with
historical discourses, they also reflectively comment on the present social
realm and contemporary discourses, reimagining the Nordic/Eastern
border/boundary both backward and forward.

What the films reimagine is not simply stereotypes and 'grand narratives' about Russians and East Europeans, but also the dominant Nordic (national) discourses and self-conceptions – both within and beyond the Eastern noir narrative. Although this narrative encapsulates an ahistorical and solidified image of Russia and Eastern Europe, its specific manifestations are embedded in their own historical moments, reflecting upon the Nordic societies in transition. This dual optics is inherent to the concept of border/boundary outlined in the Introduction. This leads us to the question raised in the Introduction: what is Nordic about the representations of Russia and Eastern Europe in Nordic cinemas? First of all, while this physically close but imaginatively distant space is being transformed from a single screen for negative projections into a plurality of nuanced and complex places and (hi)stories, the Nordic selves are also renegotiating their own histories and positions in the region, both in relation to Europe and the wider transnational global reality. Problematising the exceptionalist self-image of 'better' societal models, the anxiety of becoming Europe's periphery, challenging the fantasy of stable and nationally defined spaces embracing welfare state values by imagining them as spaces that have never been 'purely' national and that are open to transnational exchange, Nordic renderings of the eastern neighbours seek to grasp the ongoing developments affecting their own societies. By invoking specific geopolitical and cultural contexts, including the specifically Nordic relations with Russia and Eastern European countries, the films reimagine the hegemonic East/West border as a more complex North/East boundary. Nevertheless, many Nordic films also expose the particularly Nordic hierarchies and divisions pervading the Nordic cultural imagination – such as those instigated by exceptionalist self-conceptions of being the northern 'top of the world'.

Moreover, just as *Sauna* both thematises and activates strong emotions – primarily guilt and fear – in its viewers, emotions also play an important role in imagining and reimagining Russia and Eastern Europe in Nordic films. As we have seen, these emotions are anchored in specifically Nordic cultural contexts and include the deep-rooted fear of Russians, guilt and shame related to Nordic privilege, as well as shame resulting from submissiveness towards the powerful neighbour, and not least 'Nordic nostalgia' for the past world (specifically European) order. However, rather than being simply enacted, these feelings are often critically approached. It is worth reflecting on nostalgia again here. Unlike what Rosalind Galt has observed in relation to post-Wall European cinema (2006: 239), nostalgia – and especially what Svetlana Boym has defined as 'restorative nostalgia', oriented exclusively towards the past (Boym 2001)[1] – is not a dominant modality in Nordic renderings of the eastern neighbours; indeed, the eastern neighbours are not depicted as capable of recovering the past. Rather, the films that reach beyond the Eastern noir modality express an urge to represent and rethink stories of the past and historical issues which could not be expressed earlier (mainly due to the self-censorship), as well as an urge to abandon nostalgia for past national discourses and instead turn toward the eternally changing present moment, as well as toward future connections.

Indeed, these discourses of boundary entail optimistic prefigurations of common transnational futures (as in *Upperdog* or *Four Weeks in June*). Moreover, a new trope for a future Nordic/Eastern connection is signalled in several Nordic films (of which *Occupied* is an example analysed in this book; similarly, this is apparent in *Sauna*) related to environmental consciousness, with the ecosphere incarnating the boundary resisting divisions. *Sauna* offers a fantasy of the future without human-imposed borders, its Eastern noir atmosphere – in line with the convention of the horror genre – inciting and thus epitomising the fear of a world without borders, absorbed by an all-encompassing boundary. But the film does not provide easy solutions. If seen from the non-anthropocentric perspective promulgated by its narrative, foregrounding nature rather than human-erected structures, this vision offers the fantasy of a better world.

Importantly, *Sauna*'s contestation of borders, not only in relation to theme but also as regards representation – including the seamless combination of the horror genre with art cinema – conveys a discursive and philosophical complexity found most often in artistically oriented films. This type of cinematic constellation – combining hegemonic and marginal perspectives in ways that cannot leave one or the other intact – is able to complicate not only cinematic but also social realms, and thus provide a space for reimagining the hegemonic discourses shaping our imagination.

Similar approaches, deliberately employing genre conventions to communicate complex content specific to marginal domains, are rare when considering the spectrum of Nordic films engaging with Russia and Eastern Europe. Rather, the Eastern noir modality spreads to documentary and other minor forms, infecting them with its dichotomous structures – although, as I have also argued, the border discourse rarely remains unchallenged by an inner boundary. *Sauna*, representing what Tommy Gustafsson and Pietari Kääpä identify as new Nordic genre film (2015: 4), implements a reversed direction of impact, 'infecting' Eastern noir with a philosophical complexity, thus offering a cinematic pattern potentially capable of contributing to a more widespread reimagining of the common border. But whereas *Sauna* may seem quite removed from the present day, despite its conceptualisation of a transnationality clearly embedded in the present moment, a fully-fledged reimagining of the Nordic/Eastern border, with a more profound impact on the popular imaginary, would require that films with wider audience appeal enact nuanced boundary discourses relating to contemporary realities – a strategy unsuccessfully pursued in the ambitious Norwegian television series *Struggle for Life* or more successfully in the Finnish series *Bordertown*.[2] The characteristic feature of today's dynamically evolving Nordic genre cinema lies in the promulgation of synergies between art and genre, combining 'the politics of the welfare state in transition with thematic areas familiar for international counterparts' (Gustafsson and Kääpä 2015: 13). 'Transplanting' both boundary discourses and the Eastern noir narrative into new Nordic genre cinema would offer hope both for a more profound reimagining of this narrative and for a greater impact upon the popular imaginary.

In the early 1990s, the Baltic Sea provided an imaginative repository for a 'new space' that could replace the Nordic identity with a Baltic identity, uniting all the countries that border on the Baltic Sea in one dynamic and horizontally (rather than hierarchically) structured region (Wæver 1992). Although these hopes proved to be utopian, such ideas pointed to the impending necessity to reconfigure the former spatial constellations. Today, borders in Europe are again solidifying, whereas the growing distance towards Russia's foreign policies in both *Norden* and the West encourages a revival of dichotomous discourses, and it seems at the time of writing that this tendency is on course to being reinforced. However, as the films analysed in this book show, social reality is not reflected, but rather refracted in the cinematic imagination. Cinematically rendered spaces can offer a 'third' space, where it is possible to resist socially and hierarchically produced meanings – a space defined by boundary, providing common ground for new forms of exchange and dynamic neighbourliness.

At the same time, one must hope that, despite the escalating polarisations in the present social realm, the neighbours across the former Iron Curtain will not fade from the Nordic consciousness – and will continue to inspire Nordic directors and produce a plurality of perspectives, provoking not only cinematic, but also real-life involvement, leading to effective mutual reimaginings of both distant and close neighbours. The idea of strengthening such mutual involvement could be helped along by a scholarly investigation that takes Russia and Eastern Europe as its starting point. An analysis of representations of *Norden* in the neighbouring Russian and Eastern European film cultures, showing us how *Norden* is being reimagined in their rich cinematographies, could yield further insights into how common Nordic/Eastern boundaries can be imagined in, and for, the future.[3]

Notes

1. As opposed to 'reflective nostalgia', which combines longing with critical thinking and is future-oriented (see Boym 2001).
2. *Bordertown* has been sold to several countries and was widely watched in Finland, see https://en.wikipedia.org/wiki/Bordertown_(Finnish_TV_series) (accessed 29 September 2017).
3. For an investigation of how *Norden* is narrated in contemporary Polish literature, see Czapliński (2016).

Bibliography

Aas, Sigmund and Thomas Vestgården (2014), *Skammens historie. Den norske stats mørke sider 1814–2014*, Oslo: Cappelen Damm.

Agger, Gunhild (2016a), 'The development of transnationality in Danish Noir – from *Unit One* to *The Team*', *Northern Lights*, 14: 83–101.

Agger, Gunhild (2016b), 'Nordic noir – location, identity and emotion', in Alberto N. García (ed.), *Emotions in Contemporary TV Series*, Basingstoke: Palgrave Macmillan, pp. 134–52.

Ahmed, Sara (2014), *The Cultural Politics of Emotion*, 2nd edn, Edinburgh: Edinburgh University Press.

Alexievich, Svetlana (2016), *Chernobyl Prayer. A Chronicle of the Future*, trans. Anna Gunin and Arch Tait, Harmondsworth: Penguin Books.

Alm, Martin (2008), 'Ryska revolutionen i svenska ögon 1917–1920', in Kristian Gerner and Klas-Göran Karlsson (eds), *Rysk spegel: svenska berättelser om Sovjetunionen – och om Sverige*, Lund: Nordic Academic Press, pp. 113–49.

Antunes, Luis Rocha (2016), *The Multisensory Film Experience. A Cognitive Model of Experiential Film Aesthetics*, Bristol and Chicago, IL: Intellect.

Arvas, Paula (2011), 'Next to the final frontier: Russians in contemporary Finnish and Scandinavian crime fiction', in Andrew Nestingen and Paula Arvas (eds), *Scandinavian Crime Fiction*, Cardiff: University of Wales Press, pp. 115–27.

Ashcroft, Bill, Gareth Griffiths and Helen Tiffin (eds) (1998), *Key Concepts in Post-Colonial Studies*, London and New York: Routledge.

Assmann, Aleida and Sebastian Conrad (eds) (2010), *Memory in a Global Age: Discourses, Practices and Trajectories*, Basingstoke: Palgrave Macmillan.

Augé, Marc (2008), *Non-places. An Introduction to Supermodernity*, 2nd edn, London and New York: Verso.

Baczko, Bronisław (1994), *Wyobrażenia społeczne. Szkice o nadziei i pamięci zbiorowej*, trans. Małgorzata Kowalska, Warszawa: Wydawnictwo Naukowe PWN.

Bakøy, Eva (2011), 'Migrasjon på film: fra ensomme gjestearbeidere til diasporatrøbbel', in Eva Bakøy and Tore Helseth (eds), *Den andre norske filmhistorien*, Oslo: Universitetsforlaget, pp. 168–83.

Bal, Mieke (ed.) (1996), *Double Exposures. The Subject of Cultural Analysis*, New York and London: Routledge.

Ballesteros, Isolina (2015), *Immigration Cinema in the New Europe*, Bristol and Chicago, IL: Intellect.

Bartram, David (2007), 'Conspicuous by their absence: why are there so few foreign workers in Finland?', *Journal of Ethnic and Migration Studies*, 33: 5, 767–82.

Bastiansen, Henrik G. and Rolf Werenskjold (eds) (2015), *The Nordic Media and the Cold War*, Göteborg: Nordicom.

Baudrillard, Jean (1983), *Simulations*, transl. Paul Foss, Paul Patton and Philip Beitchman, New York: Semiotext(e).

Beller, Manfred (2007), 'Perception, image, imagology', in Manfred Beller and Joep Leerssen (eds), *Imagology. The Cultural Construction and Literary Representation of National Characters. A Critical Survey*, Amsterdam and New York: Rodopi, pp. 3–16.

Beller, Manfred and Joep Leerssen (eds) (2007), *Imagology. The Cultural Construction and Literary Representation of National Characters. A Critical Survey*, Amsterdam and New York: Rodopi.

Bhabha, Homi K. (2004), *The Location of Culture*, London and New York: Routledge.

Billig, Michael (1995), *Banal Nationalism*, Los Angeles, London, New Delhi, Singapore and Washington, DC: Sage.

Bjerke, Paul (2015), '"The Most Disgraceful of All Crimes". Critical journalism during the Cold War? A Norwegian spy case study', in Henrik G. Bastiansen and Rolf Werenskjold (eds), *The Nordic Media and the Cold War*, Göteborg: Nordicom, pp. 193–214.

Boletsi, Maria (2013), *Barbarism and its Discontents*, Stanford: Stanford University Press.

Bondebjerg, Ib (2012), *Virkelighedsbilleder. Den moderne danske dokumentarfilm*, København: Samfundslitteratur.

Bondebjerg, Ib (2005), 'Det sociale og det subjektive. Tómas Gislason og dokumentarfilmen', in Anne Jespersen og Eva Jørholt (eds), *Som i et spejl. Om film og filmkunst*, København: Ries, pp. 86–106.

Bondebjerg, Ib (2002), 'Det sociale og det poetiske blik. Den nye danske dokumentarfilm', *Kosmorama*, 229: 18–40.

Bonsdorff, Pauline von (2005), 'Beauty and truth in *The 3 Rooms of Melancholia*', in Claes Entzenberg and Simo Säätela (eds), *Perspectives on Aesthetics, Art and Culture*, Stockholm: Thales, pp. 20–40.

Booth, Alan R. (1991), 'The development of the espionage film', in Wesley K. Wark (ed.), *Spy Fiction, Spy Films and Real Intelligence*, London: Frank Cass, pp. 136–60.

Bordwell, David and Kristin Thompson (2008), *Film Art. An Introduction*, 8th edn, Boston: McGraw Hill.

Boym, Svetlana (2001), *The Future of Nostalgia*, New York: Basic Books.

Boym, Svetlana (1994), *Common Places. Mythologies of Everyday Life in Russia*, London and Cambridge, MA: Harvard University Press.

Brown, William (2010), 'Negotiating the invisible', in William Brown, Dina Iordanova and Leshu Torchin (eds), *Moving People, Moving Images. Cinema and Trafficking in the New Europe*, St Andrews: St Andrews Film Studies, pp. 16–48.

Browning, Christopher (2007), 'Branding Nordicity. Models, identity and the decline of exceptionalism', *Cooperation and Conflict*, 42: 1, 27–51.

Brundtland, Arne Olav (1966), 'The Nordic balance. Past and present', *Cooperation and Conflict*, 1: 4, 30–63.

Brunow, Dagmar (2010), 'The language of the complex image: Roy Andersson's political aesthetics', *Journal of Scandinavian Cinema*, 1: 1, 83–6.

Brzezińska, Marta (2014), *Spektakl – granica – ekran. Mur berliński w filmie niemieckim*, Wrocław: Oficyna Wydawnicza ATUT.

Casey, Edward S. (2011), 'Border versus boundary at La Frontera', *Environment and Planning D: Society and Space*, 29: 3, 384–98.

Chambers, Ross (2001), 'Narrative and the imaginary: a review of Gilbert Durand's *The Anthropological Structures of the Imaginary*', *Narrative*, 9: 1, 100–9.

Churchill, Winston (1946), 'Iron Curtain speech', www.historyguide.org/europe/churchill.html (accessed 28 January 2017).

Clemmensen, Jesper (2012), *Flugtrute Østersøen. Historien om 'den usynlige mur' mellem DDR og Danmark under den kolde krig*, København: Gyldendal.

Coates, Paul (2000), 'Shifting borders: Konwicki, Zanussi and the ideology of "East-Central Europe"', *Canadian Slavonic Papers*, 42: 1–2, 87–98.

Coxe, Brinton Tench (2010), 'Playground – graveyard: violence, the body and borderline urban space in *Lilja 4-Ever*', *Ulbandus Review*, 13: 29–40.

Creeber, Glen (2015), 'Killing us softly: investigating the aesthetics, philosophy and influence of *Nordic Noir* television', *Journal of Popular Television*, 3: 1, 21–35.

Cronqvist, Marie (2008), '*Vi går under jorden*: kalla kriget möter folkhemmet i svensk civilförsvarsfilm', in Erik Hedling and Mats Jönsson (eds), *Välfärdsbilder. Svensk film utanför biografen*, Stockholm: Statens ljud-och bildarkiv, pp. 166–81.

Cronqvist, Marie (2004), *Mannen i mitten. Ett spiondrama i svensk kallakrigskultur*, Stockholm: Carlssons.

Csoma, Emőke (2012), 'War', in Pietari Kääpä (ed.), *Directory of World Cinema: Finland*, Bristol and Chicago, IL: Intellect, pp. 85–8.

Czapliński, Przemysław (2016), *Poruszona mapa. Wyobraźnia geograficzno-kulturowa polskiej literatury przełomu XX i XXI wieku*, Kraków: Wydawnictwo Literackie.

Dancus, Adriana Margareta (2014), 'Ghosts haunting the Norwegian house: racialization in Norway and *The Kautokeino Rebellion*', *Framework*, 55: 1, 121–39.

Dancus, Adriana Margareta (2011), 'Diasporic feeling and displaced nostalgia. A case study: import-eksport and blodsbånd', *Scandinavian Studies*, 83: 2, 247–66.

Davidsen, Leif (1988), *Den russiske sangerinde*, København: Lindhardt og Ringhof.

Derrida, Jacques (1994), *Specters of Marx. The State of the Debt, the Work of*

Mourning and the New International, trans. Peggy Kamuf, New York and London: Routledge.

Eder, Klaus (2006), 'Europe's borders: the narrative construction of the boundaries of Europe', *European Journal of Social Theory*, 9: 2, 255–71.

Eichler, Maya (2012), *Militarizing Men: Gender, Conscription, and War in Post-Soviet Russia*, Stanford: Stanford University Press.

Engelstad, Audun (2016), 'Sensation in serial form: high-end television drama and trigger plots', *Kosmorama*, 263, www.kosmorama.org/artikler/sensation-in-serial-form.aspx (accessed 2 November 2016).

Enquist, Per Olov [1968] (1973), *The Legionnaires. A Documentary Novel*, trans. Alan Blair, London: Jonathan Cape.

Falicka, Krystyna (2002), 'Potęga świata wyobrażeń, czyli archetypologia według Gilberta Duranda', in Krystyna Falicka (ed.), *Potęga świata wyobrażeń czyli Archetypologia według Gilberta Duranda*, Lublin: Wydawnictwo UMCS, pp. 5–11.

Ferguson, Tamara J., Daniel Brugman, Jennifer White and Heidi L. Eyre (2007), 'Shame and guilt as morally warranted experiences', in Jessica L. Tracy, Richard W. Robins and June Price Tangney (eds), *The Self-Conscious Emotions. Theory and Research*, New York and London: The Guilford Press, pp. 330–48.

Forshaw, Barry (2012), *Death in a Cold Climate. A Guide to Scandinavian Crime Fiction*, London and New York: Palgrave Macmillan.

Foucault, Michel (1995), *Discipline and Punish. The Birth of the Prison*, trans. Alan Sheridan, New York: Vintage Books.

Foucault, Michel (1980), *Power/Knowledge. Selected Interviews and Other Writings 1972–1977*, ed. Colin Gordon, trans. Colin Gordon, Leo Marshall, John Mepham and Kate Soper, New York: Pantheon Books.

Foucault, Michel (1971), 'Orders of discourse. Inaugural lecture delivered at the Collège de France', *Social Science Information*, 10: 2, 7–30.

Furhammar, Leif (2003), *Filmen i Sverige, en historia i tio kapitel och en fortsättning*, 3rd edn, Stockholm: Dialogos.

Gajewska, Katarzyna (2013), *Transnational Labour Solidarity: Mechanisms of Commitment to Cooperation within the European Trade Union Movement*, 2nd edn, London: Routledge.

Galt, Rosalind (2006), *The New European Cinema. Redrawing the Map*, New York: Columbia University Press.

Garsztecki, Stefan (2008), 'Poland', in Martin Klimke and Joachim Scharloth (eds), *1968 in Europe. A History of Protest and Activism, 1956–1977*, New York: Palgrave Macmillan, pp. 179–87.

Gerner, Kristian (2000), 'Svenskars syn på Sovjetryssland: myten om antisovjetismen', in Klas-Göran Karlsson and Ulf Zander (eds), *Östersjö eller Västerhav? Föreställningar om tid och rum i Östersjöområdet*, Karlskrona: Östersjöinstituttet, pp. 33–46.

Gerner, Kristian and Klas-Göran Karlsson (eds) (2008), *Rysk spegel: svenska berättelser om Sovjetunionen – och om Sverige*, Lund: Nordic Academic Press.

Gullestad, Marianne (2006), *Plausible Prejudice: Everyday Experiences and Social Images of Nation, Culture and Race*, Oslo: Scandinavian University Press.

Gustafsson, Tommy and Pietari Kääpä (eds) (2015), *Nordic Genre Film. Small Nation Film Cultures in the Global Marketplace*, Edinburgh: Edinburgh University Press.

Hansell, Sven (2004), 'Du är inte normal! Kön, norm och frihet i Lukas Moodyssons filmer', *Kvinnovetenskaplig tidskrift*, 1–2: 99–112.

Hansson, Per Albin (1982), 'Folkhemmet, medborgarhemmet', Per Albin Hanssons tal i andra kammarens remissdebatt, 1928, in Per Albin Hansson, *Från Fram till folkhemmet: Per Albin Hansson som tidningsman och talare*, ed. Anna Lisa Berkling, Solna: Metodica Press, pp. 227–34.

Harvey, David (2009), *Cosmopolitanism and the Geographies of Freedom*, New York: Columbia University Press.

Hedling, Olof (2007), 'Smilende gyldenbrune øjne. De politisk korrekte indvandrerportrætters dominans i svensk film', *Kosmorama*, 240: 33–49.

Hedling, Olof (2004), 'Om *Lilja 4-ever*: en svensk film', in Bibi Johnsson, Karin Nykvist and Birthe Sjöberg (eds), *Från Eden till damavdelingen*, Lund: Absalon, pp. 323–34.

Hendrykowski, Marek (2000), *Film jako źródło historyczne*, Poznań: Ars Nova.

Henlin-Stromme, Sabine Brigitte (2012), *Nature, Nation and the Global in Contemporary Norwegian Cinema*, PhD dissertation, Iowa: University of Iowa.

Hight, Craig (2010), *Television Mockumentary. Reflexivity, Satire and a Call to Play*, Manchester: Manchester University Press.

Hilson, Mary (2008), *The Nordic Model. Scandinavia since 1945*, London: Reaktion Books (Kindle edn).

Hjort, Mette (2010), 'On the plurality of cinematic transnationalism', in Nataša Ďurovičová and Kathleen Newman (eds), *World Cinemas, Transnational Perspectives*, London: Routledge, pp. 12–33.

Hjort, Mette (2005), *Small Nation, Global Cinema. The New Danish Cinema*, London and Minneapolis: University of Minnesota Press.

Hollender, Pål (2006), 'Interview on *Buy Bye Beauty*, 2006', www.hollender.se/05_text/bbbtext.htm (accessed 2 August 2016).

Hollender, Pål (2005), 'Sanning', '.doc', www.hollender.se (accessed 5 February 2016).

Holm, Ingvar (1975), *Roman blir film*, Lund: Bo Cavefors Bokförlag.

Houellebecq, Michel (2015), *Soumission*, Paris: Flammarion.

Huyssen, Andreas (2003), *Present Pasts. Urban Palimpsests and the Politics of Memory*, Stanford: Stanford University Press.

Iversen, Gunnar (2012), 'From trauma to heroism: cultural memory and remembrance in Norwegian occupation dramas, 1946–2009', *Journal of Scandinavian Cinema*, 2: 3, 237–48.

Iversen, Gunnar (2001), 'Folkets erfaring – om Knut Erik Jensens fjern-synserie *Finnmark mellom øst og vest*', in Sara Brinch and Gunnar Iversen (eds), *Virkelighetsbilder. Norsk dokumentarfilm gjennom hundre år*, Oslo: Universitetsforlaget, pp. 203–18.

Iversen, Gunnar (1998), 'Norway', in Tytti Soila, Astrid Söderbergh Widding and Gunnar Iversen, *Nordic National Cinemas*, London and New York: Routledge, pp. 102–41.

Iversen, Gunnar and Ove Solum (2010), *Den norske filmbølgen. Fra Orions belte til Max Manus*, Oslo: Universitetsforlaget.

Jacobsen, Alf R. (1991), *Iskyss. Om spionasje og kjærlighet i den kalde krigens tid*, Oslo: Aschehoug.

Jazdon, Mikołaj (2016), 'Rosja – Polska. Nowe spojrzenie? Młodzi dokumentaliści wobec tradycji polskiej szkoły dokumentu', in Tadeusz Szczepański and Małgorzata Kozubek (eds), *Polski dokument w XXI wieku*, Łódź: Wydawnictwo Uniwersytetu Łódzkiego, pp. 125–48.

Jazdon, Mikołaj (2011), 'Marian Marzyński – autobiografia dokumentalisty', *Kwartalnik Filmowy*, 73: 42–52.

Jensen, Bent [1984] (2002), *Stalinismens fascination og danske venstreintellektuelle*, 2nd edn, København: Lindhardt og Ringhof.

Jerman, Helena (2004), 'Russians as presented in TV documentaries', *Global Review of Ethnopolitics*, 3: 2, 79–88.

Johansson, Jorgen (2001), 'Bye, bye ethics', *The Baltic Times*, www.baltictimes.com/news/articles/4642/ (accessed 2 August 2016).

Jørgensen, Thomas Ekman (2008), 'Scandinavia', in Martin Klimke and Joachim Scharloth (eds), *1968 in Europe. A History of Protest and Activism, 1956–1977*, New York: Palgrave Macmillan, pp. 239–52.

Jørholt, Eva (2007), 'Perkere og andet godtfolk. De "fremmede" i dansk film', *Kosmorama*, 240: 7–32.

Kahn, Aaron Seth (2012), 'Creating the safe harbour: depictions of Swedish refugee assistance actions in wartime propaganda film', *Journal of Scandinavian Cinema*, 2: 3, 217–30.

Karaś, Dorota (2017), 'Kajakiem, pontonem, czasem wpław. Tak uciekli z PRL-u na wyspę wolności', *Gazeta Wyborcza*, 28 January, www.trojmiasto.wyborcza.pl/trojmiasto/7,35636,21295698,mt-ucieczki-na-wyspe-wolnosci.html#BoxLokPozImg (accessed 11 February 2017).

Karlsson, Klas-Göran and Ulf Zander (eds) (2000), *Östersjö eller Västerhav? Föreställningar om tid och rum i Östersjöområdet*, Karlskrona: Östersjöinstituttet.

Kaskinen, Saija (2012), 'The tale of Finland's eastern border', *Folklore: Electronic Journal of Folklore*, 52: 124–9.

Katzenstein, Peter (2005), *A World of Regions: Asia and Europe in the American Imperium*, Ithaca, NY: Cornell University Press.

Kimmel, Michael S. (2003), 'Toward a pedagogy of the oppressor', in Michael S. Kimmel and Abby L. Ferber (eds), *Privilege. A Reader*, Boulder: Westview Press, pp. 1–10.

Kirby, David (1995), *The Baltic World 1772–1993. Europe's Northern Periphery in an Age of Change*, London and New York: Longman.

Koivunen, Anu and Tytti Soila (2005), '*Melancholian 3 huonetta. The 3 Rooms of Melancholia*', in Tytti Soila (ed.), *The Cinema of Scandinavia*, London: Wallflower Press, pp. 253–60.

Kott, Matthew (2015), 'Rysskräck and Sweden's ambivalence', *New Eastern Europe*, www.neweasterneurope.eu/articles-and-commentary/1537-rysskrae ck-and-sweden-s-ambivalence (accessed 14 February 2017).

Kristensen, Lars (2007), 'Divergent accounts of equivalent narratives: Russian-Swedish *Interdevochka* meets Swedish-Russian *Lilya 4-ever*', *PORTAL Journal of Multidisciplinary International Studies*, 4: 2, www.epress.lib.uts.edu.au/ojs/index.php/portal (accessed 8 May 2015).

Kääpä, Pietari (2015), 'A culture of reciprocity: the politics of cultural exchange in contemporary Nordic genre film', in Tommy Gustafsson and Pietari Kääpä (eds), *Nordic Genre Film. Small Nation Film Cultures in the Global Marketplace*, Edinburgh: Edinburgh University Press, pp. 244–61.

Kääpä, Pietari (2014), *Ecology and Contemporary Nordic Cinemas. From Nation-building to Ecocosmopolitanism*, London: Bloomsbury (Kindle edn).

Kääpä, Pietari (ed.) (2012), *Directory of World Cinema: Finland*, Bristol and Chicago, IL: Intellect.

Kääpä, Pietari (2011), 'Born American? Renny Harlin and global Hollywood', *Film International*, 9: 2, 55–70.

Laderman, David (2002), *Driving Visions: Exploring the Road Movie*, Austin: Texas University Press.

Laine, Kimmo (2012), 'Military comedy, censorship and World War II', *Journal of Scandinavian Cinema*, 2: 3, 257–61.

Laine, Tarja (2015), *Bodies in Pain. Emotion and the Cinema of Darren Aronofsky*, New York and Oxford: Berghan.

Laine, Tarja (2007), *Shame and Desire: Emotion, Intersubjectivity, Cinema*, Brussels: Peter Lang.

Lakoff, George and Mark Johnson (2003), *Metaphors We Live By*, Chicago, IL and London: University of Chicago Press.

Larsen, Leif Ove (2015), 'New voices, new stories: migrant cinema and television in Norway', in Ib Bondebjerg, Eva Novrup Redvall and Andrew Higson (eds), *European Cinema and Television. Cultural Policy and Everyday Life*, Basingstoke: Palgrave Macmillan, pp. 169–91.

Larsson, Mariah (2010), 'Representing sexual transactions: a national perspective on a changing region in three Swedish films', in Erik Hedling, Olof Hedling and Mats Jönsson (eds), *Regional Aesthetics: Locating Swedish Media*, Stockholm: National Library of Sweden, pp. 21–41.

Larsson, Mariah (2006), 'Om kön, sexualitet och moral i *Ett hål i mitt hjärta*', in Erik Hedling and Ann-Kristin Wallengren (eds), *Solskenslandet: svensk film på 2000-talet*, Stockholm: Atlantis, pp. 245–66.

Lauridsen, John T., Rasmus Mariager, Thorsten Borring Olesen and Poul

Villaume (eds) (2011), *Den kolde krig og Danmark*, København: Gads Leksikon.

Lavik, Erlend (2015), *Forfatterskap i TV-drama. Showrunnermodellen, one vision – og Kampen for tilværelsen*, Bergen: Universitetsforlaget.

Leontieva, Alexandra N. and Karin Sarsenov (2005), 'Russian women in the Scandinavian media', in Ildikó Asztalos Morell, Helene Carlbäck, Madeleine Hurd and Sara Rastbäck (eds), *Gender Transitions in Russia and Eastern Europe*, Eslöv: Förlags AB Gondolin, pp. 137–58.

Linna, Väinö (2016), *Unknown Soldiers*, trans. Liesl Yamaguchi, Penguin.

Loshitzky, Yosefa (1997), 'Constructing and deconstructing the Wall', *Clio*, 26: 3, 275–96.

Lounasmeri, Lotta (2015), 'A careful balancing act. Finnish culture of self-censorship in the Cold War', in Henrik G. Bastiansen and Rolf Werenskjold (eds), *The Nordic Media and the Cold War*, Göteborg: Nordicom, pp. 83–100.

Ludvigsson, David (2003), *The Historian-Filmmaker's Dilemma. Historical Documentaries in Sweden in the Era of Häger and Villius*, PhD dissertation, Uppsala: Uppsala Universitet.

Lundén, Thomas and Torbjörn Nilsson (eds) (2010), *1989 med svenska ögon. Vitnesseminarium 22 oktober 2009*, Stockholm: Samtidshistoriska instituttet, CBEES, Centre for Baltic and East European Studies.

Lundén, Thomas and Torbjörn Nilsson (eds) (2006), *Sverige och Baltikums frigörelse. Två vittnesseminarier om storpolitik kring Östersjön 1989–1994*, Stockholm: Samtidshistoriska instituttet, CBEES, Centre for Baltic and East European Studies.

Lyotard, Jean-François (1984), *The Postmodern Condition: A Report on Knowledge*, trans. Geoff Bennington and Brian Massumi, Manchester: Manchester University Press.

Mąka-Malatyńska, Katarzyna (2012), *Widok z tej strony. Przedstawienia Holocaustu w polskim filmie*, Poznań: Wydawnictwo Naukowe UAM.

Malia, Martin (1999), *Russia under Western Eyes. From the Bronze Horseman to the Lenin Mausoleum*, London and Cambridge, MA: Harvard University Press.

Malmborg, Mikael af (2001), *Neutrality and State-Building in Sweden*, Basingstoke: Palgrave.

Mankell, Henning [1992] (2012), *The Dogs of Riga*, trans. Laurie Thompson, London: Vintage Books.

Marklund, Anders (2010), 'Beyond Swedish borders: on foreign places in Swedish films 1980–2010', in Erik Hedling, Olof Hedling and Mats Jönsson (eds), *Regional Aesthetics: Locating Swedish Media*, Stockholm: National Library of Sweden, pp. 81–104.

Marks, Laura U. (2000), *The Skin of the Film. Intercultural Cinema, Embodiment, and the Senses*, London and Durham, NC: Duke University Press (Kindle edn).

Marusek, James A. (2010), 'A chronological listing of early weather events', http://www.breadandbutterscience.com/A_Chronological_Listing_of_Early_Weather_Events.pdf (accessed 7 January 2017).

Marx, Karl and Friedrich Engels [1848] (2012), *The Communist Manifesto*, ed. Jeffrey C. Isaac, New Haven and London: Yale University Press.

Mathisen, Stein R. (1998), 'Det farlige naboskapet i nord. Eksplisitte og implisitte fortellinger på en "ny" grense', *Tradisjon*, 28: 2, 11–23.

Mazierska, Ewa (2010), 'Eastern European cinema: old and new approaches', *Studies in Eastern European Cinema*, 1: 1, 5–16.

Mazierska, Ewa (2009), 'In search of freedom, bread and self-fulfillment: a short history of Polish emigrants in fictional film', in Kathy Burrell (ed.), *Polish Migration to the UK in the 'New' European Union*, London and New York: Routledge, pp. 107–27.

Mazierska, Ewa, Lars Kristensen and Eva Näripea (eds) (2014), *Postcolonial Approaches to Eastern European Cinema: Portraying Neighbours On-Screen*, London and New York: I.B. Tauris.

Meinander, Henrik (2013), *A History of Finland*, trans. Tom Geddes, New York: Oxford University Press.

Meinander, Henrik (2011), 'A separate story? Interpretations of Finland in the Second World War', in Henrik Stenius, Mirja Österberg and Johan Östling (eds), *Nordic Narratives of the Second World War. National Historiographies Revisited*, Lund: Nordic Academic Press, pp. 55–77.

Michelet, Jon (1977), *Orions belte: en roman fra Svalbard*, Oslo: Forlaget Oktober.

Miller, Laura (2010), 'The strange case of the Nordic detectives', *The Wall Street Journal* (Europe), 15 January.

Mohnike, Thomas (2007), *Imaginierte Geographien. Der schwedischsprachige Reisebericht der 1980er und 1990er Jahre und das Ende des Kalten Krieges*, Würzburg: Ergon Verlag.

Mrozewicz, Anna Estera (2017), 'Ciało i miejsce. Obrazy współczesnej Rosji w polskich i szwedzkich filmach dokumentalnych', *Panoptikum*, 17: 24, 146–69.

Mrozewicz, Anna Estera (2016), 'Embodying transnational shared space. Pirjo Honkasalo's *The 3 Rooms of Melancholia*', *Journal of Scandinavian Cinema*, 6: 2, 119–35.

Mrozewicz, Anna Estera (2014), 'At vende tilbage til ukendte steder. Posthukommelse og sted hos Jacob Dammas, Jacob Kofler og Maja Magdalena Swiderska', *K&K*, 42: 117, 113–30.

Mrozewicz, Anna Estera (2013a), 'Between the two shores of the deep blue sea: crossing the Baltic on the Scandinavian screen', *Journal of Scandinavian Cinema*, 3: 2, 125–40.

Mrozewicz, Anna Estera (2013b), 'Porous borders. Crossing the boundaries to "Eastern Europe" in Scandinavian crime fiction', *Academic Quarter*, 7: 350–65.

Mrozewicz, Bolesław (2004), *Obrachunek z mitem Fina w twórczości Väinö Linny i Paavo Rintali*, Poznań: Wydawnictwo Naukowe UAM.

Mulari, Heta (2013), 'Transnational heroines: Swedish youth film and immigrant girlhood', in Raita Merivirta, Kimmo Ahonen, Heta Mulari and Rami Mähkä (eds), *Frontiers of Screen History. Imagining European Borders in Cinema, 1945–2010*, Bristol and Chicago: Intellect (Kindle edn).

Musiał, Kazimierz and Dominika Bartnik-Światek (2016), 'Rozmrażanie Wschodu. Najnowszy duński dyskurs o Polsce', in Tomasz Zarycki (ed.), *Polska jako peryferie*, Warszawa: Scholar, pp. 254–67.

Naarden, Bruno and Joep Leerssen (2007), 'Russians', in Manfred Beller and Joep Leerssen (eds), *Imagology. The Cultural Construction and Literary Representation of National Characters. A Critical Survey*, Amsterdam and New York: Rodopi, pp. 226–9.

Nail, Thomas (2016), *Theory of the Border*, New York: Oxford University Press (Kindle edn).

Näripea, Eva, Ewa Mazierska and Lars Kristensen (2016), 'Gazing at the Baltic: tourist discourse in the cinema of the Baltic Sea countries', in Simo Mikkonen, Pekka Suutari (eds), *Music, Art and Diplomacy: East-West Cultural Interactions and the Cold War*, Farnham and Burlington, VT: Ashgate, pp. 49–66.

Necef, Mehmet Ümit (2003), 'De fremmede og Det Onde: Fra kitsch til hybrid-itetens glæder', in Anders Toftgaard and Ian Hawkesworth (eds), *Nationale spejlinger: Tendenser i ny dansk film*, København: Museum Tusculanums Forlag, pp. 167–91.

Necef, Mehmet Ümit and Henning Bech (2013), 'Racistiske repræsentationer?', in Søren Frank and Mehmet Ümit Necef (eds), *Indvandreren i dansk film og litteratur*, København: Spring, pp. 256–95.

Németh, Ágnes (2015), 'Watching the other across the border: representations of Russia and Estonia on Finnish national television', *Journal of Borderlands Studies*, 30: 1, 37–52.

Nestingen, Andrew (2013), *The Cinema of Aki Kaurismäki. Contrarian Stories*, London and New York: Wallflower Press.

Nestingen, Andrew (2008), *Crime and Fantasy in Scandinavia. Fiction, Film, and Social Change*, Seattle: University of Washington Press; Copenhagen: Museum Tusculanum Press.

Nichols, Bill (2010), *Introduction to Documentary*, 2nd edn, Bloomington: Indiana University Press.

Niskanen, Eija (2012), '*The 3 Rooms of Melancholia. Melankolian 3 huonetta*', in Pietari Kääpä (ed.), *Directory of World Cinema: Finland*, Bristol and Chicago, IL: Intellect, p. 232.

Oisalo, Niina (2016), 'Cinematic worlding: animating Karelia in *Santra and the Talking Trees*', *Journal of Scandinavian Cinema*, 6: 2, 153–68.

Olsen, Kåre (2005), 'Under the care of Lebensborn: Norwegian war children and their mothers', in Kjersti Ericsson and Eva Simonsen (eds), *Children of World War II: The Hidden Enemy Legacy* (1), London: Berg Publishers, pp. 15–34.

Oxfeldt, Elisabeth (ed.) (2016), *Skandinaviske fortellinger om skyld og privilegier i en globaliseringstid*, Oslo: Universitetsforlaget.

Paasonen, Susanna (2015), 'Heavy skies and a cold Soviet feel: Helsinki as a Cold War cinematic body double', *Journal of Scandinavian Cinema*, 5: 1, 5–18.

Peeren, Esther (2014), *The Spectral Metaphor. Living Ghosts and the Agency of Invisibility*, London: Palgrave Macmillan.

Piirimäe, Pärtel (2011), 'Baltiska provinser eller en del av Norden?', in Jenny Björkman, Björn Fjæstad and Jonas Harvard (eds), *Ett nordiskt rum. Historiska och framtida gemenskaper från Baltikum till Barents hav*, Göteborg, Stockholm: Makadam Förlag.

Piotrowski, Piotr (2009), *In the Shadow of Yalta. Art and the Avant-garde in Eastern Europe, 1945–1989*, trans. Anna Brzyski, London: Reaktion Books.

Pomerantsev, Peter (2014a), *Nothing is True and Everything is Possible. The Surreal Heart of the New Russia*, New York: Public Affairs.

Pomerantsev, Peter (2014b), 'Russia and the menace of unreality. How Vladimir Putin is revolutionizing information warfare', *The Atlantic*, www.theatlantic.com/international/archive/2014/09/russia-putin-revolutionizing-information-warfare/379880/ (accessed 27 February 2017).

Przylipiak, Mirosław (2011), 'Kino Paladino, albo schyłek wielkich narracji', in Mikołaj Jazdon and Katarzyna Mąka-Malatyńska (eds), *Zobaczyć siebie. Polski film dokumentalny przełomu wieków*, Poznań: Zamek, pp. 31–49.

Ringgaard, Dan (2010), *Stedssans*, Århus: Aarhus Universitetsforlag.

Romney, Jonathan (2003), 'Last Exit to Helsinki', *Film Comment*, 39: 2, 43–7.

Ronström, Owe (2009), 'Är du ryssk, sork? Ryssar och rysskräck i Sverige', in Åke Sandström (ed.), *Ryss'n kummar! Symposium om ryssar och rysskräck på Gotland från Bodisco till Nordstream*, Visby: Gotland University Press, pp. 121–31.

Roscoe, Jane and Craig Hight (2001), *Faking It: Mock-Documentary and the Subversion of Factuality*, Manchester and New York: Manchester University Press.

Rosello, Mireille (1998), *Declining the Stereotype. Ethnicity and Representation in French Cultures*, Hannover and London: University Press of New England.

Rosello, Mireille (1996), *Infiltrating Culture. Power and Identity in Contemporary Women's Writing*, Manchester: Manchester University Press.

Rosenberg, Henrik (1995), *Från Runar Schildts novell 'Köttkvarnen' till filmen Den stulna döden. En adaptations tillkomst och tidsnivåer*, Åbo: Åbo Akademi.

Rossel, Sven Hakon (2009), 'The Baltics in Danish and Swedish literature. A foray into research possibilities', in Imbi Sooman and Stefan Donecker (eds), *The 'Baltic Frontier' Revisited. Power Structures and Cross-Cultural Interactions in the Baltic Sea Region*, Vienna: S.n., pp. 283–305.

Rumford, Chris (2012), 'Towards a multiperspectival study of borders', *Geopolitics*, 17: 4, 887–902.

Rydzewska, Joanna (2012), 'Ambiguity and change: post-2004 Polish migration to the UK in contemporary British cinema', *Journal of Contemporary European Studies*, 20: 2, 215–27.

Said, Edward (1978), *Orientalism*, New York: Vintage Books.

Salokangas, Raimo (2015), 'The shadow of the bear. Finnish broadcasting, national interest and self-censorship during the Cold War', in Henrik G. Bastiansen and Rolf Werenskjold (eds), *The Nordic Media and the Cold War*, Göteborg: Nordicom, pp. 67–82.

Sandberg-Fries, Yvonne and Peter Althini (2000), 'Förord', in Klas-Göran

Karlsson and Ulf Zander (eds), *Östersjö eller Västerhav? Föreställningar om tid och rum i Östersjöområdet*, Karlskrona: Östersjöinstituttet, pp. 5–5.

Sandvik, Kjetil (2010), 'Convergence of place and plot. Investigating the anatomy of the crime scene', in Jørgen Riber Christensen and Kim Toft Hansen (eds), *Fingeraftryk. Studier i krimi og det kriminelle*, Festskrift til Gunhild Agger, Ålborg: Aalborg Universitetsforlag, pp. 277–305.

Sarvig, Ole (1978), *De rejsende*, København: Gyldendal.

Schmid, David (2012), 'From the locked room to the globe: space in crime fiction', in Vivien Miller and Helen Oakley (eds), *Cross-Cultural Connections in Crime Fictions*, Basingstoke: Palgrave Macmillan, pp. 7–23.

Scribner, Charity (2003), *Requiem for Communism*, Cambridge, MA: MIT Press.

Seaton, A. V. (2000), 'The worst of journeys, the best of journeys: travel and the concept of periphery in European culture', in Mike Robinson (ed.), *Expressions of Culture, Identity and Meaning in Tourism*, Sunderland: Centre for Travel and Tourism, pp. 321–46.

Shaw, Tony (2007), *Hollywood's Cold War*, Edinburgh: Edinburgh University Press.

Shaw, Tony and Denise J. Youngblood (2010), *Cinematic Cold War. The American and Soviet Struggle for Hearts and Minds*, Lawrence: University Press of Kansas.

Sohn, Ole (2002), *Rundt om filmen Den højeste straf*, København: Forlaget Hvepsen.

Sohn, Ole (1999), *Frihedens port*, København: Vindrose.

Sohn, Ole (1992), *Fra folketinget til celle 290. Arne Munch-Petersens skæbne*, København: Vindrose.

Soila, Tytti, Astrid Söderbergh Widding and Gunnar Iversen (1998), *Nordic National Cinemas*, London and New York: Routledge.

Solum, Ove (2016), 'Nordic noir. Populærkulturell suksess og velferdssamfunnets mørke bakside', in Elisabeth Oxfeldt (ed.), *Skandinaviske fortellinger om skyld og privilegier i en globaliseringstid*, Oslo: Universitetsforlaget, pp. 133–50.

Stavning Thomsen, Bodil Marie and Kristin Ørjasæter (eds) (2011), *Globalizing Art. Negotiating Place, Identity and Nation in Contemporary Nordic Art*, Århus: Aarhus University Press.

Stenport, Anna Westerståhl (2015), 'The threat of the thaw: the Cold War on the screen', in Scott MacKenzie and Anna Westerståhl Stenport (eds), *Films on Ice. Cinema of the Arctic*, Edinburgh: Edinburgh University Press, pp. 161–75.

Stenport, Anna Westerståhl (2012), *Lukas Moodysson's Show Me Love*, Seattle: University of Washington Press; Copenhagen: Museum Tusculanum Press.

Stjernfelt, Frederik (2003), 'The ontology of espionage in reality and fiction: a case study on iconicity', *Sign Systems Studies*, 31: 1, 133–62.

Stålhammar, Mall (1997), *Metaforernas mönster i fackspråk och allmänspråk*, Stockholm: Carlssons.

Sundholm, John (2013a), 'Stories of national and transnational memory: renegotiating the Finnish conception of moral witness and national victimhood', in Simo Muir and Hana Worthen (eds), *Finland's Holocaust. Silences of History*, London: Palgrave Macmillan, pp. 31–45.

Sundholm, John (2013b), 'Finland at war on screen since 1989: affirmative historiography and prosthetic memory', in Conny Mithander, John Sundholm and Adrian Velicu (eds), *European Cultural Memory Post-89*, Amsterdam: Rodopi, pp. 209–39.

Sundholm, John (2007), '"The Unknown Soldier": film as a founding trauma and national monument', in Conny Mithander, John Sundholm and Maria Holmgren (eds), *Collective Traumas: Memories of War and Conflict in 20th-Century Europe*, Brussels: Peter Lang, pp. 111–41.

Sørenssen, Bjørn (2015), 'Frozen kisses. Cinematographical reflections on Norway's role in the Cold War', in Henrik G. Bastiansen and Rolf Werenskjold (eds), *The Nordic Media and the Cold War*, Göteborg: Nordicom, pp. 333–46.

Sørensen, Øystein and Bo Stråth (eds) (1997), *The Cultural Construction of Norden*, Oslo: Scandinavian University Press.

Šukaitytė, Renata (2015), 'Lithuania redirected: new connections, businesses and lifestyles in cinema since 2000', in Michael Gott and Todd Herzog (eds), *East, West and Centre. Reframing Post-1989 European Cinema*, Edinburgh: Edinburgh University Press, pp. 175–90.

Tartakovskaya, Irina (2000), 'The changing representation of gender roles in Soviet and post-Soviet press', in Sarah Ashwin (ed.), *Gender, State and Society in Soviet and Post-Soviet Russia*, London and New York: Routledge, pp. 118–36.

Taylor, Gabriele (1985), *Pride, Shame, and Guilt. Emotions of Self-Assessment*, Oxford: Clarendon Press.

Tigervall, Carina (2005), *Folkhemsk film – med 'invandraren' i rollen som den sympatiske Andre*, PhD dissertation, Umeå: Umeå universitet.

Totaro, Donato (1992), 'Time and the film aesthetics of Andrei Tarkovsky', *Canadian Journal of Film Studies*, 2: 1, 21–30.

Trägårdh, Lars (1997), 'Statist individualism: on the culturality of the Nordic welfare state', in Øystein Sørensen and Bo Stråth (eds), *The Cultural Construction of Norden*, Oslo: Scandinavian University Press, pp. 253–85.

Tybjerg, Casper (1999), 'Red Satan: Carl Theodor Dreyer and the Bolshevik threat', in John Fullerton and Jan Olsson (eds), *Nordic Explorations: Film before 1930*, London: John Libbey, pp. 19–40.

Tygstrup, Frederik (2013), 'Affekt og rum', *K&K*, 11: 17–32.

Urry, John and Jonas Larsen (2011), *The Tourist Gaze 3.0*, Los Angeles: Sage.

Van Heuckelom, Kris (2014), 'From dysfunction to restoration. The allegorical potential of immigrant labour', in Leen Engelen and Kris Van Heuckelom (eds), *European Cinema after the Wall. Screening East-West Mobility*, Lanham: Rowman & Littlefield, pp. 71–93.

Van Heuckelom, Kris (2013), 'Londoners and outlanders: Polish labour migration through the European lens', *The Slavonic and East European Review*, 91: 2, 210–34.

Vatulescu, Cristina (2010), *Police Aesthetics: Literature, Film, and the Secret Police in Soviet Times*, Stanford: Stanford University Press.

Vogler, Christopher (2007), *The Writer's Journey. Mythic Structure for Writers*, 3rd edn, Studio City: Michael Wiese Productions.

Volquardsen, Ebbe (2014), 'Scandinavia and "the Land of UnSwedish Freedom": Jonathan Franzen, Susanne Bier and self-conceptions of exceptionalism in crisis', in Kristín Loftsdóttir and Lars Jensen (eds), *Crisis in the Nordic Nations and Beyond. At the Intersection of Environment, Finance and Multiculturalism*, Farnham: Ashgate, pp. 31–50.

Williams, Linda (1999), *Hard Core: Power, Pleasure, and the 'Frenzy of the Visible'*, Berkeley: University of California Press.

Winston, Brian (1988), 'The tradition of the victim in Griersonian documentary', in Larry Gross, John Stuart Katz and Jay Ruby (eds), *Image Ethics. The Moral Rights of the Subjects in Photographs, Film, and Television*, New York: Oxford University Press, pp. 34–57.

Wolff, Larry (1994), *Inventing Eastern Europe: The Map of Civilization on the Mind of the Enlightenment*, Stanford: Stanford University Press.

Wright, Rochelle (2005), '"Immigrant film" in Sweden at the millennium', in Andrew Nestingen and Trevor Elkington (eds), *Transnational Cinema in a Global North: Nordic Cinema in Transition*, Detroit: Wayne State University Press, pp. 55–72.

Wright, Rochelle (1998), *The Visible Wall: Jews and other Ethnic Outsiders in Swedish Film*, Carbondale and Edwardsville: Southern Illinois University Press.

Wæver, Ole (1992), 'Nordic nostalgia: northern Europe after the Cold War', *International Affairs*, 68: 1, 77–102.

Zaremba, Maciej (2008), *Polski hydraulik i inne opowieści ze Szwecji*, trans. Wojciech Chudoba, Katarzyna Tubylewicz, Jan Rost and Anna Topczewska, Wołowiec: Wydawnictwo Czarne.

Żmuda-Trzebiatowska, Magdalena (2012), 'Styvbarnen i folkhemmet? Utanför-skap i svenska barndomsskildringar', *Folia Scandinavica*, 14: 157–77.

Öhman, Anders (2007), 'Norrland and the question of cultural identity', in Bjarne Thorup Thomsen (ed.), *Centring on the Peripheries. Studies in Scandinavian, Scottish, Gaelic and Greenlandic Literature*, Norwich: Norvik Press, pp. 59–67.

Östling, Johan (2013), 'Realism and idealism: Swedish narratives of the Second World War. Historiography and interpretation in the post-war era', in John Gilmour and Jill Stephenson (eds), *Hitler's Scandinavian Legacy. The Consequences of the German Invasion for the Scandinavian Countries, Then and Now*, London: Bloomsbury, pp. 179–97.

Østergård, Uffe (1997), 'The geopolitics of Nordic identity – from composite states to nation-states', in Øystein Sørensen and Bo Stråth (eds), *The Cultural Construction of Norden*, Oslo: Scandinavian University Press, pp. 25–71.

Filmography

This filmography is chronological and applies the following format:
English title or *standard English translation as used in the book* (*original title* if other than the English title, director or directors, country or countries of production, year of first release, genre if other than feature-length fiction [documentary, short documentary, short fiction, animation, TV series]).

1910s

The Daughter of the Revolution (*Revolutionens datter*, Ottar Gladtvet, Norway, 1918)

Heroes of Our Time (*Vor tids helte*, Peter Lykke-Seest, Norway, 1918)

Jeftha's Daughter (*Jefthas dotter*, Robert Dinesen, Sweden, 1919)

1920s

Christian Wahnschaffe (Urban Gad, Germany, 1921)

Leaves from Satan's Book (*Blade af Satans Bog*, Carl Theodor Dreyer, Denmark, 1921)

When Millions Roll . . . (*När millionerna rulla . . .*, Lasse Ring, Sweden, 1924)

Karl XII (John W. Brunius, Sweden, 1925)

The Bothnians (*Pohjalaisia*, Jalmari Lahdensuo, Finland, 1925)

Battleship Potemkin (*Броненосец «Потёмкин»*, Sergei Eisenstein, USSR, 1925)

Fugitives from Murmansk (*Muurmanin pakolaiset*, Erkki Karu, Finland, 1927)

The Highest Victory (*Korkein voitto*, Carl von Haartman, Finland, 1929)

1930s

One Night (*En natt*, Gustaf Molander, Sweden, 1931)

Outlaw (*Fredlös*, George Schnéevoigt, Sweden, Denmark, GB, 1935)

We Are from Kronstadt (*Мы из Кронштадта*, Efim Dzigan, USSR, 1936)

The Stolen Death (*Varastettu kuolema*, Nyrki Tapiovaara, Finland, 1938)

Soldier's Bride (*Jääkärin morsian*, Risto Orko, Finland, 1938)

The Activists (*Aktivistit*, Risto Orko, Finland, 1939)

The February Manifesto (*Helmikuun manifesti*, Yrjö Norta, T. J. Särkkä, Finland, 1939)

The Great Wrath (*Isoviha*, Kalle Kaarna, Finland, 1939)

1940s

The Secret Weapon (*Salainen ase*, Theodor Luts, Erkki Uotila, Finland, 1943)

A Day Will Dawn (*En dag skall gry*, Hasse Ekman, Sweden, 1944)

The Russians are Leaving Bornholm (*Russerne forlader Bornholm*, Denmark, 1946, documentary footage)

Two lives (*To liv*, Titus Vibe-Müller, Norway, 1946)

1950s

The Reconstruction of Rønne and Neksø (*Rønne og Neksøs genopbygning*, Poul Bang, Denmark, 1954, documentary)

The Unknown Soldier (*Tuntematon Sotilas*, Edvin Laine, Finland, 1955)

1960s

The Boys (*Pojat*, Mikko Niskanen, Finland, 1962)

Ivan's Childhood (*Иваново детство*, Andrei Tarkovsky, USSR, 1962)

The Spy Who Came In From the Cold (Martin Ritt, US, 1965)

Andrei Rublev (*Андрей Рублёв*, Andrei Tarkovsky, USSR, 1966)

I Am Curious – Yellow (*Jag är nyfiken – gul*, Vilgot Sjöman, Sweden, 1967)

Workers in Moscow (*Arbejdere i Moskva*, Tørk Haxthausen, Denmark, 1968, documentary)

USSR on the Way to Communism (*USSR på vej til kommunisme*, Tørk Haxthausen, Denmark, 1968, documentary)

A Letter from St. Lawrence to Poland (*Et brev fra Skt. Lawrence til Polen*, Marian Marzyński, Denmark, 1969–70, documentary)

1970s

The Ship (*Skibet*, Marian Marzyński, US, 1970–2010, documentary)

A Baltic Tragedy (*Baltutlämningen*, Johan Bergenstråhle, Sweden, 1970, fiction/documentary)

Stalin. Portrait of a Dictator (*Stalin. Porträtt av en dictator*, Olle Häger, Hans Villius, Sweden, 1970, documentary)

A Berliner Family (*En berliner familie*, Tørk Haxthausen, Denmark, 1971, documentary)

GDR – Middle Class and Socialism (*DDR – middelstand og socialisme*, Tørk Haxthausen, Denmark, 1971, documentary)

Tomorrow, My Darling (*I morgen, min elskede*, Finn Karlsson, Denmark, 1971)

Solaris (*Солярис*, Andrei Tarkovsky, USSR, 1972)

Under a Stone Sky (*Under en steinhimmel*, Knut Andersen, Igor Maslennikov, Stanislav Rostotsky, Norway, USSR, 1974)

Stalker (*Сталкер*, Andrei Tarkovsky, USSR, 1979)

Two Forces (*Kainuu 39*, Pirjo Honkasalo, Pekka Lehto, Finland, 1979, fiction/documentary)

1980s

Nostalgia (*Nostalghia*, Andrei Tarkovsky, USSR, Italy, 1983)
The Ninja Mission (Mats Helge, Sweden, 1984)
Orion's Belt (*Orions belte*, Ola Solum, Norway, 1985)
Finnmark between East and West (*Finnmark mellom øst og vest*, Knut Erik Jensen, Norway, 1985, documentary)
The Unknown Soldier (*Tuntematon sotilas*, Rauni Mollberg, Finland, 1985)
Born American (*Jäätävä polte*, Renny Harlin, Finland, US, 1986)
Seppan (Agneta Fagerström-Olsson, Sweden, 1986)
After Rubicon (*Etter Rubicon*, Leidulv Risan, Norway, 1987)
Russians on Bornholm (*Russerne på Bornholm*, Ole Askman, Denmark, 1987, documentary)
The Winter War (*Talvisota*, Pekke Parikka, Finland, 1989)
Codename Coq Rouge (*Täcknamn Coq Rouge*, Pelle Berglund, Sweden, 1989)
300 Miles to Heaven (*300 mil do nieba*, Maciej Dejczer, Poland, 1989)
The Last Ferry (*Ostatni prom*, Waldemar Krzystek, Poland, 1989)

1990s

Lithuania, Spring 1990 (*Litauen foråret 1990*, Sonja Vesterholt, Denmark, 1990, documentary)
The Birthday Trip (*Kajs fødselsdag*, Lone Scherfig, Denmark, 1990)
Enemy's Enemy (*Fiendens fiende*, Thomas Borgström, Lars Bill Lundholm, Sweden, 1990, TV series)
Russian Terminator (Mats Helge, Sweden, 1990)
Mysterion (Pirjo Honkasalo, Eira Mollberg, Finland, 1991, documentary)
Hotel Russia (Kristoffer Nyholm, Denmark, 1993, short documentary)
The Russian Singer (*Den russiske sangerinde*, Morten Arnfred, Denmark, 1993)
My Dear Friend (*Min kjære venn*, Knut Erik Jensen, Norway, 1994, documentary)
Take Care of Your Scarf, Tatjana (*Pidä huivista kiinni, Tatjana*, Aki Kaurismäki, Finland, 1994)
The Dogs of Riga (*Hundarna i Riga*, Pelle Berglund, Sweden, 1995)
Burnt by Frost (*Brent av frost*, Knut Erik Jensen, Norway, 1997)
Screwed in Tallinn (*Torsk på Tallinn*, Tomas Alfredson, Sweden, 1999)
You Can't Eat Fishing (Kathrine Windfeld, Denmark, 1999, short fiction)

2000s

The Eclipse of the Soul (*Sielunpimennys*, Marja Pensala, Finland, 2000, documentary)
Maximum Penalty (*Den højeste straf*, Tómas Gislason, Denmark, 2000, documentary)
Cool and Crazy (*Heftig og begeistret*, Knut Erik Jensen, Norway, 2001, documentary)
The Voice of Ljudmila (*Ljudmilas röst*, Gunnar Bergdahl, Sweden, 2001, documentary)

Executive Protection (*Livvakterna*, Anders Nilsson, Sweden, 2001)
Buy Bye Beauty (Pål Hollender, Sweden, 2001, documentary)
Lilya 4-ever (*Lilja 4-ever*, Lukas Moodysson, Sweden, Denmark, 2002)
The Cuckoo (Кукушка, Alexandr Rogozkhin, Russia, 2002)
Virgins (Jerzy Śladkowski, Finland, 2003, documentary)
War Children (*Sotalapset*, Erja Dammert, Ulla Simonen, Finland, 2003, documentary)
The 3 Rooms of Melancholia (*Melancholian 3 huonetta*, Pirjo Honkasalo, Finland, Denmark, Germany, Sweden, 2004, documentary)
Stateless (*Statsløs*, Jacob Kofler, Denmark, 2004, documentary)
Popular Music (*Populärmusik från Vittula*, Reza Bagher, Sweden, 2004)
The Eagle: A Crime Odyssey (*Ørnen: En krimi-odyssé*, Denmark, 2004–6, TV series)
Four Weeks in June (*Fyra veckor i juni*, Henry Meyer, Sweden, 2005)
Mother of Mine (*Äideistä parhain*, Klaus Härö, Finland, Sweden, 2005)
In Transit (Lisa Aschan, Denmark, 2005, short fiction)
The Queue (*Jono*, Kimmo Yläkäs, Finland, 2005, short documentary)
Ljudmila & Anatolij (Gunnar Bergdahl, Sweden, 2006, documentary)
Baba's Cars (*Babas bilar*, Rafael Edholm, Sweden, 2006)
The Monastery: Mr. Vig and the Nun (*Slottet*, Pernille Rose Grønkjær, Denmark, 2006, documentary)
Revolution (*Kenen joukoissa seisot*, Jouko Aaltonen, Finland, 2006, documentary)
Dresser (*Kredens*, Jacob Dammas, Denmark, Poland, 2007, short documentary)
The Border (*Raja 1918*, Lauri Törhönen, Finland, 2007)
The Killing (*Forbrydelsen*, Denmark, 2007–12, TV series)
Ice Kiss (*Iskyss*, Knut Erik Jensen, Norway, 2008)
Sauna (Antti-Jussi Annila, Finland, 2008)
Coffee in Gdańsk (*Kaffe i Gdańsk*, Per-Anders Ring, Sweden, 2008, short fiction)
The Wild Hearts (*De vilde hjerter*, Michael Noer, Denmark, 2008, documentary)
Volga – a Russian River (*Volga – venäläinen joki*, Marja Pensala, Finland, 2009, documentary)
The Photographer from Riga (*Fotografen från Riga*, Maud Nycander, Sweden, Finland, Latvia, 2009, documentary)
The Interrogation (*Kuulustelu*, Jörn Donner, Finland, 2009)
Upperdog (Sara Johnsen, Norway, 2009)
Millennium trilogy (Sweden, 2009):
The Girl with the Dragon Tattoo (*Män som hatar kvinnor*, Nikolaj Arcel)
The Girl Who Played with Fire (*Flickan som lekte med elden*, Daniel Alfredson)
The Girl Who Kicked the Hornets' Nest (*Luftslottet som sprängdes*, Daniel Alfredson)

2010s
The Naked of Saint Petersburg (*De nøgne fra St. Petersborg*, Ada Bligaard Søby, Denmark, 2010, short documentary)

Nastja's Heart (*Nastyas hjerte*, Lise Birk Pedersen, Denmark, 2010, short documentary)

Berik (Daniel Joseph Borgman, Denmark, Russia, 2010, short fiction)

Tank City (*Tankograd*, Boris Bertram, Denmark, 2010, documentary)

Norwegian Ninja (*Kommandør Treholt & Ninja troppen*, Thomas Cappelen Malling, Norway, 2010)

Beyond the Border (*Gränsen*, Richard Holm, Sweden, 2011)

Those Who Kill (*Den som dræber*, Denmark 2011, TV series)

Look of a Killer (*Tappajan näköinen mies*, Lauri Nurkse, Finland, 2011, TV series)

The Bridge (*Bron / Broen*, Sweden, Denmark 2011–15, TV series)

Between Dreams (Iris Olsson, Finland, Russia, France, 2011, short documentary)

Icebreakers (Maximilien Van Aertryck, Sweden, 2012, short documentary)

Two Lives (*Zwei Leben*, Georg Mass, Germany, Norway, 2012)

Hamilton – In the Interest of the Nation (*Hamilton – I nationens intresse*, Kathrine Windfeld, Sweden, 2012)

An Enemy to Die For (*En fiende att dö för*, Peter Dalle, Sweden, 2012)

Putin's Kiss (*Putins kys*, Lise Birk Pedersen, Denmark, 2012, documentary)

The End of the Road (*Vägens ände*, Maud Nycander, Sweden, 2013, documentary)

1989 (Anders Østergaard, Erszébet Rácz, Denmark, 2014, documentary)

The Escape (*Flugten fra DDR*, Jesper Clemmensen, Denmark, 2014, documentary)

I am Kuba (Åse Svenheim Drivenes, Norway, 2014, documentary)

Me and My Moulton (Torill Kove, Norway, Canada, 2014, short animation)

A Pigeon Sat on a Branch Reflecting on Existence (*En duva satt på en gren och funderade på tillvaron*, Roy Andersson, Sweden, 2014)

Struggle for Life (*Kampen for tilværelsen*, Norway, 2014–15, TV series)

Occupied (*Okkupert*, Norway, 2015–, TV series)

Seamstress (*Ompelijatar*, Ville Suhonen, Finland, 2015, documentary)

The Look of a Killer (*Tappajan näköinen mies*, Lauri Nurkse, Finland, 2016)

Bordertown (*Sorjonen*, Finland, 2016–, TV series)

World War Three: Inside the War Room (Gabriel Range, GB, 2016, documentary)

Zealand in the Cold War (*Sjælland i kold krig*, Denmark, 2016, documentary)

Small Town Killers (*Dræberne fra Nibe*, Ole Bornedal, Denmark, 2016)

Strawberry Days (*Jordgubbslandet*, Wiktor Ericsson, Sweden, Poland, 2017)

The Unknown Soldier (*Tuntematon sotilas*, Aku Louhimies, Finland, 2017)

Index